DATE DUE

#47-0108 Peel Off Pressure Sensitive

A SHORT HISTORY
OF THE FUTURE

FU

A SHORT HISTORY
OF THE FUTURE

W. WARREN WAGAR

Afterword by IMMANUEL WALLERSTEIN

THE UNIVERSITY OF CHICAGO PRESS

Chicago and London

W. WARREN WAGAR is Distinguished Teaching Professor in the Department of History at the State University of New York at Binghamton. In
addition to writing numerous articles and science fiction short stories,
and editing several collections, Wagar is the author of seven books,
including *Terminal Visions: The Literature of Last Things; Good Tidings:
The Belief in Progress from Darwin to Marcuse; The City of Man: Prophecies of a World Civilization in Twentieth-Century Thought;* and *H. G. Wells
and the World State.* He is on the editorial board of *Futures Research
Quarterly* and is a vice president of the H. G. Wells Society in London.

The University of Chicago Press, Chicago 60637
The University of Chicago Press, Ltd., London
© 1989 by the University of Chicago
All rights reserved. Published 1989
Printed in the United States of America

98 97 96 95 94 93 92 91 90 89   5 4 3 2 1

Two of the poems in chapter 3 are reprinted, with permission, from pages
174 and 178 of W. Warren Wagar, *Building the City of Man: Outlines of
a World Civilization* (New York: Grossman Publishers, 1971), © 1971 by
World Order Models Project, New York. The excerpt from *The Shape of
Things to Come,* by H. G. Wells, is reprinted by permission of A. P. Watt
Ltd. on behalf of The Literary Executors of the Estate of H. G. Wells.

Library of Congress Cataloging-in-Publication Data

Wagar, W. Warren.
   A short history of the future / W. Warren Wagar.
      p.   cm.
   Bibliography: p.
   Includes index.
      1. Twenty-first century—Forecasts.   2. Twentieth century—
Forecasts.   3. Imaginary histories.   I. Title.
CB161.W24   1989
.303.49′09′05—dc20   89-32019
ISBN 0-226-86901-6 (alk. paper)   CIP

♾ The paper used in this publication meets the minimum requirements of the
American National Standard for Information Sciences—Permanence of Paper for
Printed Library Materials, ANSI Z39.48-1984

To the many friends, and especially one, who have helped

[What follows] is, or at least it professes to be,
a Short History of the World for about the next
century and a half. (I can quite understand that the
reader will rub his eyes at these words and suspect
the printer of some sort of agraphia.) But that is
exactly what this manuscript is. It is a Short History
of the Future.

H. G. Wells,
The Shape of Things to Come
New York: Macmillan 1933, p. 4

CONTENTS

FOREWORD   by W. Warren Wagar

From molecular biophysics to women's studies, the appearance of a rich profusion of inter-, multi-, and pandisciplinary fields on university campuses has caused a great uproar in the second half of our century. Trend watchers and academic doomsters wonder if the traditional disciplines can survive the assaults of these rude interlopers of mixed and dubious descent. What will become of classic literary criticism if it is repeatedly ravaged by philosophy and psychology? Can history preserve its Rankean identity in the face of demands to take on board a heavy freight of sociology and anthropology? Are biology, chemistry, and physics in danger of irretrievable scrambling?

Among the most outrageous of the interlopers, although so far it has won only a modest following in academe, is futures studies—outrageous because it borrows freely from every traditional discipline, has no methods peculiar to itself, and claims knowledge of what is unknowable. How can one "study" what has not yet happened, what does not yet exist and perhaps never will?

Obviously, one cannot, at least not in the usual sense. But one can do something. This book is an outgrowth of my many years of teaching undergraduates what I call the "history of the future."

Although *history of the future* is an oxymoron, the human race does have only one future. That single inevitable future will unroll along a single line of time in one way and no other, just as the nineteenth century happened in one way and no other. The problem is that we cannot conceivably know what that "way" will be, even for so short a time as a decade or a century. The number of perspectives and variables is too vast, and our knowledge too imperfect, to make possible anything like scientific prediction of the future.

For that matter, we cannot retroactively predict the nineteenth century. The quality of our evidence is better than for the twenty-first, but no scholar has the power to reconstruct even a small fragment of that lost time. All our histories are nothing more than models of a reality infinitely more complex than any human mind can encompass. They are not the past itself, but paintings of selected scenes.

So, if it is not really possible to write the history of the nineteenth century, we need not be embarrassed or inhibited by our inability to know the future. Some of the raw evidence that later historians will use to explain the twenty-first century presumably exists right now, just as we need data from before 1800 to assemble our images of the nineteenth century. For the rest, scholars must rely on their limited understanding of humankind and its natural environment to assemble their images of the future. These images will almost certainly be "wrong."

But the assumption of futures studies is that responsible efforts to see what lies ahead give *Homo sapiens* more control over its destiny than if the attempts were never made. Based on the best knowledge available in every science and scholarly craft, each serious history of the future draws attention to possibilities. Awareness of these possibilities improves the chance that public planning, policy-making, and personal decision will bring the real future into congruence with the desired future, whatever that might be.

Thus far most futurists have shown a commendable reluctance to prophesy. The typical essay by a scholar in futures studies explores a welter of alternatives, thickly hedged with qualifiers. Possibility A may occur in the next few decades, but possibilities B, C, D, and E must also be considered, along with F and G, or any two or three, depending on circumstances A^1, B^1, C^1, and D^1.

The difficulty with such prudence is that, again, there is only one future and it will happen in only one way, year after year, for as long as humankind persists. To capture the sense of the *historicity* of the future, the sense of a historically conditioned interactive process propelling the whole human race into coming times, a few futurists have chosen the device of the "scenario," the story line of an imaginary but plausible future in which one set of possibilities is fully elaborated. Paul Hawken, James Ogilvy, and Peter Schwartz of SRI International drafted seven such scenarios for the 1980s and 1990s in their *Seven Tomorrows* (1982). Brian Stableford and David Langford have written an imaginary history of the next thousand years, *The Third Millennium* (1985). The prototype of all their efforts is H. G. Wells's *The Shape of Things to Come* (1933), which inspired his 1936 film, *Things to Come*.

A *Short History of the Future* falls into this curious subgenre of futures studies. Presented as an informal general history of the years 1995–2100 with supporting documents, it blends analysis and narrative in the style of history textbooks. The story it tells has not happened, and almost surely never will. Scenarios make no predictive claims.

But a scenario can teach us something about the future that discursive essays cannot. Above all, scenarios demonstrate how events are shaped by other events occurring at earlier points in time. The twenty-first century will reveal itself to our distant descendants not as a synchronic hodgepodge of alternatives but as a *chronology*, a line of development, an ongoing and ever-changing temporal context in which only certain choices could be made and only certain paths could be taken, for better or worse, at any given moment in history. Inventing imaginary chronologies is a good way to remind ourselves of the consequences of our actions and the irreversibility of time.

A scenario such as the one offered here has other values. Working out one set of future prospects in plausible detail tests a hypothesis, not unlike the hypothesis that initiates an experiment in chemistry or physics. In this case, the working hypothesis is the Marxian expectation of the future demise of world capitalism, leading to proletarian socialism and finally pure communism. Following the example set by Marx and Engels, most latter-day Marxists shy from explicit forecasting for fear of discouraging hard analysis of present-day realities, but such pious scruples need not deter the futurist.

In a larger sense, the threefold schema of *A Short History of the Future* also replicates the apocalyptic paradigm in Christian eschatology, whether the Armageddon, Millennium, and New Jerusalem of *Revelation* or the Inferno, Purgatory, and Paradise of *The Divine Comedy*. It may just as well call to mind the late Arnold J. Toynbee's vision of the transition from tribal prehistory to the age of civilizations and from the age of civilizations to "the next ledge" of world spiritual and political integration. Readers may even find echoes of the utopian tradition in book 3, "The House of Earth," where most of the problems that have beset humankind since earliest times trouble it no more. But like Wells's *The Shape of Things to Come,* this book offers no static utopia. Problems of one kind are succeeded by problems of another, and, although there may be cumulative progress, emphasis falls on the ceaseless self-actualization of *Homo sapiens,* not its elevation to deity.

Viewed from a different angle, this book is also a conventional inventory of alternatives. To be sure, the "alternatives" are strung out along a single time line, but there are so many! The reader is invited to pluck them out of their various contexts and test the plausibility of each.

Perhaps, for example, we are slated for half a dozen of the major calamities surveyed in book 1, but not the rest. We may have an epidemic of addictive designer drugs, but not the greenhouse effect. We may have superpower solidarity in managing the Third World, but not a Third World War. We may have no more catastrophic business recessions, but an even faster disintegration of the old twentieth-century middle class. In any case, there is enough raw material in these chapters for a plethora of global futures, all equally conceivable to someone working and writing in the late 1980s.

Finally, I intend *A Short History of the Future* as a challenge: a challenge to specialists in every field. This book is the work of a professional historian who has applied the methods and mind-set of historians to the task at hand. But there is no intrinsic reason why scholars initially trained in other disciplines could not profitably follow the example set here. A case in point is Dougal Dixon's engaging *After Man: A Zoology of the Future* (1981). Dixon draws on research in biology to foresee the possible future evolution of animal life on earth after the extinction of *Homo sapiens.*

Such exploits enlarge our understanding of what we already know about the world of the present day, just as essays in "counterfactual" history (what if the Roman Empire had not fallen, what if there had been no railroads in the nineteenth century, what if Hitler had been killed in the putsch of 1923?) help us fathom the real past. They would also enable us to chart the human future more efficiently, and they might well save us from a multitude of foreseeable disasters. Why not imaginary geologies of the twenty-first century, or accounts of future religious history, or textbooks of future genetics or future computer science?

One could call such a field "hypothetics," the production of imaginary treatises in every field of the human and natural sciences. Its aim would be not to forecast the shape of things to come but to pursue various hypotheses about the future in enough technical detail to assess their validity at levels not accessible to most students of general world futures.

For now, what we have before us is a short (actually a medium-length) history of coming times that pursues a single hypothesis as far as the author's mind can stretch. Given the frailties of human flesh, the future unscrolled in the following pages is perhaps the best we may expect during the next two centuries. But our short history is only one of imaginable millions. If you don't like it, write a better one! Nothing would please me more.

Many good people have made *A Short History of the Future* possible, and I would like to take a few lines to inscribe my thanks and heartfelt appreciation.

In the planning stages, even before the decision to cast this book in the form of a future history, I sent a prospectus of its contents to two eminent friends, Professor Saul H. Mendlovitz of the World Order Models Project and Dr. Michael Marien, editor of *Future Survey*. They replied with a number of valuable comments and suggestions.

At a later stage, the manuscript was read by Professor Immanuel Wallerstein of the State University of New York (SUNY) at Binghamton, Professor Theodore H. Von Laue of Clark University, Professor Michael Barkun of Syracuse University, and George Zebrowski, novelist and co-editor of *The Bulletin of the Science Fiction Writers of America*. They all gave me the benefit of their counsel and criticism, for which I am most appreciative. I owe a special debt to Professor Wallerstein, who wrote the afterword. John Wagar, Bruce Wagar, and Steven Wagar also read the manuscript and furnished me with many useful suggestions for making it better.

Correspondence and conversations over the last few years with several people have done much to clarify my thinking and add to my store of knowledge. I would like to express thanks, in particular, to Hudson Cattell of L&H Photojournalism, Dr. Michael Marien, Dr. Mary Warner Marien, Charlotte Waterlow, Douglas C. Garnar, and Lyman Hinckley. Still more thanks are due to the thousands of students who have taken my courses in futures studies at SUNY Binghamton since 1974. The opportunity to teach them, and to learn from them, has been priceless.

Another blessing that university authors need is time: preferably one long unbroken spell far removed from the clamor of campus life. SUNY Binghamton gave me this welcome gift of time in the spring and summer of 1987.

But authors are powerless without publishers. Several who looked at *A Short History of the Future* threw up their hands in bafflement. The University of Chicago Press responded in quite a different spirit— with unflagging encouragement, support, and advice, for which I am profoundly grateful.

Let me add that none of these people, however dear to me, bears the slightest responsibility for the views and evidence presented herein. The faults, flaws, and follies are all my own.

Vestal, New York
January 1989

A SHORT HISTORY
OF THE FUTURE

A NOTE TO THE READER

What you are about to read is a transcript of the words spoken in the holofilm presented to me by my grandfather Peter Jensen on Earth Festival Day, 2200, when I was a child of ten. It was his personal gift, and so, although you may think me selfish, I do not wish to share his image. But I have withheld no other part of what he gave me. In essence, like many works published in the twenty-first century and before, it is a book only of words. The chapter titles and subheads were inserted by Peter himself with a holoplastic laser pen. I hope that reading his book will take you back in feeling as well as thought to earlier times. In its odd way, it may even help you understand the sufferings and strivings of our common past.

Ingrid Jensen

PREFACE AND DEDICATION

My dearest Ingrid! For reasons that you will soon learn, this recording is the last of all my gifts. When you receive it, you will be celebrating Earth Festival with Mother and Father and little Dette l and the others. Do not play every spool right away. Save some for tomorrow, and even the day after tomorrow. I want you to stretch open your mind as if it were a pelican's pouch or a snake's jaw or a whale's womb. Stretch it wide, fill it full! Some day, I think, you will be a historian, as I was, and many other Jensens before me. My last gift to you is a history book.

Not the kind of history book you view in school. I have included no reenactments of romantic events, no portraits of dead leaders, no statistical abstracts, no anthology of conflicting theories. These things are all helpful, and I want you to study them well and learn your craft.

But here is something different. Something more personal and fragmented, as you might expect from your grandfather, who was 115 on his last birthday and whose cerebral enhancement surgery was performed in the previous century, when very little could be done to coax a person's mind to work better. Next to you, I am almost an imbecile, saved from irrelevance only by the wry wisdom of living.

Unlike most of the histories you study in school, this one treats just a short period. As you know, our kind arrived on earth in the form we acknowledge as our own at least thirty-five thousand years ago. There have been civilizations of farmers, herdsmen, and city dwellers for almost six thousand years.

But, in this brief book, I want to tell you something of what happened only in the past two hundred years, the time of passage from the "modern" age to the world order of today. So you may understand that this is a human story, carved on the stones of time by real people and not vast faceless forces beyond their ken or control, I have also gathered for you a few letters and other documents written through the years by members of our family.

Enjoy my gift. I hope you find it truthful. Remember, just the same, my beloved Ingrid, that it is not the past as we human beings have lived the past. The history in books, even the books of your grandfather, never happened. The best we can do is sample the past, as a sailor samples the waves of the sea. Each of us is one unique self, who sees in part, and hears in part, and knows in part, and, for all the rest, sees and hears and knows nothing.

BOOK THE FIRST
EARTH, INC.

1

THE LAST AGE OF CAPITAL

Diseases of the World System

This first book of our history concerns the fall, after one final roaring season, of the world-sway of capital.

Strange to say, what defeated the lords of capital in the end was the tireless ingenuity of their magicians. Every great corporation and national government employed thousands of these modern Merlins to keep them supplied with a steady flow of new commodities and weapons. The magicians were always glad, for a small price, to oblige.

Thanks to their yeomanly toil, by the close of the twentieth century (when this history begins) the pace of change in the world order had become unacceptably swift. One might say intolerably so.

Capital thrived, as never before. The corporate giants had devoured most of their smaller competitors in the lean years of the 1990s, when only they had been able to store enough fat to last the course. New technologies, as always, fueled quick profits. Already burdened by debt and poverty, whole countries fell into their clutches.

But in these rapidly changing times the world economic system was also perilously unstable. The headlong growth caused massive dislocations, exacted social costs, battered the environment, and wreaked injustice and misery. To use a metaphor from the technology of 2000, the system was something like a locomotive of the latest design, capable of nearly supersonic speeds, which kept running faster and faster on rails designed only for steam engines. There was never time or money to make fundamental repairs.

9

The rush and wobble of the global economy lay at the center of the predicament of modern civilization. But other problems no less lethal afflicted modern man and woman, all issuing from the same ultimate source: the pell-mell tempo of change at which the wizard-hirelings of capital forced the whole world to march.

The most obvious of these further problems was the disturbance of the equilibrium of the earth itself. At the turn of the century the mother planet remained rich and abundant. But the industries conjured up by the wonder-workers of capital, and the frantic efforts of the poor nations to reach the levels of mass consumption attained by their wealthy sisters, threatened essential components of the biosphere. Air, water, soil, climate, fertility, all were affected critically. At the time there developed—aggravated by the criminal manipulations of corporate oligarchs—true shortfalls of strategic resources, as furiously multiplying populations settled like locusts on the good things of the earth.

Yet another problem was the ever-widening gulf between defensive and offensive weaponry. In the world wars of the early twentieth century, all the bombs and shells and bullets in all the world's armies had been virtually powerless against the brute obduracy of armor plate, brick walls, and warm flesh. Warriors rolled up their guns and fired away, to no avail. Airmen dumped tons of high explosives on their targets, but the cities and factories absorbed them as a boxer absorbs blows and refused to break. Waves of troops, columns of tanks, wolf packs of submarines, all did their worst, and killed and killed, but it was never enough. Eventually, one side or the other wearied, and victory—of a sort—ensued. The fabric of civilization emerged more or less intact.

As you know, this situation changed profoundly after 1945. Offensive weaponry advanced far beyond any nation's capacity to defend itself. Quixotic visions of "invincible shields" lingered and for a time obsessed policymakers, especially in the Western alliance. We all remember the fiasco of the American "strategic defense initiative," which cost $1.75 trillion (measured by the purchasing power of the American dollar in 2000) and resulted in a cumbersome system that one critic described as "three rows of orbiting tin ducks in a celestial shooting gallery."

Meanwhile, the tools of attack continued to improve. Battle plans kept pace. The nations, despite the erosion of their sovereignty by the exploits of world capital, never quite managed to disarm. The summer of 2044, when it finally came around, should have brought surprises to no one, although—of course—it did.

There was also a more intangible problem, equally grave, and equally chargeable in the last analysis to the magicians of capitalist technology, even if they had no direct connection with it and may have seemed entirely innocent. Simply put, this was the problem of belief: specifically, the death of belief. One might call it "credicide."

Credicide was the killing off or the dying out—it hardly matters which—of the moral, spiritual, and metaphysical values that modern civilization inherited from the immemorial past. Such wholesale massacres had been attempted before, as during the eighteenth-century Enlightenment, when the great Voltaire urged his friend d'Alembert to "crush the infamous thing." But they had been only partially successful. What the fully modern man and woman of the twentieth century achieved was to cut the foundations away from belief itself, to make all professions of faith mere exercises in creaturely catharsis, of no greater relevance to the Good, the True, and the Beautiful than the grunt of a pig or the bray of an ass. From Carnap to Derrida, this was the whole task of twentieth-century philosophy. The task was executed in a sequence of clean surgical strokes that beheaded all our totems and left us with nothing but bare plains and empty sky.

Yet none of this would have happened, or mattered, had the magicians not simultaneously laid waste, with their fatal powers of invention, to nearly all the social, economic, and political institutions and mores of traditional civilization. As late as 1900, many of those old structures still thrived, especially in Asia and Africa. By 2025, they were either dead or so transformed from within by the merciless assault of modernization that only their outer walls remained standing. The common assumption of the times was that the traditional institutions had been propped up by their fundamental belief systems, but in fact it was just the other way round. The "fundamental" belief systems were validated by the institutions they had evolved to justify, and, when the institutions perished, the beliefs perished with them. Carnap and Derrida and all their clever confreres merely administered the last rites.

Then came the greatest question of all. Could modern men and women live productive, harmonious lives without shared beliefs, without even the power of belief?

Given the blessings of hindsight, we know the answer, but such knowledge would have done modern men and women no good. In

2000, or 2025, or even July 2044, they were still intractably resolved
to drive the "adventure of modernity" to its logical conclusions thousands of years hence. Gazing forward, they saw their corporate logos,
their tribal flags, and their shiny array of polychrome commodities
flinging into the future without resistance or pause. As the high com-
missioner of the newly formed Global Trade Consortium intoned in
Zurich in 2008, "My friends, nothing can stop us now!"

In a sense, he was right. Certainly nothing contrived by men and
women could have stopped them. Not in 2008. When the high com-
missioner spoke, capital was king of the world. A popular weekly
news magazine made him its man of the year and dubbed his realm
"Earth, Inc."

The Global Economy

An exhaustive analysis of the world economic system would have to
begin in the sixteenth century with the first encroachments of Western capital outside the traditional boundaries of Western civilization. Piece by piece, the system organized itself, from century to
century, until by the year 2000 it was nearly complete.

It bore three distinguishing marks. First, it was a planetary system,
a densely interwoven fabric of exchanges in a single world market.
Every region was closely tied to every other by investment, trade,
migration, and communications. Indeed, the well-being of every region hinged on what other regions could buy or sell or lend or borrow. In effect, if not in form, there was one world currency, one
world bank, and one reigning system of exchange of commodities,
services, and capital. The rules of the global game were quite clear.
All the players understood them well.

In the light of what followed in the second half of the twenty-first
century, it is easy to forget the breadth and depth of world economic
interdependence already achieved in this era. But the lords of capital
had been building their empire for five hundred years. They knew
what they were doing, and they built on the grandest scale possible.

A second distinguishable mark of the world economic order was
its articulation into three distinct zones or sectors. In the model
constructed by the late twentieth-century American sociologist
Immanuel Wallerstein, these were the "core," the "periphery," and
the "semiperiphery," terms that defined in a rough but serviceable
way the place of each sector in the global industrial process and its

division of labor. The nations of the core, whose members changed from century to century, composed the world haute bourgeoisie; those of the periphery functioned as an international proletariat; and those of the intermediate sector, the semiperiphery, acted as a buffer zone between the two, both exploiting and exploited, not unlike the petty bourgeoisie in the class structure of capitalist societies.

In the core, the level of technology, profits, and wages was high. In the periphery, low. And in the semiperiphery, sometimes high, sometimes low, sometimes midway between the two extremes. In the year 2000, for example, the core included the United States, the Soviet Union, Japan, and the Federal Republic of Germany. The periphery was occupied by countries such as Colombia, Ethiopia, and Bangladesh. In the semiperiphery, among many others, were Spain, Poland, Saudi Arabia, Iran, China, and Brazil.

Although individual countries could rise or fall in this planetary pecking order, the outcome was always much the same. At any one time, some parts of the world (core and rich semiperiphery) fared well and enjoyed a vastly disproportionate share of its wealth, and other parts (periphery and poor semiperiphery) fared miserably. Economists charted a gross and steadily growing inequality between the rich and the poor nations more pronounced than the inequality found within most capitalist societies.

In purely statistical terms, disregarding the place of each country in the international division of labor, the thirty richest nations, with only 22 percent of the world's population, accounted for 79 percent of its production of goods and services in the year 1985. In 2030, the same thirty countries, reinforced by five others that had scrambled into the ranks of the affluent (notably the Republic of Korea), had only 15 percent of the world's population but produced 89 percent of its goods and services.

Finally, the world economic order was indelibly and irreversibly capitalist. No one doubts this today, but, in the late twentieth and early twenty-first centuries, it was a difficult thesis to maintain. Apologists for so-called market economies agreed with apologists for so-called socialist economies that the world was divided into two camps. Politically and ideologically this may have been true, except for the working alliance between the United States and China, on the one hand, and the Soviet Union and India, on the other.

But in a larger sense the division of the world into "capitalist" and "socialist" camps was a mirage. Party leaders in the Soviet Union, in

China, in Poland, and elsewhere could boast of the building of socialism all they pleased: in fact, their economies were fully integrated
into the capitalist world order. For whether capital was owned privately or by organs of state, what mattered most was how the capital
was employed and for what ends.

Measured by such criteria, capital in the Soviet Union functioned
the same way as it functioned in the United States. In both countries,
and in all countries, it financed production for profit, not for use; the
commodities so produced were exchanged in the same unique world
market according to the same rules with the same unequal result;
and the working class (brain workers and hand workers alike) was
systematically excluded from the direction of economic affairs. What
prevailed, then, in the allegedly socialist countries was not socialism
at all but state capitalism. Whatever else it may have been, for better
or worse, state capitalism was capitalism.

One simple index to the correspondence of the two capitalisms
could be found in the distribution of wealth within the so-called
socialist countries and those that styled themselves capitalist. The
richest fifth of the people of socialist China, for example, earned incomes in 1985 eight times greater than the poorest fifth, but so also
did the richest fifth of the people in capitalist America. The ratio between the richest and the poorest fifths in the Soviet Union was significantly lower, four to one, but in capitalist Japan it was also four to
one and in capitalist West Germany five to one.

Two generations later, on the brink of the great depression that
buckled the world economy in 2032, the disparity between the haves
and the have-nots had grown even wider, following trends that could
be traced back as far as the 1970s. In mature countries of the inner core such as the United States, a radically stratified society had
emerged with virtually no true middle class. This can be seen most
easily by dividing the population into thirds rather than fifths. In
2030, the top third of the American people received 76 percent of the
national income, the middle third 15 percent, and the bottom third
9 percent. But, again, conditions were not much different in the leading "socialist" countries. Although precise income statistics for the
2030s and 2040s are not available, economic historians agree that
the richest third in the Soviet Union in this period earned at least 70
percent of the national income.

To the myth of a separate "socialist" world that attempted to coexist in peaceful competition with capitalism should also be added other, less pervasive delusions of the age. From time to time, some countries imagined that they could isolate themselves from the world economic order. This came to be known, ironically, as the "Cambodian" strategy, after the disastrous experiment in top-to-bottom social reconstruction mounted by the government of the soi-disant Marxist Pol Pot in 1975–78. At least a dozen small to medium-sized countries with varying ideologies and economic systems took strangely similar paths during the next seventy years. All were sooner or later recaptured by the world economy.

The saddest of delusions afflicted the Muslim world near the close of the twentieth century and for some years thereafter. The model, in this instance, was the revolutionary Islamic republic of Iran, established by a small, resolute elite of fundamentalist clerics. Their goal was nothing less than the erection of a fraternal community of nations living by the Koran that would shield the people of God from the exploitation of capitalists and socialists alike.

Politically, Islamic fundamentalism scored remarkable successes; but, in its economic policies, it failed categorically. To achieve its goals, it needed an army. To fight its enemies, beginning with the Iraqis, its army needed modern weapons. To pay for these weapons, its merchants and bankers and state agencies had to sell Iranian products such as crude oil in the capitalist marketplace. To produce the oil, keep the weapons in working order, and train the troops, it needed the same technologies and social infrastructure as any capitalist country. For every step the ayatollahs took backward into neomedieval purity, they took two others forward into the welcoming arms of world capital. In the end, they were fully reabsorbed into the global economy, although one wonders if they had ever, to any significant degree, managed to leave it.

Not that the ownership of the means of production made no difference at all. On the whole, the market-oriented elements in all countries, whether the country was nominally capitalist or socialist or Islamic, tended to extract more and better work from workers than the centrally planned elements. A case in point was the privatization of the postal systems of Canada and the United States in the late 1990s, a move that led to a 250 percent increase in the productivity of the postal labor force. On a still larger scale, and with comparable gains in efficiency, came the decollectivization of large segments of Soviet agriculture in 2002, after the example set decades earlier by socialist Hungary. No one should have been surprised. In an age of capital, capitalist incentives worked better than others, for reasons that were as much psychocultural as economic.

The Rise of the Megacorps

Overshadowing the failures of public enterprise was the blind inexorable process by which capital itself, in its most advanced and sophisticated forms, careened along the course charted centuries ago by the political economists of the Industrial Revolution.

Marx and Engels, for one crucial instance, had foreseen that capital would agglomerate in the hands of an ever-dwindling number of ever bigger corporate entities. In the main, and despite opportunities for small entrepreneurs at the cutting edge of high technology in concerns not initially requiring massive infusions of investment capital, this is precisely what took place. Wholesale and retail commerce, transport, communications, manufacturing, mining, agriculture, and most services (from inn keeping and catering to legal, medical, and financial services) fell increasingly under the control of highly diversified corporations organized and operating on a world scale. Once called "multinational corporations" or MNCs, by 2010 they were universally known, in all languages, as "megacorps."

The process was most visible in manufacturing. As of 1940, before America's entry into the Second World War, two-thirds of all manufacturing assets in the United States were owned by the largest one thousand companies. A quarter century later, the same fraction was owned by the largest two hundred companies. In the year 1995, the number of these companies had dropped to 140 and then, after the corporate bloodletting of the depression of 1995–2001, to thirty-six.

But this was only the beginning. As the diversification and globalization of the megacorps hurried along in the first decades of the new century, the market-oriented economies became the playground of a small cluster of giants—by 2015, only twelve in number—with combined annual sales of nearly U.S. $20 trillion, far higher than the gross national product (GNP) of any nation on earth.

A representative megacorp, in some ways the prototype of them all, was the Japanese-American behemoth General Industries (GI), formed in 2003 as the result of the "supermerger" of three oil com-

panies, two electronics companies, and two automobile manufacturers. General Industries' sales topped U.S. $1 trillion in its first full
year. Within five years, it had also acquired a controlling interest
in several worldwide chains of hotels, banks, hospitals, and news-
papers, had invaded the petrochemicals industry on a large scale,
and become a leading producer of industrial robots. General Industries illustrates quite well how capital performed in its last great
heyday. With its immense capital reserves and holdings in many different enterprises, it could weather any financial storm and crush its
competition by underselling or buying them out. The bigger it grew,
the bigger it could grow.

Giantism in capitalist industry was nothing new. But this time
around the lords of capital sensed, and promptly seized, opportunities that too often had slipped through their fingers. They used their
stranglehold on the world economy and their vast influence in the
corridors of political power to drain the national governments, little
by little, of their capacity to govern. In effect, they became the new
rulers of earth.

The process never reached its logical end point. The national governments did not beat their swords into ploughshares or abandon
their claims to sovereign power. The lords of capital left them alone
whenever possible, avoiding head-on confrontations. But, in all matters directly pertaining to the world economy (as most matters did),
they made the major decisions and relied on their stooges in government to shape policy accordingly. Regimes that proved uncooperative
usually fell, either immediately or after economic sanctions applied
from behind the scenes by the international banking and business
community.

To mobilize their collective strength, the directors of the leading megacorps established the Global Trade Consortium (GTC) in
Zurich in 2008. At first only six firms (including General Industries)
formally belonged to the GTC, but by 2015 it had enlisted all twelve
of the true megacorps, the so-called Dirty Dozen. Facilities familiarly
known as branch offices were set up in Moscow, Warsaw, Prague,
East Berlin, Beijing, Hanoi, and elsewhere to enable GTC commissioners to work closely with their opposite numbers in the principal
state-operated enterprises of the socialist world. When the first GTC
branch office, located in Moscow, was raided by the Soviet secret police in 2013, the GTC acted swiftly to cut the flow of imports from

the market-oriented economies to the Soviet Union by 50 percent
and threatened to take even more drastic measures if the office were
not allowed to reopen within two weeks.

It reopened in three days. From that time forward, relations between the panjandrums of the GTC and their comrades in the planned
economies proceeded smoothly, often more smoothly than relations
between the megacorps and the smaller fry of the "free" world. When
giants sit down to dinner, they understand one another's needs and
purposes instinctively.

In point of fact, the state enterprises in the socialist sphere were
nothing more than advanced forms of the megacorps themselves,
forms that had actually attained the goal pursued with such passion by every capitalist, to monopolize sales in one or more markets.
The world outlook of their managers was nearly identical to that of
the board members of the megacorps, all the more so because two
of the megacorps based in Western Europe were wholly or partly
state owned, a number that in the hard times of the late 2030s rose
to four.

As state ownership grew more common in the West, private ownership became widespread in the East. Western and Pacific corporations, whether from the GTC or smaller concerns, were invited to set
up shop in many socialist countries and played a steadily larger role
in their economies.

A striking illustration is provided by Hollings-Gray, the only megacorp that invested heavily in agriculture. The specialty of HoG (the
self-deprecating acronym cheerfully adopted by the firm itself) was
"chain" or "franchise" farming. Hollings-Gray bought the land, supplied standardized high-quality equipment and training, and contracted with agribusinessmen to produce crops and livestock at a
guaranteed minimum price, sharing the profits with their franchise
holders.

The system worked well in North America, where half the remaining family farms had vanished during the downturn of the late 1990s.
Soviet agronomists were impressed. In the first decade after decollectivization, Hollings-Gray set up more than five thousand large chain
farms and ranches in the Soviet Union equipped with the latest Western agricultural technology. Citing Joseph Stalin's old war against the
kulaks of nearly a century before, party purists grumbled, to no
avail. The high profits earned by the new farms smothered all criticism. Although Hollings-Gray farms were less productive than well-

managed family farms, their sheer size and capital resources allowed them to survive and prosper and eventually bankrupt many of their smaller rivals in the private sector of Soviet agriculture.

The Last Long Wave

In short, it was a glorious age for capital. Exuberant futurists foresaw more of the same in the decades and centuries to come, until, by the year 2200, the whole world would be "developed" and "free." (So it is, but not—of course—as they used the words.)

Some economists were even convinced, right up to the spring of 2032, that capital had finally learned how to regulate its affairs without the harsh purgations of the age-old business cycle charted by the Russian economist Nikolai Kondratieff. The megacorps, so their argument ran, were too powerful to need or tolerate a significant downturn in production. In the past, depressions had actually helped capital by getting rid of inefficient producers and disciplining the labor force, which needed periodic reminders of its abject dependence on the employment that only capital could offer. For twenty or twenty-five or thirty years, prices generally rose, GNPs grew, and handsome profits were taken. Then, time and again, the world economy tumbled. For the same number of years, growth was sluggish or even negative, jobs were scarce, and many businesses failed, only to be followed by a new boom as technological innovation and the opening of new markets sparked revival.

Kondratieff, who wrote in the mid-1920s, identified three such cycles or "long waves" in world economic history, the first running from the time of the French Revolution to the 1840s, the second from the 1840s to the 1890s, and the third beginning at the turn of the century, with a new worldwide depression imminent. The events that followed the stock market crash of 1929 confirmed his judgment. So did the rest of economic history in the capitalist era. The depression of the 1930s was followed by a strong upturn in the 1940s and 1950s. A further downswing occurred in 1970 and thereafter, with the world economic order touching its lowest point during the severe depression of 1995–2001.

The last of the great long waves commenced in the second quarter of 2001, when the economies of all the core countries recorded vigorous growth for the first time in six years. Thereafter, with only brief and no less predictable interruptions, capital flourished as never before. The chief engine of its recovery was a series of remarkable breakthroughs in technology, including the new IIRs (intelligent industrial robots), critical advances in the exploitation of renewable energy sources, and, after several false starts, biotechnology.

In each instance, innovation took the same course: rapid development of new products, discovery of the cheapest and most efficient ways of manufacturing them, and, finally, what the economist Mary Kaldor termed the "baroque" stage, characterized by extensive dysfunctional differentiation, overproduction, falling profits, and collapse. Product lines became monstrously complex, sporting costly improvements of negligible utility that led to frequent breakdowns and expensive repairs.

But while it lasted the boom was exhilarating, if you happened to be one of the lords of capital or a wizard of technology in their employ or some other favored underling. Even (or perhaps especially) in the poorest countries, life at the top had never been better. For most people in the middle and lower strata of the rich countries it remained at least tolerable, until the 2030s. Only the masses in the periphery and less affluent portions of the semiperiphery gained nothing.

More to the point, capital furnished the incentives required at this stage of history to gather the human race under a single system of trade and production for the first time in thirty-five thousand years. The world economy of capital wrested unprecedented wealth from the earth, in part because capital mobilized and rewarded invention. At the peak of its last long wave, capital had carried our species to the threshold of universal abundance, freedom from manual labor, lifelong health, and mastery of outer space. No other system of social relations of production could have performed such services in the centuries after 1500. We do not honor capitalists today, any more than we honor politicians or generals. Nor should we. Yet, of the three, it was always the capitalists whose power best revealed the cunning of history. Without them, most of us would still be slaves and peasants, living our brief lives under a harsh, remorseless sun.

This is to take the long view. Few people alive in the late 2030s and early 2040s would have shared it. The depression of those years was the most brutal in history. At the low point, reached in 2038 and again in 2043, half the workers in the core countries and more than half in the periphery had no work. Unemployment was less severe in the semiperiphery but still unusually high. The gross world product fell by 25 percent in just the first two years of the depression. A short-lived recovery in 2040–41 was followed by a second deep plunge in the winter of 2041–42. In the summer of 2044, things looked a little brighter, but it was too late. Catastrophe of another sort intervened.

The basic structural causes of the downturn after 2032 were the usual ones. The system produced more than it could sell, by paying workers less than the true value of their labor in order to squeeze out more profits and fuel more growth. Growth became cancerous, not to say "baroque."

But special problems arose in this last long wave, most of which I have already cited. The pace of technological innovation and the rate of economic growth were unprecedentedly high, allowing the system to reach peaks from which any fall might be fatal. The extremes of rich and poor were also greater, leading to increased social instability on a world scale and to a multiplicity of hidden costs for which the price eventually had to be paid: theft, banditry, welfare and relief programs, debt and bankruptcy, broken homes, growing irresponsibilty in the workplace, provinces or entire nations in receivership, and the ever-rising expense of regulating and policing the system by bureaucrats. Other costs came from the environment, ravaged unscrupulously by generations of short-sighted profiteers. Dying forests and ecosystems, fields turning to desert, superheated skies melting ice caps that flooded lowlands, exhausted mines, wells, and aquifers, all presented their bills.

Compounding the woes of the flesh was the sense of meaninglessness and purposelessness fostered by credicide. In earlier downturns, sufferers could look to this or that traditional faith or belief system for solace. Not in the 2040s.

Whether the world economic order would have finally collapsed under its own weight in the middle of the twenty-first century or staggered to its feet, marking the beginning of yet another long wave, no one knows. My instincts tell me that it was strong enough to survive, in spite of everything. But, as people used to say, the question is academic. In the bag of tricks held by the magicians was one trick they had never played, although tens of trillions of dollars had been spent by governments to ensure its readiness in case of need.

On July 5, 2044, a spasm of fear seized the politicians. Unimaginable commands flashed around the globe. The trick came out of the bag.

For a time the world economy ceased to exist. When it did return to life, it belonged to the lords of capital no more.

INTERLUDE

I promised to read you some letters now and again, written by members of our family. Here is my first group. It is also the oldest. The author, Jens Otto Jensen, was a cousin of my grandfather. He emigrated from Denmark to the United States with his parents in 1995. I know very little of "Bob," but I believe he was Robert Luczycki, an old school friend and confidant. Jens Otto graduated from a university college of business and spent most of his life working for WT&T, one of the twelve megacorps I discussed earlier. I have collected several hundred letters written by Jens Otto, but I shall read only these few.

20 January 2016

Dear Bob:

Regards from Tokyo! My flight from Teheran was uneventful, which is always the best kind. The new SSTs are a lot uglier, but they get you there in a hurry, and they look safer. I understand from friends on the inside that Boeing-Mitsubishi has made a killing on the 240s already, and that's not counting at least a dozen orders still unfilled. At this rate, B-M will be a mega before the decade's out. Well, maybe not a mega. But on its way. Indubitably on its way.

I'll stay in Tokyo for another week, before shuffling back to L.A. The reason I'm writing, to be honest with you, is Lonnie. She's scheduled to take a sales trip of her own starting about six hours before I land in L.A., so we're going to miss each other again. Ships that don't even pass in the night, for Christ's sake! She's booked for Rio, São Paulo, Buenos Aires, and I think Capetown and Perth. Her boss wants her to try some high pressure on one of the new optical hardware lines, I don't even know what the hell it is anymore.

But the thing is this. I can video her from Tokyo, and I will. HomeFort is minding Jeepers Creepers and the house, and Norah will stay with her grandmother, that's no problem. What would help, though, is if you could just find the time to drop in and say hello and let her know how much I'm missing her. She trusts you. She even believes you, which I don't think is true any more where I'm concerned. We haven't been any good at communication since I took the Asia region job. She thinks I did it to spite her. She takes it personally. Well, you know the story. I'm not even sure she isn't half right, although I'd never admit it to her. But the bottom line is I love this woman, I love Norah, I even love the god-damned slinky alley cat, and I want to protect this marriage.

Help me, buddy. She'll be home until the afternoon of the 27th. Bring Sue along. She likes Sue, too, at least I hope so. Thanks for everything, as always. I'll owe you.

Best,

Jens

♠

9 March 2016

Dear Bob:

I've never taken the chance to thank you properly for seeing Lonnie back in January. I wish it could have done some good, but you tried your best, and I want you to know I won't forget it.

It's been hectic around here. Either I'm in Asia or I'm at home staring at screens, trying to figure out the next strategies, but nothing seems to work with Lonnie. She says she wants me home more, but when we're both here, she goes out shopping and I wind up spending most of my time with Norah and the cat. We haven't slept together this whole censored year.

The next crisis is my trip to Islamabad. I asked Moe to make sure it would coincide with hers to Bogotá, but at the last minute her boss moved Bogotá back a week. That bitch has hot pants for Lonnie, I'm con-vinced of it more and more. I have nothing against lesbians. Some of my best friends are lesbians, etc. But when one of them tries to move in on your wife, what do you do? Lonnie is straight, but she's also mad at me, and she knows she's at a crucial stage in her career. She may just be vulnerable.

Incidentally, I should have listened to your warning about HomeFort. The house was empty for two days last week, and on the second, a couple of poppers broke into the den and took some stuff, including the laser theater and my whole collection of live concert discs and Norah's simul-doll. HomeFort had a wagon there within ten minutes, but the poppers got away. It's the same problem you mentioned. The alarm system is foolproof, but knowing is not enough. If the service doesn't have mobile units on the spot and ready to respond immediately, anybody can get in and out of your house before the wagon arrives.

Damn the Democrats! They have the whole country bleeding its heart dry for the New Poor, and meanwhile the New Poor are living high (oh, literally!) and stealing the paint off our walls. We have to bring the death penalty back for dealing crack and pop. It worked pretty well, and now things are worse than they were in the 1990s.

I've met an interesting woman in our Tokyo office. She's with GI and does liaison work between us and them. She's Irish of all things, and we've had dinner a couple of times. Her name is Faren. No, I haven't taken her to bed. I won't, either. But it's a nice change to be sociable and close with a woman who doesn't want to collect your scalp. The tension with Lonnie is almost too much. Take care of yourself. Or better yet, let Sue! Count thy blessings.

Best,

Jens

♦

18 July 2016

Dear Bob:

Since our last video talk, Lonnie finally did what she's been threatening to do all summer. She packed her bags, grabbed Norah, and went to live with her sister in Philadelphia. She insisted that I get reassigned to a home desk job, or at least something that would keep me parked in L.A. As I expected, my executive "family" at WT&T invited me to place my reproductive organ in the lower part of my digestive tract. Then I said she should apply for a transfer so she could at least have a different boss, and she repeated the advice I got from WT&T. But she did apply for a transfer, and that's one reason she's in Philadelphia. (Her new job's in New York, but it's only a twenty-minute commute now that the mono system is up.)

We have more problems than jobs and bosses. You know that as well as anyone. Still, they can make an already mediocre situation intolerable. I was sorry, by the way, to hear about your own difficulties. Sue is crazy if she thinks you guys could have a better life selling your house and going to work for WT&T in Toronto. Tell her I said so. They're bloodsuckers and they don't give a shit for anybody. The money's good, if you like to spend your life riding lions who eat small children for breakfast and countries in Africa for lunch. But take it from one who knows. It isn't a life.

In my case, I think I've had it. Maybe it's better for Norah that we split now. At least she's getting to know her aunt, who's a first-class human being. Families are so far apart these days. Norah has met most of her family, on both sides, but there's no substitute for living with somebody or being in the same town, day in, day out. The typical menage nowadays consists of a husband on business in Nairobi, a wife on business in Seoul, a kid in boarding school in Boston, and an empty house (except for the burglars) in Houston. Grandma #1 is in Tampa, Grandma #2 is in Hong Kong, Grandpa #1 is in Barcelona, Grandpa #2 is in Sydney, and no two uncles or aunts or cousins live within 500 miles of one another, or the kid.

But it hurts, buddy, it hurts and hurts. When I walk into that empty bedroom and realize that Lonnie may never again share a bed or a house or even a meal with me as long as we live, when I realize that I may become a stranger to my own little girl, I can't handle it. I turn around and go downstairs and bunk on the sofa.

As ever,
Jens
♦

23 September 2016
Dear Bob:

The divorce will be final some time next month. We're not going to battle about anything. I don't have any fight left in me, and I think that's true for Lonnie, too. Lonnie's boss, the old dyke, got her transferred back to L.A., but we had to dispose of the house anyway. Neither one of us could afford the damned thing.

I will be able to see Norah as often as I want, within reason. She's processing the divorce pretty well, I think. She's a little more quiet than usual, but she doesn't cry.

I've been seeing Faren, the woman I met in Tokyo. I'm too burned out for the time being to play Romeo, which she understands, but I think it's for real. She's pretty, she's fun to be with, and we have a lot in common. We get together every time I'm in Tokyo.

In fact I'll be there for three days starting on the 30th. How about giving me a call? I'll be at the usual hotel, and you can always get me around eight a.m. local time. I'd like to hear more about Sue and her negotiations with WT&T. Tell me you're not interested! When a man and *wife both work for the same mega, it's like adding a leash to a tether. They have more ways to keep you under their thumb than you could ever imagine.*

As ever,

Jens

◆

10 November 2016

Dear Bob:

Faren and I are engaged! It's just great. She thinks she can get a new posting in L.A. I would have called, but I forgot where you said you'd be traveling this week.

Old buddy, it's hard to believe. She's as happy as I am, and I know this is going to work, although it would help a lot if she could get the L.A. assignment. I'd be glad to base in Tokyo, if only the "family" could arrange it. Moe made sympathetic noises, more than usual, but he said it's no go.

Anyway, nothing is going to rain on this parade. I feel like I'm twenty years old again.

Your resurrected pal,

Jens

◆

20 December 2016

Dear Bob:

Thanks for your calls. I hope you two don't get screwed. Just remember what I told you about how they use wives against husbands and husbands against wives. They don't care what happens to people as long as WT&T winds up in the black at the end of each quarter.

In my own situation, nothing has changed since we talked. Faren is still a little numb, but what can she do? Getting to be GI's assistant supervisor for the whole West Soviet market at the age of thirty is not the kind of opportunity that knocks every day or every decade.

So the engagement is on hold. She'd have to be in Moscow or Leningrad or Kiev 90% of her time. Moe would authorize a transfer to Russia for me, but only if I gave up my seniority in the sales division and started over again in megacorp liaison. It's like asking a pool hustler to become a diplomat. I'm crazy about Faren, but she won't let me even think of it. And somehow, I get the sick feeling in the pit of my stomach, where I often do my best thinking, that this god-damned promotion means much more to her than marrying me. I'll keep you posted.

Best,

Jens

♦

5 February 2017

Dear Bob:

I apologize for not staying in touch with you. I've been depressed lately. I even took a holiday with myself in the Caribbean last week. The sun felt unusually warm. I've never been so tempted to try a little pop. It's all over the islands these days, at bargain basement prices. But I didn't succumb. Even cheap chemical highs cost a lot more than the solar variety, and the only risk you run with sunshine is skin cancer.

Faren took the Russian job. She gave me an affectionate call from Leningrad last night. But I had to tell her my news. This will blow you away. I've just been transferred to Buenos Aires, effective 15 March. It's permanent, no appeal. I'll try to touch base with her next month, but she's terrifically busy and excited. Her face fell a little when I mentioned Argentina. Then two minutes later she was effervescing about a new product line of seabed mining robots that GI plans to introduce in 2017. It could double GI's sales in her district since none of the Soviet government corporations manufactures anything like it, and GI has a two-year lead on the other megas.

You will tell me to hang in there and fight the good fight, but how the hell can I do anything stashed away in Buenos Aires?

Best,

Jens

♦

Things never quite came together for Jens Otto. The letters to Bob continued for a long time, but they became routine and impersonal. In the archive is a clipping mounted in plastic from a newspaper in Leningrad, dated 1 July 2018, announcing the marriage of Faren Flaherty to Dmitri Dmitrievich Liadov. Both were employed by General Industries. Jens Otto eventually married a dull, comfortable widow from Montevideo.

2

RULING CIRCLES

The World System as a Polity

My task in this chapter is to sketch the political history of "Earth, Inc.," which in a sense I have already done. To paraphrase an American president of the early twentieth century, the business of humanity (until 2044) was business; and its business was also its politics. The megacorporate web enclasped every country, snaring the domestic and foreign policy of every government in its threads. The Global Trade Consortium and its twelve members all had elaborate "liaison divisions" further divided into intercorporate and governmental sections, which helped coordinate the policies of states and megacorps alike. Politicians seldom acted without consulting the GTC, and the GTC seldom failed to anticipate their every move.

But in the first chapter I examined the world system of this time as an economy, as a market in which goods, services, and capital were produced and consumed, bought and sold, borrowed and lent, in a tireless quest for material gain. The world system was also a polity, or, rather, a cluster of polities, in which public power was wielded by politicians, in a tireless quest for something quite different: glory, fame, the hallucinogenic pleasures of power itself. The corporate wire-pullers presented the politicians of the twenty-first century with a meager menu of options from which to formulate policy. But as the social psychologist Fernándo Diego López of Santander writes, "Within their sphere they had real choices to make, and invariably the men and women in power were cunning sociopaths who governed because they enjoyed watching their subordinates squirm and their followers fawn."

It might be added that the public, by and large, was composed of psychosocially immature, almost childish personalities, who craved surrogate fathers and mothers and dwelled obsessively on the minutiae of their masters' tedious lives. Most of what passed for news (and even history) in the twentieth century and the first half of the twenty-first was gossip about the whims, fancies, and posturings of politicians.

A good index to this addiction may be found in the encyclopedias of the two centuries. Turn to any specimen published before 2044, and you discover the same absurd imbalance. Political entities such as France or the Soviet Union, rulers such as de Gaulle or Kravchenko, and political ideologies such as liberalism or socialism received long articles. But you will look in vain for an entry on Volkswagen or Royal Dutch Shell or General Industries or Hollings-Gray. The GTC itself went unnoticed in any major encyclopedia until 2031.

All the same, we must not let our own prejudices and perceptions color the past more than we can help. The fact remains that politics and politicians did flourish in the last age of capital, and not always purely in the service of capital.

The Management of Democracy

Nor should we forget that the process of modernization that began in the sixteenth century entailed not only the coming of capital, the mechanical revolution in industry, and the rise of an integrated world economy but also a measure of authentic democratization. Those of us who despise the "modern" world and everything it stood for cannot escape the evidence at hand. Political power gradually but inexorably spread from the minuscule band of clerics, princes, and merchants who monopolized it in the sixteenth century to ever-widening circles of society during the next five hundred years. With local exceptions now and then, rulers fell increasingly under the constraints imposed by parliaments, laws, civil services, media, and electorates. Opportunities to penetrate ruling circles from below multiplied.

Most citizens failed to make productive use of the power that had come their way. But if, in order to fill the numberless jobs essential to the functioning of a complex industrialized modern economy, governments educate their citizens and lift the majority of the population to a standard of living well above subsistence, some of these fortunate new arrivals in the higher strata of society will translate their educational and economic power into political power.

The only available alternative strategy, adopted for years by the magnates of several countries in Latin America, was to refuse to educate and enrich. The magnates paid a heavy price for their obduracy. Their countries remained more or less medieval, at the mercy of every corporation and superstate in the developed world.

At the turn of the millennium, therefore, those who ruled the earth found themselves in an odd situation. On the one hand, never before in modern history had wealth and might been so concentrated in so few institutions. The rising megacorps and the major industrial and nuclear states dominated the planet. On the other hand, no member of the ruling class could take a step without considering its impact on that great formless entity, "the people," and their tribunes in the press, the courts, and the representative assemblies. If the people failed to govern, at least they could, sooner or later, force the removal of the men and women who did. A special thorn and threat was the demagogue, like Mussolini or Ibn Jihad, who played the body politic as if it were a violin and could, for a time, divert the whole course of world history.

The solution found to the problem of democracy was a judicious blend of "public information management" and "enhanced data control." Armed with less formidable technologies, both had been tried throughout history, but in the early twenty-first century both were raised to unprecedented heights of efficiency by the megacorps and their subalterns in government.

Public information management began with a concerted effort by the megacorps to gain full mastery of the mass media. Big newspaper chains, television networks, and publishing companies were already well known in the twentieth century. They had all conspired informally to shape news to protect capital and the state. Corporate sponsorship even of public radio and television in the United States became so obtrusive in the 1970s and 1980s that one political humorist nicknamed PBS (Public Broadcasting Service) the "Petroleum Broadcasting Service." Throughout Western Europe, vigorous forays into radio and television by private entrepreneurs challenged traditional public ownership and control of the media. At the other end of the spectrum, the once heavy-handed Soviets developed a new style of "open" journalism that purveyed official truths as if they were the carefully considered personal views of lovable mavericks.

The skills honed in the late twentieth century were then applied on a far grander scale in the twenty-first, with help from advances in technology. Over the years, three megacorps, including WT&T, managed to buy up nearly every metropolitan and national news paper, private television network, and major publishing house of books and periodicals in the market-oriented world. Two of them also invested heavily in the film and video industries. What before had been imperfect and hit or miss now became all but total control of what the public heard and what it was meant to think. The liaison divisions of these corporations also made certain that government-owned media throughout the world, even to some degree in the socialist countries, followed much the same line and promoted the same consensual values.

By the 2020s, it made little difference whether one read a news-weekly in Berlin, heard bulletins over the radio in Havana, or caught a television newscast in Melbourne. A single homogenized electronic news and entertainment culture spanned the earth. Thanks to the proliferation of communications satellites coordinated by Intelsat from its old-fashioned glassy headquarters in Washington (dating back to the 1980s), the same stories were read and the same programs seen or heard everywhere, massaged by the same corporate information managers and distributed by the same trio of global news and entertainment services.

The other face of megacorporate policy in dealing with the problem of democracy was less amiable. The experts called it data control, a euphemism for the use of widely gathered and centrally collated information about citizens to keep them loyal, industrious, and quiet. In fact, it was a euphemism for legalized blackmail.

The heart of the world data control system was the International Data Storage Center (IDSC), established in 2012 in Zurich by the GTC. Many individual corporations and national governments had already created their own central data banks by this time, but what the GTC achieved transcended anything attempted hitherto. Computer technology had reached the point where all the information pertaining to every living person could be stored on a few microchips and made instantly available to any subscriber anywere in the world.

At first, all the data gathered came from corporations. But, since

corporate personnel records were quite detailed, nothing else might
be required. Firms demanded vast amounts of verifiable information
from job applicants and kept careful watch over the lives and work
of their employees. They had records of birth, family history, education, medical care, religious affiliations, community and military
service, court appearances, previous employment, performance on
the job, marital partners, finances, credit history, purchases, travel,
memberships, publications, citations in publications by others—
whatever data had been entered into computers linked to a centralized system, which soon came to include the great majority of all
computers except those used by governments.

The GTC, however, was not satisfied with this exception. It applied pressure on the United Nations to build a parallel public data
storage center. Housed in New York, the center opened its doors
in 2027. Into this great bank poured still more data: tax and arrest
records, security clearances, license and passport applications, even
files of "geneprints," computerized models of each citizen's unique
genetic structure, which by 2010 had largely replaced the fingerprint
in police work.

The center made its treasures available on demand to any state
official of the country in which the individual under investigation
held citizenship, to any state official of another country with the approval of the individual's national data control bureau, and to any
authorized representative of the GTC after receiving the same approval and an endorsement (seldom withheld) by U.N. staff. In practice, anyone's life was an open book. For most people, this had been
true for decades, but now the last fugitives were ferreted out and
their secrets laid bare to the cold eyes of authority.

Armed with the information supplied by data storage centers,
governments and corporations hired, fired, arrested, threatened, rewarded, persuaded, penalized, monitored, and generally controlled
whomever they pleased. A politician who showed demagogic tendencies could be ruined by a tawdry revelation. A corporate executive who opposed her fellows on a matter of policy could be whipped
into line with a suggestion that certain credit records itemizing the
expenses of a week spent in Hawaii with a lover might fall into the
hands of her husband. A technician who loafed on the job could
be shown the results of computer surveillance of his equipment minute by minute, day by day. A broadcast journalist who began airing

structural analyses of the evils of the world economy could be extradited and jailed for arguable infractions of the law committed years ago in another country. Few miscreants escaped the net, and who among us has never been a miscreant?

The problem of democracy, in short, was reduced to manageable proportions. At the same time, the lords of capital received further support from the new distribution of wealth discussed earlier. As the middle class disappeared and most people received a dwindling share of the gross world product, they had less opportunity to be heard, less self-esteem, and less leverage. Upward mobility was diminished. More time was spent struggling simply to preserve life and dignity.

But the same process that eroded the middle class not only created a larger number of poor: it also added significantly to the ranks of the well-to-do. When we speak of the "lords of capital," we do not mean the directors and chief executive officers of the megacorps alone. True, a relatively small group of men and women—perhaps two hundred—perched at the top of the biggest corporations and states effectively ruled the world, in the sense that the responsibility to decide every major question confronting the world system was ultimately theirs. But they would not have lasted long had they made such decisions arbitrarily.

In fact, the new ruling class was fairly large, comprising not only megacorporate moguls and heads of state but also a considerable body of managers, engineers, bureaucrats, scientists, publicists, and experts of every kind, without whose expertise the system would have collapsed overnight. Compared to what it had been in the nineteenth or early twentieth centuries, the world economy was now almost inconceivably complex. Its dependence on advanced capital-intensive technology was profound. Government had also grown more complex, especially in the areas of surveillance and defense— hence the need for a close working alliance with managerial and technical elites, who, in any case, could not be ignored because they enjoyed considerable wealth and a high opinion of their worth.

It might even be argued that Earth, Inc., was a technocracy, a great world republic of experts, fulfilling the steely dreams of Auguste Comte and Thorstein Veblen. The "leading" men and women of the period were often figureheads, dancing to the tunes piped by their advisers and the powerful professional associations to which these advisers belonged. The leaders were still needed, if only to furnish the public with suitable heroes, but the experts ran the show.

The World Crisis of 1997

Having said all this, I must now review the principal events of the time so that you may see how, operating on the basis of these underlying economic and political structures, late modern civilization fared. We are inclined to think too much of the Catastrophe of 2044 and dismiss the half century that preceded it as a gray and ominous foretaste of the horror to come.

What stands out most prominently in the period is the relative easiness of relations between the major powers in the industrial core and the anger, breakdown, and subjugation of the lands in the periphery. In this sense, the period from 1995 to 2044 recalls the period from 1871 to 1914, when the major powers annexed most of the non-Western world without fighting, more than a little, among themselves.

The root cause of this change of fortunes is obvious from all we have said before: the surging power of the megacorps, usually at the expense of the balanced economic growth of the peripheral and poor semiperipheral countries. Just as the indigenous cultures of these countries were ravaged by Westernization, so their economies were badly distorted to accommodate the immense purchasing power and limitless profit hunger of the people in the core. In effect, they became the hands, feet, and backs of the rich countries. Their raw materials and labor were routinely undervalued and subject to the ruinous vicissitudes of the global price system, which could devastate whole countries almost as easily as it wiped out the family farms of North America in the 1990s.

The year 1995 makes a convenient starting point, as the point at which the already slumping world economy took a spectacular downward plunge triggered by the near collapse of the Soviet and Polish economies and by the chronic inability of various debtor nations in the Latin American semiperiphery to pay interest on their massive international loans. The hardest hit country was Mexico. Intolerable poverty and unemployment finally persuaded the various factions on the Mexican left to form a united front, which quietly gathered strength all during the darkest years of the new depression.

Although seeds of future conflict had been well planted, no major political events roiled the surface of life in Latin America between 1995 and 2001. Trouble came first to the Philippines. After decades of bitter struggle in many parts of the archipelago, Communist guerrillas seemed at last on the verge of victory. The Philippine army and bourgeoisie were appropriately terrified. In February 1997, they called on their allies, the United States, for armed assistance. Ever since the fall of the corrupt Marcos regime in 1986, the media had made the defense of American-style democracy in the Philippines a favorite cause. With significant corporate and military interests at stake and the public primed for intervention by a noisy campaign in the press, Washington did not hesitate to deploy its Pacific fleet and a sizable force of marines against the insurgents.

The American administration made a point of taking into consideration "the lessons of history" as it prepared its response to this new challenge. Unfortunately, the policymakers, like policymakers everywhere, had short memories. They resolved not to let the Philippines become another "Vietnam," meaning that, instead of introducing American forces piecemeal and running the risk of a long, dirty, confusing war, they would immediately send into battle all the troops and hardware required for a quick, clean victory.

The victory did not come. After six murderous months, the situation stabilized enough to permit the United States to save face by withdrawing. No longer vital to its military interests in the Pacific, the two American bases in the Philippines were abandoned. With generous supplies of American arms and advisers, the Philippine army continued the struggle, but it was obviously only a matter of time until the rebels prevailed. The American troops returned home, fifteen thousand of them in body bags.

Meanwhile, on the other side of the world, a crisis unfolded in the Balkans, which might have followed an entirely different course had there been no war in the Philippines. It began with the death of the Rumanian party chief Nicolae Ceauşescu after almost thirty years in office. Ceauşescu had presided over one of the most repressive governments in Eastern Europe, and his death uncorked explosive forces in Rumanian society. A reformist faction of the ruling party took power in Bucharest. At first, Rumania's neighbors did not react, but, in April 1997, the Soviet leader made a personal visit to the Rumanian capital and demanded an immediate halt to liberalization.

Change would be endorsed, but only "measured" change. To Western observers it seemed like a replay of what had happened in Czechoslovakia in 1968, when liberalization in the spring prompted armed intervention by the Soviet Union and its allies in the summer.

With American forces committed in the Philippines, the Soviet leadership assumed that it would be allowed a free hand. So it would have been, but for the involvement of the Yugoslavs. In an unusual gesture for a Balkan nation, Rumania appealed to long neutral Yugoslavia for moral, diplomatic, and, if necessary, military assistance in its struggle against the Soviets. One by one, the leaders of East Germany, Czechoslovakia, Hungary, and Poland indicated (with fulsome regrets and excuses) their intentions not to commit troops if the Soviet Union deemed it necessary to invade Rumania. The Bulgarians hedged. Clearly, 1997 was not 1968. Under the circumstances, Yugoslavia saw the Rumanian affair as an irresistible opportunity to deal a fatal blow to Soviet hegemony in the Balkans.

At this point, in July, it was still not too late to avoid a showdown. The new Rumanian leaders flew to Moscow for urgent talks, bringing concessions. But the Soviets were so disconcerted by the disloyalty of their Warsaw Pact allies and the threatened meddling of Yugoslavia that they declined to bargain. Soviet troops massed on the Soviet-Rumanian border. Five Yugoslav divisions crossed the Rumanian frontier and were greeted by delirious crowds and garlands of flowers as they rolled with a Rumanian military escort eastward through Craiova, Bucharest, Braila, and on to the Soviet-Rumanian border. The Rumanians concentrated virtually their whole army in the east and north against the Russians.

The game plan of the Yugoslav-Rumanian alliance was, of course, not to engage the Soviets in a shooting war but to demonstrate to their big brothers that an invasion would be costly, embarrassing, and not worth the effort.

For a month the two sides squared off against one another nervously, along a vast frontier that stretched from the Carpathians to the Black Sea. By then it was late August. The United States was just then disengaging from the Philippines, in part to turn its undivided attention to the Balkan crisis. The president's national security advisers in the White House conceived the plan of compensating for America's humiliation in the Pacific by dispatching some of its battle-hardened marines to the aid of Yugoslavia, on the pretext that, with many of their best troops in Rumania, the Yugoslavs needed help to defend their own borders. There was no question of sending American forces to Rumania, still a Warsaw Pact nation and thus nominally an ally of the Soviet Union. But, as a country without treaty obligations to other powers, Yugoslavia could issue an invitation to the United States to render "fraternal aid." In the end it agreed to do so. American warships carrying a modest force of marines supported by a wing of naval aircraft entered the Adriatic and discharged their passengers at the port of Rijeka.

The Soviets made a great outcry against the presence on Yugoslav soil of "counterrevolutionary marauders with bloody hands." The Hungarians, still refusing to commit their own troops, had no choice but to let the Soviets concentrate several armored divisions on the Hungarian-Yugoslav border, where they soon found themselves eye to eye with American marines as well as regular Yugoslav army troops.

Early in the morning on 29 September, the first shots were fired across this border, by Soviet artillery responding to what they wrongly construed as an attack by the United States. In the skirmish that ensued, a dozen Americans were killed. Naval aviators were ordered to cross into Hungarian air space to bomb and strafe the Soviet guns. By noon, the generals on both sides were urging their respective governments to authorize full-scale operations. Both sides had tactical nuclear weapons at their disposal; the Americans, in particular, were eager to use their neutron shells against the greatly superior Soviet armor. The temptation grew almost overwhelming shortly after three o'clock, when forty Soviet tanks entered Yugoslav territory near Beli Manastir.

At five, however, orders arrived from Washington and Belgrade to draw back and see what the Russians would do next. For their part, the Soviet forces were ordered to retreat behind the frontier and ignore, as long as possible, any further provocations by the "marauders." All three governments concerned simultaneously demanded an emergency meeting of the U.N. Security Council and issued declarations of their unswerving devotion to the cause of peace.

By the next day it became apparent from the sudden cessation of hard news that something theatrical was about to happen. The general public everywhere expected war. But instead the American and Soviet leaders agreed to a summit meeting in Vienna, which took place in mid-October and laid the diplomatic groundwork for the Vienna Conference of 1998. Within a month of the summit, the marines were sailing home from Rijeka, the Soviet armored divisions returned to their usual bases in Hungary and the Soviet Union, the Yugoslav divisions in Rumania went back to Yugoslavia (without a fresh round of flowers), and the Rumanians demobilized.

The Vienna Conference was almost surely the most important peace conference of the twentieth century. While it led to no formal treaty, something far more useful emerged: an understanding, almost an entente cordiale, between the United States and the Soviet Union.

The two "superpowers," we know now, had been frightened nearly witless by the events of September 1997. The Balkan crisis of 1997 was, in fact, a salutary experience for the whole world and no doubt the best thing that could have happened at the time. It supplied the physical jolt necessary to finish building a world order more congruent with political and economic realities.

Those realities were basically twofold: first, the obsolescence of war between countries with nuclear arms as an instrument of policy because of the near impossibility of limiting conflict to acceptable levels of death and destruction; and, second, the shift in the balance of power from the state system to the corporate system, which had more to lose than it had to gain from a continuation of old-fashioned world politics. The United States, Western Europe, and the Soviet Union went on attempting to perfect defensive shields against nuclear attack, and weapons to disable the shields, and still other weapons to disable the disabling weapons, all of which meant high profits for the arms industry. But they stopped thinking seriously of war among themselves as an instrument of state policy. Nonsense about "limited" or "protracted" nuclear war, "counterforce" strategy, and the like was heard no more in defense ministries.

For this change, the Balkan crisis deserves only part of the credit. By acting out their fantasies, the Soviet and American leaders taught themselves a valuable lesson. Much the same thing had already happened once before as a result of the Cuban missile crisis of 1962, which helped lead to a fifteen-year interlude of superpower "détente."

But now there was a new quantity in the equation: the growing sophistication of the lords of capital and their counterparts in the Soviet economy. Many had already concluded, years earlier, that it was not in their interest to tolerate, much less encourage, the machismo of their colleagues in government. Competition for markets in the poor countries and heavy expenditure on baroque weapons systems had justified superpower rivalry in their eyes at first, but the situation was clearly spinning out of control. They understood that a radical overhaul of the world system was imperative.

Overhauling the System

The turning point came in November 1997, when several prominent corporate executives from the United States and Japan met with the president at Camp David. They convinced the president and his secretary of state to formulate an unconventional agenda for the conference in Vienna, headed by a proposal to divide the world into spheres of domination. Some of the same moguls held a secret meeting in Stockholm in mid-December with a delegation of Soviet trade officials and directors of state enterprises, a meeting whose outcome may have influenced Soviet thinking as much as the weekend at Camp David influenced American.

With the ground thus prepared, the Vienna Conference held early in the next year achieved precisely what the lords of capital hoped it would. All parties—the two superpowers and their allies in Europe and East Asia—agreed to a comprehensive arms limitation protocol regulating the numbers of all major weapons systems, nuclear, chemical, and conventional. The delegates deliberately refrained from converting the protocol into a treaty in order to exclude the world press and the American Senate from any part in shaping or modifying the new policy.

Under the arms control regime established at the conference, weapons research and upgrading would continue, together with a brisk trade in arms worldwide, but no longer would there be in any real sense an arms "race." The powers concurred, without benefit of a public announcement, that the purpose of weapons for countries in the developed world was not to fight or bully one another but to stimulate the global economy and promote their vital interests in South Asia, Africa, and Latin America.

To the end of promoting such interests, and to minimize friction among the developed powers, the family of rich nations further resolved at Vienna to carve the planet into "zones of legitimate special influence." It took them three long months of hard bargaining and haggling to agree on the details, but agree they finally did.

To the Soviet Union and its partners were assigned the Middle East (excluding Israel), Cuba, and the Indian subcontinent. Japan,

soon to be a nuclear power, and China, working together, received
Southeast Asia. The United States assumed responsibility for the
Pacific islands, Latin America (excluding Cuba), and Israel. Its Eu-
ropean allies were awarded the entire continent of Africa. Finland,
Sweden, Switzerland, Austria, and Yugoslavia remained outside any-
one's zone, and the removal of all foreign armed forces from the two
Germanies was also arranged, to lessen the chance of another direct
confrontation between American and Soviet troops.

What did all this mean? It is not entirely clear what the Vienna
conferees expected it to mean in the years ahead, but in practice the
partition of the world into zones of special influence gave the various
industrial powers a free hand to exploit and dominate the poor nations with impunity. Playing the superpowers off against one another
was no longer, for the most part, a feasible strategy for politicians in
these countries.

Nor could these countries count on the greed of foreign corporations to supply them with the weapons, food, machinery, and loans
that had kept them going in the past. The corporations were greedier
than ever, but they saw where their long-term best interests lay, and
they enforced informal trade embargoes against any poor country
whose leaders failed to collaborate with the government of the rich
country assigned to "influence" them. The GTC made the tactic work
with terrifying competence. Although nationalism in the so-called
Third World was far from extinct, in the end it proved powerless
against the united front now presented by the corporate and political
leaders of the developed world.

Gratifying results (from the megacorporate point of view) were
not long in coming. In 1999, Syria and the Soviet Union occupied all
of Lebanon, massacred most of the leaders of the factions that had
been contending for a quarter century, executed the rest after show
trials, and transformed the country into a province of Syria. The loss
of life was hideous. Many grand old Christian families fled to the
West. But eventually Lebanon became once again a prosperous land,
and the anarchy of its brief existence as a sovereign state troubled
the Middle East and the world economy no more.

Then, in the spring of 2001, a fundamentalist coup in Cairo established the Arab Islamic Republic. The new Egyptian state promised
to annex Libya, eradicate Israel, and make Iran's Ayatollah Khomeini
of blessed memory look by comparison like a pawn of Western capitalism. The megacorps called for a complete trade embargo, which

was not wholly successful. But, with the approval of Moscow and Washington, a joint Anglo Franco Israeli airborne task force struck Cairo in January 2002, routed the Egyptian army, and captured most of the fundamentalist leaders. Egypt remained the Arab Islamic Republic in name, but it was no longer anti-Western, and many of the chief "advisers" of the new government in Cairo were Europeans.

Once the pattern had been established, it became easier and easier for the rich countries to do as they pleased in the Third World. The United States intervened to suppress revolutions in Mexico and Brazil. When a soldier of vast charisma named Ibn Jihad ("Son of Struggle") overthrew the Saudi royal house in 2016, occupied Jordan, and later marched on Israel, a joint force of Soviet, American, and Israeli troops crushed his army in three days. A second Mexican revolution, more radical than the first, prompted the occupation of all of Mexico by American forces in 2022. Later that same year, the Soviet Union annexed Iran. A fierce border war between the Soviet Union and China ended when the GTC, now supported by an official resolution of the United Nations, quarantined China.

Only once did the system appear to swing leftward in defense of the oppressed. The blacks of the old Republic of South Africa, who had received savage treatment at the hands of the ruling Afrikaner minority after an abortive uprising in 2003, rose again in 2013. Given the rigid discipline and immeasurably superior fire power of the Afrikaner army, a great slaughter of black freedom fighters was inevitable, which would have destabilized the whole continent.

But the European governments jointly responsible for Africa stepped in swiftly. An Anglo-Franco-German mobile force engaged the South African regulars at three beachheads, threatened every city in the country with devastation, and compelled the government in Pretoria to enfranchise its black majority. With their ten-to-one demographic advantage, the blacks had no difficulty winning internationally supervised elections in 2014. They also drafted a new constitution for the country and renamed it the Southern African Republic: a slight but symbolically important change.

Yet, apart from the color of the skins of the ruling class, nothing else really changed in the southernmost country of Africa. The megacorps and the European senior powers continued to exploit the region as they saw fit. The whites who stayed on, although deprived of political power, lost only a small fraction of their wealth and privilege, and life went on almost as before.

To give the system of zones of special influence more legitimacy and to reexamine its details in the light of all that had happened since the now historic 1998 agreement, the Vienna conferees met again in the same city in 2026. They now elected to take a step toward true world government by reconstituting the United Nations as the Confederated States of Earth (CSE) and the countries within the various zones of special influence as trust territories of the CSE. Although the CSE mandated legal and administrative reforms, the so-called trust territories remained under the control of the same great powers as before.

In the eighteen years between the Second Vienna Conference and the Catastrophe of 2044, the domination of the poor countries by the rich was so complete that no significant military operations were required to keep it functioning smoothly. Most of the poor countries grew poorer, most of the rich grew richer, and all, as we have seen, were affected adversely by the depression that started in 2032.

In effect, the trustee system completed the "global revolution of Westernization" delineated in a book of the late twentieth century by the American historian Theodore H. Von Laue. Modern Western civilization, together with its largely Westernized allies in East Asia, had swallowed the world. The system was well built and could have lasted much longer than it did. But, as Von Laue also foresaw, it nourished in its entrails the fanged worms of strife and resentment that would one day strike it dead.

The Dissenters

The single real problem that confronted the new political order, so far as anyone in authority knew at the time, was the rapid proliferation of protest movements from within the core countries themselves in the 2030s and early 2040s. Given the mechanisms of control available to the new governing class, the rise of political dissent even in the throes of a depression may have seemed remarkable. It still seems remarkable, to some scholars.

A few of the movements were eccentric, marginally rational, and no threat to anyone but the people in them. One, the Sons and Daughters of Liberty, was frankly reactionary, demanding the restoration of a laissez-faire economy and full national sovereignty, but headed by a woman of charm and erudition who won a large following in North

America until her assassination in 2042. Also noteworthy on the American scene was the Church of the Purification, a popular anti-modernist religious sect. Its bands of self-styled Crusaders advocated nonviolent resistance to state authority and a return to primitive Christianity and rustic simplicity. Founded in 2038, it produced thousands of martyrs each year.

In the Soviet Union, the crafty and indefatigable party boss, Vassily Borisovich Kravchenko, became the object of a vitriolic personal attack by a faction of the ruling party known familiarly as the Old Bolsheviks, who accused him of corruption, Stalinist megalomania, and even murder. Having held office longer than any Soviet leader since Stalin himself, he had his share of enemies. But the Old Bolsheviks used their campaign against Kravchenko only as a pretext for mounting a fundamental assault on the whole Vienna system. In Soviet political discourse, personal attacks no matter how vigorous were within the pale; attacks on policy, or worse yet on political and economic structure, were beyond the pale and quite dangerous. But a resourceful antisystemic faction that disguised its structural criticisms as rebukes of someone who happened to embody the system ran fewer risks.

By far the most radical of the dissenting movements hatched in the years after 2032 was a formation known simply as the World party. Organized in Hicksville, New York, in the autumn of 2035 by a young graduate of the State University Center at Binghamton named Mitchell Greenwald, it started as a study group among former State University of New York classmates to examine the causes of the world depression and soon flowered into a true political party operating both in the open and underground, with the aim of building that most improbable of polities, a democratic socialist world republic.

From the beginning, the World party refused to attack the megacorporate establishment frontally, always arguing that it represented the "highest stage in the evolution of capital." Until at least 2039, there is no evidence that anyone in Washington or Zurich or elsewhere perceived anything seditious in the activities or program of the young party. Its emphasis on the need for a rational world order, for peace and justice, and for full integration of the global economy, together with its scathing denunciations of what it called "the rust-rimmed parties of nostalgia" such as the Sons and Daughters of Liberty, gave the authorities the impression that it represented a spontaneous attempt by the heavily indoctrinated youth of America to show their loyal support of the system and their hope for its even greater future.

In time, of course, these authorities did grow suspicious. They began collecting the underground publications of the World party as well as the reasonably innocuous materials it distributed at open meetings. As the party spread into Latin America, Western Europe, and even the Soviet Union, where it formed an uneasy alliance with elements of the Old Bolsheviks, CSE intelligence agents learned much more. Arrests were made, directives were issued, and the World party was proscribed. As of 2044, it had no more than fifty thousand members worldwide, many of them in prison, the others operating under cover. Greenwald himself was working as a robot's helper in a small factory in Christchurch, New Zealand, when the megacorporate world came to its abrupt end.

He had chosen a fortunate latitude.

INTERLUDE

These letters are quite different from those of Cousin Jens Otto. Indeed, the first document is not a letter at all but a review of an important book by my own great-grandfather, the historian Carl Jensen, one of the chief theoretical mentors of Mitchell Greenwald and the World party. Carl took exception to some of the remarks of the reviewer, Theodora Snell, and shared his dismay with the readers of the journal that had published the review. The editors invited the reviewer to reply to Carl's letter, Carl replied to the reply, and the result was a small war in the venerable pages of the *American Historical Review*. Such things happened regularly at that time in the groves of academe. As you will see, however, this was much more than a squabble between pundits about ideas and methods. Snell, I should add, was a well-known social scientist in her own right and holder of the Herman Kahn Professorship of Future Studies at Duke University.

[From the *American Historical Review* 139, no. 4 (Winter 2034): 1122–23.]

CARL JENSEN. Technocracy as the Highest Stage of Capital. *Wash-ington, D.C.: Federated Universities Press, 2033. Pp. xvii, 411; $77.75 (cloth). .961 MB; $49.50 (disc).*

Most familiar as a trenchant historian of utopian thought, Carl Jensen in this new work ventures into the muddy waters of philosophy of his-tory, coming through the experience with his ego intact but his scholarly reputation badly soiled. Exceptions spring to mind, such as Arnold J. Toynbee and Paolo Orsini, but historians have generally failed egre-giously when they tried to play the prophet or the inventor of grand speculative theories. Jensen's confused efforts fail as well.

The underlying thesis of his book is not unpromising. If the highest stage of capital from the economic point of view is monopoly (sic dixit Marx) and from the political point of view imperialism (sic dixit Lenin), "so in sociological terms," writes Jensen, "the highest stage of capital is technocracy, the inheritance of supreme power from entrepreneurs and politicians by a new global mandarinate of managers, experts, and pub-lic administrators" (p. 11). The parallels with Marx and Lenin are at least clever and allow Jensen to offer himself as the third member of a new triumvirate of socialist gurus. In place of the decadent Marxism-Leninism still honored in its dotage as the official ideology of the Soviet Union, Jensen gives us Marxism-Leninism-Jensenism.

Or so one might imagine, from his first chapter and its wealth of in-nuendos and bleak sarcasms. But, at the beginning of the second chapter, Jensen states explicitly that he does not hold himself out as a socialist. He does not presume to criticize capital or the new ruling class that he finds presiding over its "highest stage." Whereas, for Marx and Lenin, "highest" also meant "last" (with the further implication of "soon to fall"), for Jensen it simply means what it says, the most advanced form of capital that history has so far produced. Whether Jensen really ap-proves of it, he declines to say. "The task of the historian is to explain, not to judge" (p. 32).

The next five chapters constitute an intellectual history of technoc-racy as a utopian vision. Here Jensen revisits his own Heavens Below (2019), which treated the same theme more briefly, and Perfect Hells (2025), a study of twentieth-century dystopian fiction, which had ar-gued that some form of technocracy appears in nearly all such works. He adds a little to his earlier research, but not much. The fifth of these five chapters is perhaps the most valuable, for its lucid summing-up of the pedigree of technocratic thought, from Plato's philosopher-kings and Bacon's faint suggestions of rule by science in The New Atlantis *to the full-blown utopias of expertise in Saint-Simon, Comte, Bellamy, Wells, Burnham, and the ironic twist imparted to Burnham's ideas by George Orwell in* Nineteen Eighty-Four. *A revealing excursus on the thought of Engels provides some reason to believe that he may have been a closet technocrat, although not his better-known colleague Marx.*

The heart of Jensen's new book is his attempt in the remaining chapters to correlate technocracy as an image with the realities of governance in the present century. He leans heavily on such obscure conservative political tracts as Cedric Blaine's The New Managers *and the essays of Gertrud Escher in the* National Review, *especially "Government as Technique," which by no stretch of the imagination represent the views, much less the policies, of any state in the modern world. He also culls the speeches of commissioners of the General Trade Consortium, a ritual target of the current generation of Cassandras. The memoirs of business leaders and international civil servants supply him with further ammunition.*

He concludes that the people who really govern in the world of the 2030s are specialists in technology and management with doctorates from the top universities—Harvard and Yale, Berkeley and Binghamton, Oxford and Paris. These paragons of power have transformed our nominal rulers, whether presidents of states or chairpersons of corporate boards, into genial figureheads and, where necessary, convenient scapegoats. Our technocratic masters are still responsive to the democratically expressed will of the people, but that will itself "has been significantly weakened by the systems of persuasion" (p. 357) at the disposal of the masters.

In an epilogue, Jensen recalls the hopes of the twentieth-century sociologist Alvin W. Gouldner that the experts may somehow become centers of human emancipation, raising our world system to still greater heights of achievement in future times. "Perhaps," he says wistfully, "Gouldner's hopes have already come true, and we are too close to our saviors to see them clearly. Or perhaps not" (p. 392). On this ambiguous note, he brings his book to a close.

It is also a typical note. Jensen never quite tells us what he thinks or what he means at any point in this second half of his book. Nor does he furnish more than the wispiest evidence for his extensive claims about the nature of the governing class in the recent and contemporary world. In order to prove his case, Jensen's task should have been obvious: in-

ventory the people in positions of high authority in selected countries for a given period (say the years from 2020 to 2025), catalog their backgrounds and achievements, determine who formulated policy in a variety of similar situations, and draw the necessary conclusions. No one would have asked Jensen to try such a feat for the public life of the present decade, with so many documents still classified and so many of the leading people busy with current problems. But for the years before 2025, he could have managed nicely.

What he has done instead is to fall back on his experience as an intellectual historian and inventory an almost random assortment of ideas and images, leaving the realities to fend for themselves. He has confused thought with action, theory with practice, ideology with history. It will not do, and Technocracy as the Highest Stage of Capital should not have been published.

THEODORA SNELL
Duke University
♦

[From the American Historical Review 140, no. 2 (Summer 2035): 477–79.]

TO THE EDITOR:

I take this opportunity, for the first time in my academic career, to respond to a published review of one of my books. Professor Snell's assault on Technology as the Highest Stage of Capital (AHR 139, no. 4 [Winter 2034]: 1122–23) contains so many falsehoods and half-truths that I almost wonder if she did not read another book and confuse it with mine. But the quotations are right, even if one of the page references is not ("The task of the historian . . ." appears on pp. 32–33, not p. 32 alone). So perhaps she at least thumbed through portions of the book she was commissioned to review. For the purposes of this letter, I shall charitably assume that she did.

My charity extends no further. Let me begin by saying that I am not a latter-day Toynbee and have never pretended to be. My book offers an explanation of a body of empirical evidence. No more, no less. It is interpretive, not speculative, history. The statement that "Jensen gives us Marxism-Leninism-Jensenism" is the purest nonsense. I am sure Professor Snell knew it was nonsense when she wrote it, but presumably she loved the roll of her own rhetoric too much to press the delete button and preserve her integrity. In my book I "give us" nothing. There is no such *animal as Jensenism. In my first chapter, just as in my second, which Professor Snell may actually have read, I categorically disavow any af-filiation, ideological or otherwise, with Marxism, socialism, or any ism. If Professor Snell chooses to "imagine" (her own verb) what I offer rather than report accurately the contents of my book, that is her affair, but I would ask her not to make such imaginings public, for the sake of her own modest reputation no less than for mine.*

Professor Snell then questions the quality of my evidence for claiming that we live in a technocratic age. The obscurity of Gertud Escher is noted, for example. Yet in a single sample year, 2029, the name of this "obscure" essayist was invoked eighty-eight times in the publications of the CSE and twenty-eight times in those of the GTC, as I report in one of my notes, presumably unread by Professor Snell (n. 97, p. 299). But then she would not think much of evidence pertaining to the GTC in any case since it is a "ritual target" of my fellow Cassandras. Doubtless Pro-fessor Snell believes that the GTC is merely a public relations office for world business concerns, of no account in the governance of mankind.

Actually, so do most of my fellow Cassandras. By contrast with the celebrity of Escher, the GTC is still, twenty-seven years after its forma-tion, a little-known agency. One or two libertarian voices have loudly called attention to its real power, but, when I surveyed the citation in-dexes of the five leading so-called antisystemic periodicals in the United States and Europe, I found only 3.7 references per year to the GTC in their pages between 2010 and 2030 (n. 85, p. 262). This hardly consti-tutes "ritual" assault. Nor, for that matter, do I assault the GTC. It has done a great deal to integrate the world economy and political order, and for that service alone it may deserve our applause.

But let us get to the real point of Professor Snell's diatribe. She faults me for not showing in detail how the technocrats—the technical and pro-fessional specialists who have seized the commanding heights of power in the modern world—actually contrive to shape and dictate policy, both state and corporate.

Very good. I agree completely. As I write in the book she has only skimmed, "No one can document the process by which the decisions of the technical intelligentsia are translated into public policy because in almost every instance the 'translation' occurs behind closed doors, out of view, unrecorded and unconfessed" (pp. 374–75). From memoirs, one may see fragments of the process, but never the whole chain of events from start to finish. No politician or board chairperson is ever likely to admit that he or she was the tool of a gaggle of professional advisers, and no adviser is going to risk his or her reputation and freedom by claiming to have wielded sovereign power. The situation is further confused when a technocrat simultaneously holds political or corporate high office, as often happens and has been happening for decades. Think only of such prominent figures of the late twentieth-century world as Jimmy Carter (engineer, agribusinessman, American president), George Shultz (economist, corporate executive, American secretary of state), or Mikhail Gorbachev (agronomist, general secretary of the Communist party of the Soviet Union). And what to make of that ultimate politician, Vassily Kravchenko, who spent ten years managing aerospace factories before his dazzling ascent to the office of Soviet premier?

But one can show this much, and I have shown it: the published technical reports of qualified experts working for governments and corporations time and again reach conclusions that may later be found, paraphrased and retouched, in laws, executive orders, judicial verdicts, and corporate policies. The most obvious correlations are visible in the doings of the United Nations and now the CSE. Corporate records are far less accessible, and many national governments (see p. 333, Professor Snell) remain somewhat less technocraticized than world agencies. All the same, the pattern is clear, and the inferences I draw are sound.

CARL JENSEN
University of New Mexico

PROFESSOR THEODORA SNELL REPLIES:

The readers of the AHR owe a debt of gratitude to Professor Jensen for his vigilant detection of an erroneous citation in my review. He is quite right. The sentence that I quoted, "The task of the historian . . . ," does indeed appear on pages 32–33, not on page 32 alone. We can all rest more comfortably at night knowing that this mistake has been caught at last. Although only the last word of the sentence quoted is actually found on page 33, the principle holds good: in our profession, errors of all magnitudes must be promptly discovered, humbly recanted, and swiftly corrected.

Only one thing troubles me. If the principle applies to Theodora Snell, why does it not also apply to Carl Jensen?

For example, Jensen suggests that I called Gertrud Escher "obscure." If Professor Jensen will take the trouble to read what I wrote, he will see that I called Cedric Blaine's book obscure, not Escher's essays. Escher is a prominent scholar and journalist of the highest caliber, and often quoted. This, however, does not prove that she is right or that she wields vast influence in the so-called ruling class.

Nor does it help to drop vague hints about the "real power" of the GTC or compare the findings of a handful of published technical reports to the wording of a handful of laws, orders, and rulings. The crux of my criticism is simply that Professor Jensen does not and cannot know what he is talking about. He admits his evidence is woefully inadequate, but he jumps to his conclusions anyway.

I could just as well argue that politicians and board chairpersons adopt the recommendations of experts because they are shrewd enough to see that the experts are right. The job of policymakers is not so much to make policy as to choose the best policy from the options that specialists identify and, most important of all, to choose the right specialists in the first place. I could also just as well argue that the only technical reports normally made available to the public are those that have led to laws, orders, and rulings; the rejected reports are, sensibly enough, erased and forgotten. I do not so argue because I have no concrete evidence. But that would never stop Professor Jensen.

Teaching Professor Jensen new tricks so late in his day is probably out of the question. Still, I am glad that this exchange has taken place, for the sake of younger historians coming along, who cannot be reminded often enough that suppositions are no substitute for evidence.

THEODORA SNELL
Duke University

♦

[From the *American Historical Review* 140, no. 4 (Winter 2035): 1092.]

TO THE EDITOR:

I beg your indulgence to comment on Professor Snell's reply to my evaluation of her review (AHR, 140, no. 2 [Winter 2035]: 478–79).

On the key issue, I find myself in the position of the witness who sees one man holding a revolver pointed at a second man. The first man pulls the trigger. There is a loud bang, and the second falls to the floor dead. Has the witness seen a murder? If so, has he seen the murderer or the murder weapon? Not necessarily. The corpse may have been the victim of a heart attack. Or, if he was shot to death, the bullet that killed him may have come through an open window, and the first man may have been firing blanks or may have missed his mark.

No, we cannot ever really know anything. In this imperfect world, we must use our common sense and decide what is most plausible on the basis of the evidence at hand. Unfortunately, not all of us are gifted with common sense.

A final remark. The young historians for whom Professor Snell displays such tender solicitude have less to fear these days. Thanks to the fuss about Technocracy as the Highest Stage of Capital, fueled in part by her own review, I have lost my tenured post at the University of New Mexico and been forced to accept an early retirement. I do not blame the editors of the AHR and would still hold them blameless if they chose to exercise caution and not print this letter.

CARL JENSEN
Albuquerque, N.M.

◆

The "fuss" to which Carl refers had little to do with academic reviews of his book. The editors at Federated Universities Press in Washington who had approved his manuscript for publication were fired in the summer of 2035 for "poor judgment." At the same time, the trustees of the University of New Mexico insisted on revoking his tenure after copies of his book were brought to their attention by an anonymous vigilante, no doubt in the employ of the GTC. Subsequently, Carl was prosecuted for seditious libel and his book removed from libraries and bookstores. Such a step was unusual in the United States in this period, but the depression forced the suspension or open violation of civil liberties everywhere. Under the circumstances, Carl got off lightly. He lived in modest comfort in retirement until 2044, wrote two more (unpublished) books, and corresponded frequently with Mitchell Greenwald.

3

FOULING THE NEST

The Living Earth

It is time now to survey the consequences of the economy and politics of Earth, Inc., for that other earth: our planet, which gives us life, and will always, wherever we go, remain our sacred home. Everyone knows the story of how the Commonwealth subjected the planet to a thorough scrubbing and cleansing in the late twenty-first century. As we look back, this may have been its most lasting achievement. Why were such strenuous efforts needed in the first place? Why were the lords of capital such careless stewards of the world entrusted to them by history? Or have they been unfairly maligned?

First, I must say that earth's biosphere, more emphatically even than the global order created by capital or the order that prevails today, is a single geophysical and biochemical system, closely resembling a living organism. Within definable limits, it has the power to restore itself, but the interdependence of its parts is so complete that one cannot attack any individual part without somehow affecting the whole.

We call it the biosphere because it is the space occupied by life on this planet and because it is spherical in shape, just like one of the outer layers of an onion. As Pierre Teilhard de Chardin taught us centuries ago, the geometry of spheres always imposes certain constraints on whatever assumes this form, just as it opens many opportunities for a higher and more complex existence. When, in the ages of capital, civilization became spherical, it extruded new spheres of its own making: a sociosphere of common institutions, a noosphere of shared consciousness. But at all times modern civilization remained slavishly dependent on the material system that allows a space for life on this planet.

During the early modern centuries, from the sixteenth to the eighteenth, the equilibrium of the biosphere was not fundamentally disturbed. Here and there difficulties arose, as they had always done since the beginning of human life on earth: droughts, floods, volcanic eruptions, plagues, overcropped and overgrazed land turning to desert. But these were local disasters, of the sort that had caused the downfall of the cliff dwellers of Colorado or ancient Zimbabwe in southeast Africa.

In the nineteenth century, the voracious appetite of modern mechanized industry led to an unprecedented scramble for minerals, the burning of unprecedented quantities of fossil fuels, and a surge in the human population also without precedent in world history. The tempo of consumption accelerated throughout the twentieth century and on into the twenty-first. By the third quarter of the twentieth century, any fool could see that the biosphere was in distress, as the supply of readily accessible mineral wealth began to run low and the air, water, and soil of the planet were lethally contaminated by the copious wastes of industry. It was not unlike what happens to the human body when it is poisoned by the excreta of invading microorganisms. Moreover, the problems were not individual or local but plural and universal. The whole biosphere had come under attack.

The lords of capital and their allies in government understood the situation fairly well. Spurred by nagging environmentalists and genuinely concerned that the long-term profitability of their enterprises might be at risk, they made a serious effort to mend their ways. Some of the biggest corporations and richest countries led the fight. Science and technology were enlisted in a campaign to reduce noxious emissions, clean up waterways, safely dispose of nuclear garbage, conserve energy, curb the use of fossil fuels, develop new higher-yielding grains, shrink population growth to near zero, and much more.

As early as the 1980s, it appeared that the struggle to restore the equilibrium of the biosphere was being won. Such was not the case. Although remedies had been found for some of the most visible and pressing problems, they were too often only stopgap measures, while still other problems were not addressed effectively at all. As the years wore on, the consequences of this environmental "too-little-too-lateness" grew more and more clear, especially for the people of the poorest countries of the Third World.

People and Food

The primary need, as always in human history, was to ensure that for every person on earth enough food was available to sustain life and health every day. Nature is unforgiving in such matters. If the average human being requires a daily ration of two thousand calories derived from fats, carbohydrates, and proteins together with certain vitamins and minerals, and if eight billion people are alive, then on the table or in the bowl sixteen trillion calories must appear every day, containing the minimal quantities of each nutrient that the body demands. A world population of five billion must have ten trillion calories. A world population of one billion must have two trillion calories. Even today we have not learned to evade this fundamental equation, without suspending animation; and life in a hibertube, although it may be life, is surely not living.

Of the approximately 115 billion people who have ever lived, four billion were walking the earth in the year 1975, five billion in 1986, six billion in 1998, seven billion in 2013, and eight billion in 2032. As these figures show, the rate of world population growth did fall steadily after the 1970s. Growth reached a rate of 1.8 percent per year during the great demographic splurge of the third quarter of the twentieth century, more than twice as high as in the period from 1850 to 1950, and then tapered toward zero in a painfully slow descending curve. By 2044, the population of the planet was only 8.3 billion.

But the damage, so to speak, had been done. So many children were born in the third quarter of the twentieth century who lived to reproduce in the third and fourth quarters, and well into the 2000s, that the falling birth rate could not succeed in producing a net annual gain of zero even as late as 2044. The formidable rise in death rates in some countries was canceled out by a corresponding drop in death rates in others, as advances in medicine prolonged the lives of millions for decades. The rich and the old flourished, at the expense of the poor and the young.

Most of the population growth, as you would expect, took place in the industrially less developed parts of the world, in the zones of special influence. Among the peasants and workingpeople of these countries, child labor was still profitable, religious sanctions against birth control were more likely to carry weight, and the costs of raising and educating children were—or were perceived to be—less burdensome. Whereas the population of the richest thirty-five countries increased by only 250 million between 1985 and 2044, the population of all the rest grew by three billion. India, with three-quarters of a billion people in 1985, had 1.4 billion in 2044. Nigeria went from ninety million to 285 million in the same period.

Now it is quite true that numbers in and of themselves tell us nothing. Countries with strong economies and just policies can support a rising birth rate. The so-called overpopulation of the world in the first half of the twenty-first century was a result, not a primary cause, of the crisis of the world system in that age. It meant higher infant mortality, chronic malnutrition, occasional starvation, and increased susceptibility to disease for two or three additional billion human beings, but such suffering did not bring the global economy crashing down or, in any literal sense, destroy the biosphere.

Even if the world's population had remained at six billion for the whole first half of the twenty-first century, the course of history might have been altered only slightly. The peripheral countries would still have been poor, the core countries would still have been rich, and the biosphere might have sustained the same or even more damage. A family of five can easily squander as many resources as a family of eight, if it gets the chance. It can devour a lot more. In the year 2030, the average person in the richest countries consumed forty-five times as much of the gross world product as the average person in all the others.

Nevertheless, overpopulation did bring more troubles than the suffering of the poor. A malnourished people will more likely lapse into apathy than flare into anger—but only if they remain distributed in the traditional way, as a widely dispersed and relatively immobile peasantry. Large segments of the peasantries of the late twentieth and early twenty-first centuries did not remain dispersed and immobile. Cheap transport and the ferment of capital lured hundreds of millions of such people into the cities of the Third World, where they congregated in outrageous shantytowns and slums, looking for work, looking for food, and sometimes (but not usually) finding both.

As early as 2000, most of the metropolises of Africa, South Asia, and Latin America were already filthy human formicaries settled by uncountable millions of people: Mexico City by at least twenty-five million, Cairo by nineteen, Calcutta by eighteen, Bombay by sixteen, Manila by eleven. No one can be sure of these figures. The actual totals were probably higher.

By 2030, the congestion had become unimaginable. The best estimates fixed the population of Mexico City, including all its satellite towns and villages of squatters, at fifty-two million. Calcutta now "sheltered" thirty-eight million people and Cairo thirty-two. Lagos was a nightmarish agglomeration of fifteen million people, Kinshasa of twelve million, Abidjan of 8.5 million. In South America, giantism afflicted Rio de Janeiro, São Paulo, Bogotá, and Caracas, all with twenty million inhabitants or more. There were twenty-seven million people in Jakarta and thirteen million in its rival at the eastern end of Java, Surabaja. In all, forty cities in the Third World reported populations in excess of fifteen million people. But again, such statistics are not dependable since many immigrants from the countryside came and went, lived and died, without leaving a trace.

Inside these cities people and their wastes accumulated at an alarming rate. Densities of five thousand persons per hectare were not uncommon. Refuse collection was sporadic or, in some of the newer, unpaved quarters, nonexistent. Water and sewer systems reached only parts of each city, the water supply was contaminated, smog blackened the air, poorly built tenement houses often collapsed, burying their inhabitants, and many people lived in homemade huts fashioned from debris.

Worse yet, perhaps, was the failure of these cities to generate any sense of civic pride or tradition or responsibility. In most of them, smuggling, theft, extortion, vigilante justice, and random violence became a way of life. Drugs and tobacco were plentiful. Food riots and spontaneous work stoppages occurred with tedious regularity. People nearly comatose one day might erupt the next, ambushing a street thief or a census taker or a policeman and dismembering him on the spot. The wealthy kept to their fortified enclaves and diverted most of each city's meager revenues into their own pockets.

A typical incident was the rampage in Lagos in 2016. After a heavy rainfall that lasted three days and flooded hundreds of hectares of the city, an angry mob of homeless and unfed poor people invaded Broad Street, killed the police who stood in their path, and began systematically overturning and burning every vehicle they could find, while others looted shops and stalls along the city's main thoroughfare. A detachment of Nigerian army troops turned its machine guns on the

crowd, which melted away as quickly as it had formed. More than
five hundred people had lost their lives. The story had become so
commonplace that only one international news service bothered to
report it.

But, as time went by, the concentration of so much misery in such
relatively small spaces did play a role in the political and economic
destabilization of various poor countries. Costly attempts to clean
up the cities increased national debts. Demagogues exploited mass
unrest for their own advantage, inspiring the wealthy to hire other
demagogues to establish neofascist regimes that freely resorted to
genocidal repression. Authentic revolutions broke out, and these in
turn were ruthlessly put down or subverted by the forces of rich patron states protecting their interests in their zones of special influence.

The classic cases date from 2022, the year that the United States
took charge of Mexico and the Soviet Union incorporated Iran into
itself as the "Iranian Soviet Socialist Republic." The fact that Mexico
City at that time had forty-seven million and Teheran twenty-one
million people was far from irrelevant. Unrest in the two capitals
helped lead to the changes of government that prompted foreign
intervention.

Of more importance to the poor themselves was that old basic
equation of calories and bodies. I said earlier that starvation in the
Third World was merely "occasional." So it was. At most 200 million
people starved to death in the first forty-four years of the twenty-first
century. Seventy-five percent of these were Africans, chiefly rural
women and young children. A greater problem was severe malnutrition, from which billions suffered in many parts of the world.

Nothing could have been more absurd than hunger in the twenty-
first century, down to 2044. Often, the immediate problem was political instability in the affected countries, which impeded relief efforts;
just as often, people starved because of a lack of adequate transport
or storage facilities for the food they already had. Seldom was it a
case of a global failure of supply. Whether enlisted in megacorps like
Hollings-Gray or in lesser concerns, agribusinessmen understood
the indispensability of Third World labor and Third World markets
to the world economy and did what they could to provide enough
food, as long as they made a reasonable profit or received state sub-
sidies for their "humanitarian" efforts.

The attempt to preserve the adequacy of global food supplies in
the last age of capital is a complex story, with many ups and downs.

If one looks only at the swift progress of biotechnology and the agricultural sciences, it seems impossible that any human being could have found a way to starve in such a time. If one looks only at the plight of the biosphere, the sheer size of the earth's population, and the great gulf between rich and poor, it seems impossible that so many people were fed at all.

The strain on the biosphere was merciless. To raise food, three ingredients were essential: a clean sky, fresh water, and good soil. All three were in dwindling supply as the new century began.

The most unexpected problem was the sky. Industrial contaminants, such as oxides of sulfur and nitrogen, heavy metals, and chlorofluorocarbons, started filling the air in toxic proportions in the third quarter of the twentieth century. They depleted the ozone layer that shields us from the full force of the sun's ultraviolet radiation, they killed forests and lakes with acidic rain, they generated smog, and, directly or indirectly, they damaged crops. Remedies were at hand, such as banning the production of chlorofluorocarbons (once used for refrigeration, packaging, and insulation) and limiting the burning of coal or requiring emission control systems, but the problem unfolded more rapidly than it could be understood or managed. For every country or corporation that adopted restrictions to save the air, two others evaded or ignored them. In defense of the wrongdoers, it must be said that sometimes they had no choice. To make a profit, to pay their debts, to balance their budgets, to meet the growing demands of a growing world population, the luxury of a clean sky was something they could not afford.

As a result, the situation worsened. Deep "holes" appeared in the ozone layer, first observed over Antarctica in the 1980s. By the year 2010, the level of ultraviolet light striking the earth's surface had become quite dangerous, producing a marked increase in smog, skin cancer, and crop damage. Once confined to the wildlands of higher elevations, acidic rain, snow, and fog began to affect the whole biosphere, causing grave problems for farmers and ranchers as well as lumberjacks and fishermen. The countries that suffered the most were those in the semiperiphery, such as Brazil, Mexico, and China, who were scrambling to qualify for membership in the core and could least spare the time and the capital needed to fight pollution.

Still more vital to the traditional agriculture of the late modern world was an abundance of clean fresh water for irrigation. At the turn of the century, 40 percent of the food produced worldwide was grown on irrigated land. Here, too, industrial contaminants posed a major problem, which could be remedied only by strict prohibitions against the indiscriminate burial of untreated toxic wastes and their discharge into rivers and lakes. Once more, the poorer countries usually found such regulations forbiddingly expensive.

But fresh water was also in short supply in many parts of the planet because of overuse. Water was removed more rapidly than it could be replaced by the natural operation of the water cycle. Excessive withdrawals for irrigation, industry, and municipalities critically lowered water tables in the southern half of the Indian subcontinent, the western half of the United States, northern China, Mexico, and portions of the Soviet Union. The loss of so many forests contributed further to the shortage since runoffs that once were slowed and trapped by the root systems of trees now moved rapidly across the land, carrying precious topsoil with them. Except in wet seasons, rivers and lakes shriveled. Wells ran dry; aquifers diminished. Some of the leading grain-producing regions of the earth, which had saved millions from starvation in the late twentieth century, were threatened with conversion to dryland farming and a consequent steep fall in their productivity.

In the new century, the threats materialized. For one instance, the Ogallala Aquifer, a vast underground reservoir supplying fresh water to parts of eight American states in the Midwest and Southwest, was sucked almost completely dry by 2005. Nebraska and Kansas, in particular, found themselves bereft of water for irrigation, and the agribusinessmen, after figuring the costs of replenishing the aquifer artificially, pulled up stakes and left.

In some regions, such as northern China, it paid to replenish, and the job was done, by capturing excess runoff and diverting streams. Desalination of ocean water was another useful trick, which became more feasible in the 2020s with the development of highly efficient extractors and the lower costs of energy. But lack of accessible fresh water remained a serious problem for food producers throughout the last age of capital.

Beyond clean skies and water, agriculture also required good topsoil. Just as water tables fell faster than they could be recharged, so topsoil was lost to erosion more rapidly than it could be replaced by natural processes. Although the causes of erosion were many, in the end they reduced to one: overuse of the land. Deforestation, overgrazing, insufficient fallowing, and failure to rotate crops—responses to inexorably rising demands for food, timber, and firewood—led to the blowing and washing away of billions of tons of topsoil. The rate of net loss worldwide amounted to more than 3 percent per decade between 1970 and 2020. Almost every major food-producing country on earth contributed to the problem.

At its worst, soil erosion turned productive land into desert. From the 1970s onward, eight million hectares a year were added to the world's deserts, until, by 2030, one-third of all the land that had been arable in the year 1970 was good for little or nothing. The northern half of Africa was the area most ruinously affected, but the deserts spread in North America, Australia, Spain, China, the Soviet Union, and elsewhere as well. Once set in full motion, the process fed on itself through a complex of biological, chemical, and atmospheric interactions. For all practical purposes, it could not be reversed.

Almost miraculously, food continued to be produced in barely adequate quantities, in spite of everything. With less land, less water, and dirtier air, farmers and agribusinessmen managed to wring more nourishment from the resources at their disposal by a combination of simple cunning and advanced technology.

Some of the strategies adopted were far from glamorous. Improved crop rotation systems and the replacement of single-crop by multiple-crop fields reduced dependence on costly artificial fertilizers and pesticides and actually increased yields in the long run, not to mention profits. Varieties of grains that thrived especially well in dry soils and enjoyed a high resistance to disease and pests were planted in preference to the fat but fragile superplants of the old "Green Revolution." Merely using less fertilizer on rich soils and more on poor resulted in substantially greater total harvests, even if the rich soils no longer produced quite as much food as before. The latter was a ploy that worked with special effectiveness for the major agribusinesses, which held millions of hectares and could develop master plans for optimal use of resources.

Aided by advances in computer technology, bioengineers supplemented the new agricultural wisdom with techniques in gene-splicing and cell culturing that enabled them to play god in the plant kingdom. They radically transformed thousands of strains of existing species and created hundreds of commercially useful new ones. Plants were evolved that performed their own nitrogen-fixing and therefore no longer needed fertilizers; plants in which photosynthesis occurred at two or three times the normal rate, enabling them to grow bigger and faster; plants that were almost entirely resistant to selected microorganisms and pests; plants that required less water and less sunlight; plants that thrived in marginal soils, although their ancestors needed the best; and plants combining one or more of these qualities with vastly increased yields.

The most spectacular of the new plant species, nicknamed the "King Plant," was a tall, dark green beauty with broad edible leaves that tasted something like a cross between Bibb lettuce and spinach, a stalk that produced a strong versatile fiber much prized in the textile industry, a nitrogen-fixing root system, a red starchy tuber more flavorful than potatoes, and crisp seedpods resembling snow peas. Three vegetables in one, the King Plant thrived in many soils, had few natural enemies, and of course needed no fertilizer of any kind. Brought to the market in 2011 after extensive research and development, it was the most popular food plant in North America and Europe for decades.

The bioengineers also did some of their best work with food plants that had been largely ignored by researchers in the twentieth century, plants of special importance to farmers in Latin America and Africa, such as amaranth, millet, sorghum, cassava, beans, and yams. Greatly improved strains were produced in the laboratory and saved millions of lives in tropical and desert countries whose people either could not or would not grow wheat and rice.

A further development, which came only after 2025, was the building on wasteland of immense "tank farms," where bioengineered edible algae of four basic types were grown in vats. The algae were then trucked to food factories, processed, textured, supplemented, flavored, and sold for both human and animal consumption. These new "synthafoods," including some less successful varieties manufactured from still other microorganisms, took hold rather slowly but made their contribution to relieving world hunger.

One category of foods that made a contribution of a wholly different sort was animal food. We sometimes have difficulty imagining how people managed to eat flesh at all, but it was a staple nutrient of most of the inhabitants of the rich countries down through the twentieth century, despite steeply rising prices and the warnings of the medical community.

Traumatized by the high cost of flesh eating, the public finally heeded the advice of physicians and cut its consumption of animal food by 50 percent throughout the developed world in only five years. Improved meat, cheese, and butter substitutes made from vegetable products helped to ease the transition. Even the world-famous American hamburger, a sandwich containing a round slab of grilled chopped beef, found itself upstaged in the fast food chains by the "earthburger," a palatable concoction of lentils and tofu reinforced by vegetable adhesives that gave it the same texture and moistness as meat. The "Big Earth" made popular by one chain provided twice the nutrition of its deluxe hamburger at one-third the cost.

Even after the return of general prosperity in the early twenty-first century, the consumption of animal foods continued to decline. The result was the liberation of much of the land, water, feed, and labor hitherto devoted to livestock and the raising of crops in their place. Since seven pounds of plant food had been required to grow one pound of meat, the net gain in food production made possible by the shift of the rich countries to a primarily vegetarian diet was substantial.

Only seafood was exempt from the declining acceptance of animal foods in the twenty-first century. The price of most wild fish remained just as high as the price of red meat, but the worldwide diffusion of aquaculture brought seafood within the reach of more than half the world's people. Begun on a large scale in East Asia in the late twentieth century, fish farming progressed rapidly in the 1990s and 2000s. Trout, salmon, oysters, crayfish, and hundreds of other species raised in pens and tanks, or in cages suspended in the open sea, were a major source of protein. Fish meal processed from heads, fins, and bones became an important ingredient of the new synthafoods.

In all, according to the estimates of the agricultural historian Hu Hanbo of Xiangtan, the harvests lost between 1995 and 2044 because of the degradation of the biosphere were matched by the rising productivity of agriculture. Taking all factors into account, such as the loss of fertile soil to urbanization or the diversion of fresh capital to farming, Hu argues that people had almost as much to eat, worldwide, in 2044 as they had in 1995. The output of food came within one or two percentage points of matching the increase in population.

Progress in Energy

Clearly, things could have been much worse. One additional reason why, perhaps, they were not was the progress of energy technologies. Modern agriculture consumed not only sunlight, air, water, and soil but also prodigious amounts of energy. The manufacture and use of farm machinery, including modern computerized irrigation systems, chemical fertilizers, pesticides, and the transport required to bring equipment to the farms and the produce of farms to the market, all consumed energy. Even in much of the Third World agriculture became mechanized in the last age of capital, as agribusinessmen displaced feudal and peasant landholders.

Under the circumstances, a sound energy economy was indispensable to agriculture. It was also indispensable to industry, commerce, public services, and all the rest of life. Abundant oil, natural gas, and coal had facilitated the great boom in the capitalist world economy of the period from 1945 to 1970. The energy conservation measures put into effect in the decades after 1975 helped to keep the economic downturn of those years moderate and (until 1995 at least) manageable. Unsurprisingly, the boom of the period from 2001 to 2032 hinged in great part on advances in the production and cheapness of energy.

In the late twentieth century, forecasters had anticipated the swift phasing out of fossil fuels in the new century, as it became technologically and economically feasible to tap alternative renewable sources such as solar, wind, tidal, biomass, and geothermal power. Other, less environmentally conscious futurists fixed their hopes on nuclear energy, whether from conventional or fast-breeder fission reactors or fusion systems. But which technologies would be developed first, and would costs be slashed deeply enough to tempt manufacturers, farmers, and other consumers of energy to forego their addiction to fossil fuels?

As the years passed, the technology for exploiting renewable energy sources did improve dramatically. Costs fell—but not as precipitously as environmentalists had hoped. In 1975, shortly after governments and corporations began deliberately limiting their use of fossil fuels and searching for alternatives in the wake of the Arab oil embargo of 1973, 82 percent of the world's energy needs were met by oil, gas, and coal. In 1995, 78 percent of its needs were still met in this way and, in 2010, 74 percent. By 2030, the figure had dropped only to 71 percent.

Of the alternatives to fossil fuels on which many countries did increasingly rely, no single source gained an overwhelming advantage during the first several decades of the new century. By 2030, hydroelectric power supplied 7 percent of the world's needs, solar power in its many forms accounted for 6 percent, wind power for 3 percent, and all the rest for 13 percent. Nuclear energy did especially well, showing a fivefold increase between 1975 and 2030, as a result of the perfection of fusion generators. Most of the old-fashioned nuclear fission reactors, whether fast breeding or conventional, ceased operation in the early years of the new century. But fossil fuels remained the largest source of energy by a substantial margin.

There were essentially three reasons for the glacial velocity of the shift from fossil fuels to alternative energy technologies. First, harnessing the sun, the wind, the tides, and other renewable resources proved easier to achieve in the laboratory or test site than in the marketplace. Gigantic solar and wind farms flowered in desert areas or other wastelands. The energy they harvested poured efficiently into power grids with the help of the new warm-temperature superconductors perfected in the 1990s. But the costs of manufacturing, installing, and coaxing useful energy from the new technologies remained, at best, a little higher than the costs of fossil fuels and, at worst, prohibitively expensive.

Much the same story must be told of nuclear power. Cost overruns in production of facilities, spectacular accidents at sites like Three Mile Island, Chernobyl, and Creys-Malville, and the high price tag of keeping reactors in good repair and safely disposing of radioactive wastes ultimately doomed fission. Then, after decades of research in several countries, the first commercial nuclear fusion plant opened in Japan in 2012, exploiting the vast stores of energy in the heavy isotopes of hydrogen.

At first fusion power seemed the answer to every capitalist's dreams. It required an abundance of capital, readily available only to the megacorps. Compared to the old fission reactors, and despite the implausibly high temperatures required to ignite the fusion process, it was quite safe, with no risk of catastrophic meltdowns. Its fuels could be extracted from ordinary seawater. When they fused, all they produced besides clean energy was the inert gas helium. Within ten years of the opening of the plant in Tokyo, fifty fusion generators were in operation in eight countries, supplying as much energy as all the hydroelectric plants in the world put together.

But there were snags. Fusion generators cost a fortune to build, and another fortune to maintain. For reasons not fully understood by nuclear physicists until the discoveries of Ivan Grushkov and Jerzy Pula in 2017, they also yielded much less energy per dollar invested than anyone had foreseen. Near-hysterical overinvestment in fusion power was the direct cause of the bankruptcy of the Standard Energy Corporation in February 2032, which in turn touched off the depression of 2032–44. The Standard Energy Corporation was the only megacorp that had not taken the trouble to diversify its holdings on a broad scale, preferring to rely primarily on its preeminence in the energy industry and in fusion power above all. It paid the ultimate price.

The final reason for the tardiness of the transition from fossil fuels was a combination of plain economics and the new imperialism. All warnings of imminent exhaustion notwithstanding, the world's proven exploitable reserves of oil in the year 2000 exceeded 1.4 trillion barrels, enough to last seventy years at the average rate of oil consumption during the preceding decade. Proven exploitable reserves of natural gas exceeded the equivalent of 500 billion barrels of oil, and there was enough recoverable coal to last at current consumption rates until the second quarter of the twenty-second century.

Especially for semiperipheral countries with limited capital struggling to enter the core or stave off economic disaster, the availability and low price of fossil fuels (in particular, oil) was difficult to resist. It was almost equally irresistible for megacorps. For them, as for anyone in the world, a dollar saved was still a dollar earned, and the hard, homely truth was that fossil fuels delivered more energy for the dollar than the alternatives.

In the late twentieth century, experts had doubted that this situation could continue, thanks to the power of international oil cartels and the political instability of the Middle East. Fears of a new surge in oil prices, repeating the events of the 1970s, mingled with fears of the partial or complete breakdown of the oil trade. As reserves in the Western Hemisphere, South Asia, and the Soviet Union approached depletion, by far the largest remaining reserves of cheap exploitable oil were in the Middle East. Of the 1.4 trillion barrels known to exist in 2000, two-thirds (and 90 percent of the best and cheapest) were Middle Eastern. One-quarter of the proven reserves of natural gas were Iranian.

Weary of being held hostage by Middle Eastern potentates, the rich countries and the megacorps rose to the challenge by implementing the Vienna accords of 1998. I have already reviewed the various military actions taken in North Africa and the Middle East between 2002 and 2022; such actions were intended only to reinforce and protect a far-ranging policy of economic and political imperialism that aimed at the virtual enserfment of the whole Third World, not excluding the countries of the Middle East.

Under various pretexts, large numbers of Soviet troops marched wherever they pleased throughout the Middle East with the watchful consent of the Western powers and in intimate collaboration with the megacorps. Their methods were borrowed (as one Soviet general admitted to an Indian journalist) from Genghis Khan. At the same time, Soviet and megacorp advisers occupied key positions in Middle Eastern governments and ensured to the world energy market a plentiful supply of cheap Middle Eastern oil and gas. The low point in Middle Eastern autonomy may have been reached when it was discovered in 2029, through the indiscretions of a mistress, that the Arabian oil minister's chief aide, Faroukh al-Khalidi, was actually an American megacorporate executive named Frank Calhoun. The son of the former American ambassador in Riyadh, Calhoun had been a vice-president for liaison of the Standard Energy Corporation throughout his years of service to the Arabian government.

At any rate, the flow of fossil fuels from the Middle East did not stop or even ebb during the last age of capital. It was as if a man fatally addicted to pop had suddenly won free access to all he could use. Even if he knew he should ignore this alluring trove, or at the very least partake sparingly, what would you expect him to do?

You would expect him to dive in. And this is more or less what happened in the first half of the twenty-first century. Environmentalists shook their fists. Companies burning coal pointed with pride (when they could) to the desulfurizing filters on their smokestacks and their new fluidized bed combustion systems, which emitted relatively few pollutants. Others did convert, in circumstances where conversion was practicable, to solar or wind or tidal or fusion power. But the fact remained that whoever burned fossil fuels released into the atmosphere large quantities of carbon dioxide, not immediately harmful to anyone or anything, but in sufficient amounts to alter the climate of our beleaguered earth.

Life in a Greenhouse

In the end, it was this insult to the biosphere, rather than toxic contamination, that most threatened civilization in the twenty-first century. In the 1970s, climatologists had been sharply divided between those who expected a general warming of the earth because of the greenhouse effect and those who expected a new, if minor, ice age because of the deflection of sunlight by dust particles and industrial pollutants in the atmosphere. In the 1980s, the protagonists of the greenhouse theory generally carried the day. As it worked out, they were indeed right, but overly optimistic about the time still available to try to halt the progress of the effect.

At first climatologists thought the effect was due almost exclusively to growing concentrations in the atmosphere of carbon dioxide (CO_2). Participants at the Villach Conference in Austria in 1985—in retrospect one of the most important international meetings of scientists in world history—established that several gases were responsible, although CO_2 remained at the top of the list. The distinguishing feature of such gases was their ability to admit radiation from the sun but trap infrared radiation reflected upward from the earth's surface. In this way they prevented the escape of heat from the lower atmosphere, much like the walls and ceiling of a greenhouse. Other gases, besides CO_2, were ozone, methane, nitrous oxide, and several chlorofluorocarbons.

As you must have learned in school, scientists can ascertain the composition of the earth's atmosphere in earlier centuries by examining glacial ice cores. Such studies proved that the quantity of greenhouse gases in the air had risen phenomenally since the eighteenth century. In 1800, the amount of CO_2 in the atmosphere was 275 parts per million; in 1960, 310; and, in 2000, 365. Most of this gain was due to the burning of fossil fuels and to erosion and deforestation (because plants consume generous amounts of CO_2 during photosynthesis). By 2040, the atmosphere contained 555 parts per million.

The other greenhouse gases showed a similar or even more alarming pattern of rapid increase in the lower atmosphere. The reasons were various, from the burning of fossil and biomass fuels to the growing use of fertilizer, industrial applications of chlorofluorocarbons, and, in the case of methane, production of the gas by the decay of organic matter in rice paddies, to which many hectares were added in this period to help feed the world's rising population. It was also discovered that much of the methane resulted from atmospheric reactions involving carbon monoxide, a familiar waste product of the internal combustion engine. Climatologists in the 2030s were able to attribute two-thirds of the warming that had occurred in the past fifty years to greenhouse gases other than CO_2.

The warming itself did not come as a surprise. But the speed of its arrival did astonish the climate modelers. Between 1880 and 1980, the global mean temperature had risen by only .5 degrees Centigrade. Between 1980 and 2040, it rose by 4.2 degrees Centigrade, partly as the result of deforestation and desertification, partly as the result of the continued discharge into the troposphere of greenhouse gases, and partly as the result of unforeseen chemical multiplier effects involving these and other gases. As ice caps and glaciers melted, and as the ocean water expanded because of its warmer temperature, the sea level rose by two meters, inundating shorelines and lowlands throughout the world. Plans for great new dikes, seawalls, and inland reservoirs were laid, and engineers started work, but often not in time.

The first major disaster, although there had been small ones for several years, came in 2039. The southern delta lands of Bangladesh, fertile but vulnerable to flooding, had begun to lose their perennial struggle with the Bay of Bengal in 2037–38. In 2039, they were also struck by a disaster not uncommon in that part of the world, an immense cyclone and tidal wave. Local authorities hoped that, when the wave receded, most of the land could be reclaimed, as in the past. But, with the rise in the sea level, only a small part of it drained. Relief workers reported the death of five million people and the permanent loss to Bangladesh of 10 percent of its land.

In the early 2040s, other areas gradually went under: much of coastal Florida, the delta of the Mississippi in Louisiana, other delta land in Egypt, Pakistan, China, and Colombia, and large stretches of coastal southern Australia, Burma, Vietnam, and Mexico. Great cities, such as Karachi, Calcutta, Rangoon, Shanghai, Buenos Aires, New Orleans, Miami, and Charleston, had to fight for their lives. Some of them did not win. Even the Netherlands, with its long experience in holding back the sea, lost a few islands. Well warned by the agony of Bangladesh, only a handful of people died in the flooding of the early 2040s, but the costs of erecting artificial defenses and the property loss ran to trillions of dollars, at a time when the world economy had reached its lowest point in history.

The warming of the earth did more than flood low-lying land.

Previously temperate zones experienced tropical summers and mild winters. The suddenness of the change produced a wild array of weathers, with scorching dryness in some areas and furious storms in others. Farmers lost harvests and had to learn new methods and grow new crops or abandon their land altogether. In Louisiana, for example, fertile earth was converted by encroaching waters into salt marshes fit only for fish and shrimp. Hollings-Gray bought the land, evicted dozens of old farming families, and replaced them with aqua-culturists.

In the long run—had there been time for a "long run"—the situation might well have stabilized, but, for the time being, it was mostly a story of dislocation, confusion, and personal tragedy. Food production in 2043 fell to the lowest level of the century, at a time when more than eight billion people needed their daily rations.

If the Catastrophe of 2044 had not intervened, it is conceivable that the temperature of the planet would have continued to rise unchecked to the end of the century. The broiled inhabitants of twenty-second-century earth might have imagined themselves back in the Jurassic period with its tree ferns and dinosaurs. Fortunately, or unfortunately, they were denied this exotic pleasure. In 2044, sweltering heat gave way suddenly to arctic cold.

INTERLUDE

From these years another relative of yours was Jens Otto Jensen's sister, Regine Jensen-Brandt, who wrote short stories and poetry and exhibited tapestries at many crafts fairs. She became rather well known in middle life, but, at the time of these letters, she was the young mother of a terminally ill child and the wife of Mogens Brandt, a monitor for the GTC Environment Commission. The GTC created the commission in 2013 to make sure that its member corporations adhered to a memorandum on the ecological responsibilities of industry initialed by the directors the year before. The guidelines set forth in the memorandum were not stringent, but they no doubt helped a little and were often cited by the GTC as an example of its "good citizenship in the world community."

Hotel G.I.-Cosmos
Avenida Infante Dom Henrique
Rio de Janeiro
23 March 2019

Dear Dad,

Bless your heart for sending the flowers to Freddy for his birthday. He understood they were from you. Mogens gave him a packet of rare stamps for his collection, but I'm not sure it was a good idea. Freddy held them in his hand, and then he got the old far-away look in his eyes, and passed them back to us.

The doctors can't say when he'll be able to come home from the hospital. They say he's responding to the new drug, but it's so slow, and meanwhile his life is dribbling away. He doesn't seem to care whether he lives or dies. The only thing I feel good about is the hospital. This is a sad country, hot and dirty and hopeless, but the Brazilians are competent virologists. The doctors here understand Freddy's problem as well as anybody.

Since I last wrote to you, we've taken two rooms on the twentieth floor of this brand-new palace near the Praia do Flamengo. I'd rather be in one of the older hotels in Ipanema or Copacabana, but we must stay close to Freddy. Mogens spends about half his time with GTC executives and the rest at the Universidade Federal, government ministries, or in Cubatão.

Apparently Cubatão is the real reason Mogens was sent to Brazil. I'll tell you about it in my next letter.

It's horribly hot again today. Our rooms are air-conditioned, with the best equipment GI can buy, but when you go outside it's always broiling. Summer officially ended two days ago. Tell the sun. Until recent years the highest temperature ever recorded in Rio was 40° C., but since we've come, it's been 40 or 41 almost every day. Of course I know things aren't much better in dear old Boston.

I wrote a poem for Mogens last night. I shouldn't be able to think of poetry or love or anything good, with Freddy so sick, but it just came tumbling out of me. I had no choice.

> *Do not doubt me, dearest,*
> *For the world is doubtful,*
> *Pocked with the graves*
> *Of gods and heroes,*

> *Its banners pale*
> *In the stare of new-born suns*
> *Doubt we must all things but one:*
> *Love's well-rubbed lamp,*
> *Love's sea-worn gold.*

Mogens is well and sends his love to you and Jessie. We miss you, Dad. Please, please take care of yourself!

> All my love,
> Regine

◆

> Hotel G.I.-Cosmos
> Avenida Infante Dom Henrique
> Rio de Janeiro
> 27 March 2019

Dear Dad,

The weather broke a little yesterday, so I've been going out more. This is such a crazy city. Beggars and billionaires all together in one enormous cauldron. You can't imagine the extremes.

Freddy has a cough, which is new, but otherwise he's making progress, according to Dr. Pimenta. I trust her.

In my last letter I promised to tell you about the situation in Cubatão. The GTC had reliable reports of major infractions of the environmental memo there, but they didn't want anyone to know exactly what Mogens was up to. Otherwise we'd be living in São Paulo, which provides equally good care for patients with immunity diseases and is much closer.

The ugliness of Cubatão is stupefying. Mogens flew me there for half a day so I'd have some idea of what he's up against. The city is located near marshy land a short distance from the ocean. It became one of Brazil's leading industrial towns in the 1970s, fell apart in the 1990s, and then staged a comeback after 2001.

Dad, you just can't believe the noise and the filth and the sky. Oh, the sky! When they have a serious thermal inversion, they say it turns black and red, but the day I was there, it was bad enough, a mixture of gray and earthy yellow, with the air so full of chemicals, I couldn't breathe. Mogens kept handing me his oxygen inhaler.

In all, Cubatão has more than 200 plants, mostly petrochemical. Some keep the emission levels down pretty well, but there are just too many factories, and when all the emissions are added up, it can be brutal. In 1984 a gasoline duct set fire to a slum and killed a hundred people. In the 1990s the city had two big lethal smogs and several major industrial accidents, including the blowout of a tank of chlorine just in front of a shack settlement that housed ten or twenty thousand people. Many of them died, I can't remember the figure.

Anyway, when Brazil went broke in 1995, a lot of companies left Cubatao. Then came the American "advisers" and the megacorps, first Ford-Shell, later GI and Hollings-Gray, and they built it up again, taking a lot of shortcuts and repeating most of the mistakes of the previous generation.

Now it's a city of half a million, about five times as many as it has room for. The living and working conditions are impossible. Almost everybody's got lung problems, many people aren't protected against cancer, and immune deficiency diseases are everywhere. We know for sure that Freddy contracted his own disease back home, probably in his wrestling class at school, but he might just as easily have picked it up in Brazil. I worry for Mogens and myself, too.

Why do we do these things? I mean, build cities like Cubatão? The work itself isn't very hard, with most of the factories robotized, but there's no life here. People are suffocating in their own vomit. I don't mean to be bitter. But I am angry.

There's just been a call from the hospital, so I'll close now and get this mailed on my way.

Lots of love,
Regine

◆

Hotel G.I.-Cosmos
Avenida Infante Dom Henrique
Rio de Janeiro
15 April 2019

Dear Dad,

Freddy has taken a sharp turn for the worse. I thought you'd want to know. What I really mean is, I thought you'd rather not be spared.

He's got a bad case of fibroid pneumoencephalitis, one of those ferocious new diseases that people with Freddy's problem are encountering. It started as bronchitis, and now it's worked its way into his central nervous system. His head twitches uncontrollably. There isn't much to do for him, except hope that the radiation treatments will stun the HIV-7 long enough to let his body fight the other virus.

Either Mogens or I have been at the hospital around the clock since the 9th. GTC has put Mogens on half-time so he can take his turns.

Freddy is just barely conscious. Sometimes he lets out a croak, or a few words, but they're hard to understand.

Somehow this awful time is bringing me closer than I've ever been to Mogens. I need his love, and strength, and caring. We've always been good for each other, but especially now. Having a man like you for a father probably led me to expect a great deal from a husband. I hope you realize that. Anyway, Mogens has met my measurements.

We've been talking about leaving Brazil, even if it means resigning from GTC. You have only to live here, with the kind of access to the inner circles that Mogens' job gives him, to realize that countries like this have no future. They exist for us, for the megacorps and the United States and the United Nations, not for themselves. And they're not making it, except for a few hundred thousand super-rich people in São Paulo and Rio. God knows what will become of the place, in a few more years.

I was talking to a bright young boy the other day, only sixteen or seventeen, an orderly at the hospital on the night shift. He's one of seven children. Two died when they were young. The whole family lives in a one-room shack. The father is out of work, the mother is sick with anemia and maybe cancer, his big sister sells herself in a bar for tourists. Somewhere he learned English, probably at the hospital. He tells me with glittering eyes that next year he will cut his throat.

I believe him. As we were talking, I realized how much he looked like Freddy, except for the darker skin. What makes him so different from Freddy? What chance do either of them have? So, yes, you can imagine what I did when I went back to Freddy's room. I wrote this, and in a way, it's for both of them.

> You stand like a sapling in the wind
> Greeting the great silent storm of nothingness:
> Once your eyes were clear
> And life was love. You sang songs
> To stars, you slept in clouds.
> Once, and then no more.
> The gates of heaven closed for you,
> For me, for all mankind
> With mind's eyes sharp enough to see.
> So now I watch you speechless on the brink

> *Of speech, too young to fly,*
> *Too young to break*
> *The hour is not early: it is late.*
> *The light is not white: it is blue.*
> *The outer spaces in your eyes*
> *Are not false: they are true.*

I can't think of anything else to say. I'm glad that Jens is getting his life back in order again. The widow from Uruguay sounds like a reasonable prospect. Maybe I'll have a chance to meet her if we stay in Brazil. But I hope we don't. Be well.

> All my love,
> Regine
> ♦

> Hotel G.I.-Cosmos
> Avenida Infante Dom Henrique
> Rio de Janeiro
> 27 April 2019

Dear Dad,

Good news travels slowly. Or is it fast? Well, you probably guessed that in this case no news is the best kind. Freddy won his battle with the encephalitis! It left him almost as quickly as it arrived, thanks to the radiation treatments. I called to tell you, but you and Jessie were out of town, so we never got to talk. Where did you go?

He's fully conscious again, and looking much less pale. The turn-around started on the 21st. The doctors say this particular virus won't be back, but of course there are a dozen other familiar plagues to take its place, if he's not extraordinarily lucky. We just have to take them as they come.

Mogens made an emergency trip to Cubatão two days ago. He's still there. He says they have a problem with eroded mountain slopes behind the town, which might cause landslides, as they've done before. One of his aides, a geologist from Chile, thinks it's much worse this time.

No poem today. I've written a few since my last letter, but I don't like any of them. Already I miss Mogens. Send me the new address for Jens, also for Uncle Carl. Does he like teaching in New Mexico? It must be quite strange for him, after all those years in Maine.

> All my love,
> Regine
> ♦

Hotel G.I.-Cosmos
Avenida Infante Dom Henrique
Rio de Janeiro
9 May 2019

Dear Dad,

Thanks for all the news. I never thought Uncle Carl would adjust so easily to a new place. I'm glad for him. I don't want to be an academic, but the fact that he's published a few books gives me ideas of my own. It's not so impossible.

Freddy is much the same, still at the hospital, still very weak. He has a throat infection now, although not a bad one. Also, the doctors found some new tumors in his thigh and lasered them out.

Mogens is having a terrific war with his boss about the situation just north of Cubatão. He's recommending an immediate injunction to evacuate the plants and workers' huts and other housing nearest the mountain range, but the GTC field manager in Rio wants him to shut up. The costs would be enormous, and GTC doesn't want the responsibility. If Mogens keeps quiet, the GTC won't get the blame no matter what happens. I think he should report the whole thing to Zurich and take the consequences. He wants to, but he knows it could cost him his career. We have to think of Freddy. Without company insurance, I don't know what kind of care we could afford. We also have to think of all those people in Cubatão. What would you do? I'm very worried.

It's cooling off, at last. No days over 35 degrees since mid-April.

This one was written a week ago.

> *The world's not for seizing, holding, keeping*
> *Just the way it was and is and will be.*
> *None of it belongs to me.*
> *But we together make a moment's pause*
> *In its continuous shuttle back and forth*
> *From alpha to omega.*
> *None of it belongs to me,*
> *None is yours, but for a moment*
> *We together lie commingling in its jaws.*

Much love,
Regine

♦

Hotel Recife
Avenida Cidade de Lima
Rio de Janeiro
22 May 2019

Dear Dad,

Mogens was demoted ("reassigned") the day before yesterday. They turned us out of our palace the first thing. To save money, we took the smallest, cheapest room we could find in this crumbling old zoo in the northern part of town.

So far Freddy is allowed to stay at the hospital "for humanitarian reasons." In other words, if we don't cooperate in every way, they will evict him, too. We should consider ourselves fortunate that they have such an easy hold over us. I remember back in '17 a woman we knew died in a mysterious floater car accident in Norway shortly after leaving GTC and spilling unpleasant information to a journalist. I've always suspected that the journalist was a GTC plant.

Honestly, Dad, I'm unsure what will happen next. I can't call you. The mails are the only thing I trust (more or less), but I've taken the extra precaution of sending this to you via the agency in Chicago. You'll get it a day later than otherwise, but they won't know to intercept it.

Freddy is a bit worse. The doctors found more cancer. But he looks pretty good, and of course we haven't told him about the trouble with GTC.

Our friends here have been kind to us. Don't worry. We're not going to do anything heroic. I wanted to, but now that the giant has picked us up in his fist and started to squeeze, we're just as scared and gutless as anyone. I did this angry poem early yesterday morning. It's not about war.

> We drink the iron from
> The red maternal earth;
> We drill long corridors
> Of fire through the smiling sky.
> We burn the seas, turn the trees
> To dust, the sands to glass,
> We pave the wilderness.
> Next we must improve on war.
> The skirmishes of old
> Were little things,
> Games played for love of race and kin.
> Next let us move the universe:

> Send blood-spouts to the sun,
> Scorch the skin of Mars,
> Bend space and time
> Until they crack. We have not done
> Our best or worst. Wait!
> The Revelation's yet to come.

Don't try to answer this, not yet anyway. You know where we are if you absolutely have to, but I'd much rather you hold off until we can be sure it's safe.

Give my love to everyone.

Love,
Regine
◆

Cubatão
31 May 2019

Dear Dad,

By now you've heard about this horrible thing in Cubatão. I won't try to tell the whole story, and anyway, you must know most of it anyway. The print and broadcast media have done an adequate job, as far as they've gone. It's not a situation you could hope to keep quiet. But I want you to know this: Mogens wasn't hurt, and we're all okay for the time being.

On the 25th, Mogens got word from his Chilean friend in Cubatão, the geologist, that there had been a small landslide in the Serra do Cubatão, the mountain range behind the city. He thought there would be more soon. So Mogens, bless him, had to go down and make one more effort. I decided to come with him, even if it meant leaving Freddy for a couple of days. He's been better lately.

Anyway, we went. Mogens got in touch with the city and state government people in Cubatão, and he and Ricardo (the geologist) pleaded with them to evacuate at least some of the housing north of town. They were running a big risk, because the GTC probably has informers in the bureaucracy. But they did it. I am so proud of Mogens, Dad! He just refused to give up.

The officials promised to check everything again and even conduct some on-site inspections with geologists from São Paulo. By then it was the 27th. Too late, of course. It rained heavily all that night and on into the morning of the 28th. Mogens and Ricardo went out to see things for themselves, and about noon, as the media people reported, the earth fell. Ricardo was right at the base of one of the steepest and most eroded slopes, taking measurements, and Mogens was a kilometer away talking with engineers in a factory.

They never found Ricardo's body. Mogens says he must have died instantly, crushed by the weight of the slide. Mogens heard the roar and looked out the window of the factory, which faced north. He saw a gray-brown wave of soil swooshing down, and dust filling the sky, and buildings disappearing underneath. The media say the death toll is 15,000, but we think it's five times as many. Seven plants with all their workers inside or on the grounds, two housing developments, several thousand squatters' huts. Add it up.

Hills need trees. Jungles need trees. The earth needs trees. Brazil was once the lungs of the world, filling the atmosphere with the oxygen respired by its trees. But they cut down most of them and poisoned the rest. I should say, we did. We all did.

Mogens and I are returning to Rio tonight. There's nothing to keep us here. Then we'll take Freddy and fly home. Mogens will resign from the GTC as soon as we're back in the States again. Then we'll see what happens. But we will survive.

Here is my envoi, composed the same day that the earth fell on Cubatão.

> How many years?
> Sisters, brothers, hear me
> This one last time.
> We are dying, we people.
> The hearth of our home
> Cools. Our breath hangs grey
> And chill in the light of evening.
> We are dying, we people, hear me:
> How many years?
> Do you love the earth?
> Do you love the children?
> Do you love the trees
> The lizards the whales the wind rounding the rocks?
> Do you love lovers clasped for life's heat?
> How many years?
> All being cries to us,
> Shouts above our deafness:

How many years?
Think. Warm your wills. Strike!

All my love,
Regine

♦

Regine and Mogens did return to the States, with their son. Freddy, whose "problem" was CAIDS (casually acquired immunodeficiency syndrome, a late variant of AIDS), died in 2020. But they had two other children and later joined the World party. Readings of her poem "How Many Years?" became a familiar ritual at party meetings in the early 2040s.

4

THE MOLECULAR SOCIETY

The New Materialism

In 2011, the French anthropologist André Pagnol published his best known work, *The Molecular Society,* which has come down to us as the classic description of the sociocultural order of late capitalism. "Today," he wrote, "mankind has been reduced to the yes and no, the positive and negative charges of particle physics. We human creatures are no longer demonic forms of God but great ziggurats of dancing molecules."

Pagnol referred to a fundamental change of consciousness that transformed the perceptions of modern men and women between the 1980s and the 2010s. In many ways the change recapitulated what had happened once before, during the Enlightenment of the eighteenth century. Following the long-forgotten promptings of Julien La Mettrie, we began to look on ourselves as machines in a mechanical cosmos.

As Pagnol argued, the new consciousness was keyed to revolutions in biochemistry, genetics, psychology, and computer science. What occurred was nothing less than a radical displacement of worldviews.

Throughout the old century, the art and philosophy of the avant-garde (a reality in those days no less powerful in its own sphere than ruling elites) had celebrated the powers of unreason. Artists, intellectuals, and scholars reveled in their "dreadful freedom." A favored few made fortunes proclaiming the irrelevance of science and the absurdity of being.

For a time their accomplishments seemed unassailable. But the stock ideas of this modish irrationalism eventually wore thin. At the end of the century, a new worldview sprang into vogue, known loosely and imprecisely as materialism or neomaterialism. Materialism suffused every aspect of the high culture of the half century that preceded the Catastrophe of 2044. It inspired a revival of Zolaesque realism in letters, a silver age of art photography, sculpture in the manner of Canova and Houdon, and the "mimetic" scores of a new generation of composers who programmed their computers to fashion eerily variant simulacra of the works of the great baroque masters. As the historian Indira Desai of Jabalpur notes in her study of twenty-first-century art, "All late culture is quotation."

But the new worldview manifested itself most stridently in the realm of the natural and behavioral sciences. The impetus for change came from a suite of disciplines dubbed the "molecular sciences," consisting of three interrelated fields of study: molecular biology, molecular psychology, and molecular technology. Although we no longer group them in this way, the molecular sciences remain with us, still valid within their narrow limits as interpretations of life and its mechanisms.

The biologists discovered that virtually all characteristics, anatomical and behavioral, are produced by specific genes or combinations of genes, inherited by the individual organism. It followed that any characteristic (from height and weight to beauty, intelligence, and aggressiveness) could be altered by genetic surgery before or immediately after conception.

The psychologists supplemented the findings of the biologists by redefining states of mental health and illness in the light of genetics, by identifying the chemical agents secreted by the nervous system to regulate mood and behavior, and by developing a host of synthetic psychochemicals capable of producing almost any desired behavioral modification in organisms from birth onward.

Finally, the molecular technologists ("moltechs" or "nanotechs") invented microscopic robots no larger than protein molecules with a broad range of capabilities in computation, data storage, medicine, industry, pollution control, space exploration, and many other fields. Together, the events of the "molecular revolution" dwarf anything accomplished in the last age of capital.

It now occurred to the avant-garde that perhaps all things were, or should be, "molecular." Structuralists in the social sciences described societies, economies, and cultures as elaborate machines. Computer scientists in the quest for artificial intelligence discovered that even naturally occurring intelligence was nothing but a function of infinitesimal mechanical processes coordinated without a coordinator, "a society of mind" in the popular phrase of the American scientist Marvin Minsky. The sense of a centrally guiding and ruling self vanished. Led by the Japanese scholar Toru Hammura, philosophers announced a "molecularist" thought system that reconceived reality from the viewpoint of events in the microcosm. "Philosophy must be constructed anew, from the bottom up," he wrote. "Small is not 'beautiful' perhaps. But small alone is real."

Despite obsessive use of the words *real* and *reality,* the new materialism did not make any claims to a knowledge of final, ultimate, or transcendental reality. It explicitly refused to answer the perennial big questions dear to ontologists and theologians. But it was easy enough to reconcile with capitalism, which, as a theory of political economy, had always relied on mechanical models traceable to such eighteenth-century philosophers as François Quesnay and Adam Smith.

It proved equally compatible with Marxism. Marx himself taught a strict materialism, but the philosophy that bore his name had slipped backward, in its Leninist-Stalinist phase, to an assertion that changes in the social environment rendered all things possible. Now, as the molecular sciences made their triumphal march across the pages of world history, Marxist voices both inside and outside the Soviet Union were quick to condemn the "neoidealist deviationism" of the recent past and revel in the vindication of Marx by the progress of modern science.

Thus emerged a new vision of man and woman and nature: composed of particles, machine-like, determined at every point by the laws of biophysics, ultimately predictable, and immediately subject to limitless redesign by bioengineering. Detractors of neomaterialism charged that it reduced people to things; advocates replied that it gave people absolute power over themselves. Detractors spoke of fatalism and resignation to a mechanical destiny. Advocates spoke of freedom and liberation from the shackles of ignorance. Detractors proclaimed the death of the soul. Advocates dreamed of building better souls.

Whatever else may be said, the new worldview did not prove supportive of a stable, conserving, or nurturing social order. With its emphasis on redesign from within, it favored economic growth and technological progress at all costs. Its social philosophers argued that technology, harnessed by capital, would create a whole new race of godlike men and women and make poverty obsolete by multiplying geometrically the productivity of labor. The world economy would be overwhelmed by abundance.

Liberal concern for the plight of the environment and the suffer ings of the underprivileged atrophied, a process that had begun in the 1980s and gathered momentum steadily during the boom years after 2001. Critics bemoaned the "new callousness," but the neo-materialists counseled patience. Give us another generation, they said, and poverty, ignorance, crime, war, sickness, and perhaps even death itself will exist only in the memory of historians. In the mean-time, we must expect, as Pagnol wrote, *un déluge des petits maux,* a torrent of small troubles. The phrase became famous, then infamous.

Crime, Drugs, Poverty

The most visible sign of the underside of progress in the last age of capital was a startling rise in the crime rate. In large cities every-where gangs of alienated, unemployed, unteachable young people terrorized the streets. Behind the scenes, vast syndicates aped the capitalists by organizing international criminal empires making use of all the latest refinements in electronic surveillance, psychochemical manipulation, and invasion of computer networks. One of these syn-dicates, founded in Japan and known simply as "The Red Thumb," grew so large in the 2020s that journalists regularly described it as the thirteenth member of the Dirty Dozen megacorps composing the Global Trade Consortium. Evidence exists that from time to time Red Thumb "executives" were invited to attend informal meetings of GTC directors in Zurich between 2026 and 2032.

But, for the average citizen, the streets were the biggest problem. The number of street and residential crimes, including robberies and burglaries, increased by an average of 3 percent per year during the first quarter of the twenty-first century in the ten largest cities of North America and Western Europe and at even higher rates in many Third World cities. Residential protection services, such as the Home-Fort Company, which failed to save the belongings of Cousin Jens

Otto in 2016, sprang up everywhere. Offices, banks, and factories hired small armies of guards.

A special factor in the rise of urban crime, besides chronic unemployment and racial and ethnic tensions, was the proliferation of illegal drugs. From the late 1950s to the early 1990s, most drug users had relied on products made from naturally occurring plants, such as the opium poppy, coca, hemp, and mescal. Costs were low and profits high. But such drugs yielded a limited repertoire of effects and were often insufficiently addictive to ensure a steady growth in use and in users.

Thereafter, the syndicates directed their attention to the development of synthetic drugs by well-paid bioengineers working in underground laboratories. Such drugs could be mass produced anywhere, reducing reliance on Third World agriculture and the services of smugglers. They could be designed to provide a wide range of desired effects, from euphoria and rage to sexual frenzy. They could also be chemically bonded to substances guaranteed to make them addictive for nearly every user and, in most instances, progressively addictive.

Perfected in the 2010s, the favorite drug of many North American addicts was known on the streets as "pop." Sold in pill form, it came in fifteen colors, depending on the psychochemical effect produced. Pop seldom if ever failed to make its user fully dependent within a week. Dosages had to be raised by approximately 5 percent per month to prevent epileptic seizures. After a decade of regular incremental use, the average "popper" began to experience convulsions no matter how many pills he took, climaxing either in death or, more often, a coma from which few victims awoke. When the high medical price of "popping" became generally known, about 2023, its use fell off sharply, but milder forms of pop continued to be sold down to 2044.

The cost of such drugs pulled millions of users into criminal careers. Not a few came from "good" homes, young people with professional parents, who made the mistake of popping a single pill to see what it might do. Teen-age boys were especially vulnerable to the "venereal pink" version of pop, which gave the addict a series of simulated orgasms much more powerful than the natural experience, accompanied by an erection lasting for several hours.

Yet the importance of drugs in crime in the last age of capital is easily overstated. The root cause of crime during these years was the steady erosion of the middle class and the inexorable worldwide growth in the numbers and anomie of the urban poor. People of all classes could become addicts, but they had to take the first step. Usually the children of the well-to-do refrained, as did whole populations in cultures where strong family ties or religious faith or both counteracted the global drift to credicide. Such cultures, unfortunately, were rare; and neomaterialism, despite its virtues as a system of moral and intellectual support for capital, did not reach deeply enough into the subconscious to serve as a true surrogate for religious faith.

One particularly venomous side effect of the growing incoherence of society was the encouragement it gave to racial prejudice. In the majority of countries, one or more ethnic minorities played the part of an underproletariat, singled out for harsh exploitation and paranoid hatred and fear. The racial underproletariats proved especially useful to politicians in search of crowd-pleasing issues. Their tactics were tolerated by the ruling elites as a way of currying popular favor with a minimum of risk to social stability.

But the risk was not negligible. In every country with a serious racial problem in the first half of the twenty-first century, the ethnic underproletariat, commingled with other classes in metropolitan centers, fared badly, resented its fate, and did what little it could to subvert the established order.

The United States is an obvious case in point. In 2030, as we know, the bottom third of the population earned only 9 percent of the national income. Of this bottom third, a full 90 percent were blacks, Hispanics, and American Indians, deprived of access to the national cornucopia simply because their skins were black, brown, or red and because the premises of their cultures clashed with the relentless neomaterialism of modern civilization. Although individual members of the despised minorities discarded their heritage and rose to positions of power and prestige in society, the rest fell permanently behind. It did not help their cause that more than half the street crime, worldwide, was committed by members of oppressed ethnic minorities. Prejudice sired more prejudice, infecting even the minorities themselves.

Not surprisingly, ruling circles throughout the world rarely looked with tolerance and sympathy on the poor, the criminal, and the victimized in their midst. For one thing, the lords of capital could not afford to bribe their masses with welfare benefits as lavishly as they had once done. The welfare system did not break down entirely, but it was badly strained by high unemployment, the greater numbers of poor, a formidable increase in the retired population, and the ravages of crime. Although public (and corporate) welfare programs doled out more money than ever, funds could not stretch to include everyone; welfare expenditures per capita fell almost every year down to 2032 and after that rose again slightly, only to fall once more between 2039 and 2044.

The result was simmering urban unrest, strikes and slowdowns, racially inspired riots, and soaring crime. The system responded in the only way it could: with savage force and technological cunning. Capital punishment returned to most countries that had abolished it. Elsewhere it became far more common. Drug dealers were routinely executed, sometimes after their first conviction. Syndicate bosses seldom interfered. Many felt that dealers working for them who were incompetent enough to get caught deserved whatever punishment they received. The same fate awaited murderers, rapists, and those guilty of less serious crimes but with several prior convictions.

For addicts and other petty criminals who escaped with prison sentences, most state authorities adopted variations of the methods foretold in Anthony Burgess's harrowing novel *A Clockwork Orange*. Hopeless poppers were allowed to die. Other offenders were treated with addictive psychochemicals that converted them into human sheep. Still others were subjected to ruthless programs of behavioral conditioning followed by surgery to implant in their brains a microminiaturized, nuclear-powered "peacemaker" that caused disabling pain whenever the wearer became angry or hostile. The cost of such remedies was high, but, since the felon could be safely returned to the streets in a few months, states were spared the still higher costs of prolonged incarceration. Despite the rising crime rate, prisons were actually less crowded in 2044 than they had been in 2001.

The Automatic Workplace

Of course not everyone was miserable in these years. Far from it. Those with jobs, money, education, and status found life in the last age of capital sweetened by a profusion of technological and medical advances. We continue to benefit from some of them today. I could spend many hours describing the first levitating cars and trains (called "floaters"), the arrival of holographic cameras and television, the conversion of postal systems to electronic mail, the development of beamplanes powered by ground-based microwave transmitters, and the new robot theaters ("robocins"), whose patrons, enclosed in wired suits and helmets, experienced directly the live or recorded adventures of robots equipped with synthetic eyes and limbs similar to a human being's. And much more. But the two areas of most significant progress were computer science and health.

In many ways the key to everything achieved in the last age of capital was computer science. A field that hardly existed in the middle of the twentieth century, it grew to awesome proportions during the next one hundred years. Its role in the automation of industry, record keeping, and communications was decisive. By 2010, manual and routine office labor in the core countries, and the more affluent countries of the semiperiphery, had been virtually abolished. Factory workers became overseers and repairmen, until, as time passed, they surrendered even these functions to machines. Stenographers, file clerks, and processors of forms and data gradually followed the typical factory hand into oblivion. Computers wrote and sent letters, advised government officials, drafted blueprints, managed air traffic, designed weapons, planned advertising campaigns, conducted medical research, whatever they were needed to do.

Already quite apparent before 1990, their usefulness multiplied many times over with the perfection of artificial intelligence in the last decade of the twentieth century by Japanese and American scientists. Up to this point, despite the speed and retentiveness of computer chips, the available hardware was incapable of parallel processing and therefore could not duplicate most of the functions of the flesh-and-blood cerebrum, in which millions of neural operations are executed simultaneously. A cat is more intelligent, in vital respects, than the finest mainframe computer of the early 1980s.

With the invention of artificial intelligence (AI), however, the world changed for all time. At one stroke, scientists had at their disposal a tool that surpassed exponentially the powers of the old sequential computers. More important, they had at their disposal a tool that could make new and better tools, that could evolve by its own internal logic—with a little initial prodding and pointing by human agents—into ever-higher orders of mechanical existence.

The first great triumph of the new AI thinking machines was the development of a generation of molecular or nano-technologies, which in turn created higher-speed, more brain-like computers and robots, many of microscopic size. Complex bioengineered protein molecules or "biochips" frequently supplanted conventional silicon chips. Applications in industry, communications, medicine, scholarship, and the exploitation of interplanetary space became available more rapidly than human beings could be educated to organize their use.

It is even possible that, if there had been no economic downturn after 2032 and no global catastrophe in 2044, the opening of the floodgates by AI and molecular technology would have washed away poverty and inequality without political action. Some of our best counterfactual historians have worked on this problem, simulating the history of the world after 2032 with altered premises, and at least one, Sarvepalli Patel of Nagpur, does make a plausible case for the neomaterialists.

In any case, the world's work was now done more expeditiously and with less human toil than ever before. Even the labor of scholars in the humanities and social sciences benefited immeasurably. With the perfection of optical disc technology and the vastly enlarged memories of chips (both silicon and bioengineered), all printed materials could be made available in microcompact forms and transmitted anywhere in the world by the World Bibliotel system operated by WT&T. When a scholar wanted to examine a document, he or she had only to call it up on a home or office screen, read or copy the relevant portions, and move on to the next task.

By the year 2030, the bibliotel network served more than twenty million institutional and individual subscribers in all countries. It held electronic copies of nine-tenths of all the books, periodicals, and archival collections in the world. Supplementary fees were charged for consulting works still under copyright. Most of the world's great research libraries and archives were converted into museums, visited more by tourists than by scholars.

Had it not been for the social relations of production under capitalism, the need even for a videolibrary system would have vanished by the second quarter of the twenty-first century. Since the master microdiscs were infinitely reproducible and (with filing dividers) could have fitted into a shoe box, there was no reason, apart from the demand for profits and royalties, why the whole collection could not have been made available to any purchaser at cost. But WT&T jealously guarded its hoard, and, unless one was prepared to embark on long, expensive research trips, World Bibliotel was the only available resource.

Longer Lives

The other great area of achievement in this age was health and medicine. Aided by advances in computer science and bioengineering, medical researchers were able to defeat a fair number of the most intransigent enemies of humankind.

Two enemies that mattered especially to adults in the affluent countries were cancer and atherosclerosis, or "hardening of the arteries," the chief cause of heart attacks and strokes. Together, these maladies accounted for most premature death as of 1990. By 2015 they were rare, except among the very poor. Although some credit belongs to changes in diet, such as the sharp decline in meat eating after the depression of 1995, coupled with reduced consumption of tobacco products, atherosclerosis and cancer were brought under control primarily by advances in medicine.

Heart disease was subdued first. New enzyme-blocking drugs reached the market in the late 1980s that impeded the synthesis by overactive livers of cholesterol, the principal ingredient of arterial plaques. In 1996, another drug, derived from research on cyclic imides, made possible the shrinking of already formed plaques in many patients. At about the same time, researchers perfected safe, inexpensive techniques for imaging soft tissues that enabled physicians to identify persons with dangerously clogged arteries well before their conditions became life threatening; and heart bypass surgery, a useful stopgap in its day, was replaced by laser angioplasty, the cleaning of arteries by a laser-tipped catheter guided by an ultrasonic probe.

Cancer fell next. Long recognized as a failure of the body's immune system, cancer was a disease that might take years to produce symptoms, by which time the patient had more or less lost the battle and drugs and surgery were too late. Working along several fronts, researchers brought the enemy under control. They developed a blood test to detect cancer in its earliest stages, reinforced the body's own defenses by enrichment of naturally occurring anticancer agents, and bioengineered human monoclonal antibodies capable of destroying tumors by carrying specially designed toxins in their molecules.

All this had become standard medical procedure by 2005. In 2008, a Japanese corporation marketed the first successful immunization system, which prevented the formation of three-quarters of all cancers by correcting imbalances in the immune system. Cancer did not disappear altogether, but deaths from it were unusual after the second decade of the twenty-first century, except among those too poor to obtain state-of-the-art medical care.

The only serious conventional medical problems remaining to be solved in the early twenty-first century were, surprisingly, viral infections. For more than a century, medical science had made relentless progress against microbes of all shapes and sizes, leading futurists to forecast the end of infectious disease in human beings by the year 2010. The one family of pathogens that refused to give up the fight were the viruses. Most did capitulate, sooner or later, but, as the new century arrived, several remained at large.

The worst were transmitted venereally, such as HIV-1 and HIV-2, which caused acquired immunodeficiency syndrome (AIDS). These were both complex viruses with several genes and an unusual capacity to alter their proteins and also give rise to new species. Acquired immunodeficiency syndrome alone killed an estimated 200 million people between 1980 and 2000. In the early 2000s, several other closely related viruses, probably mutations of HIV-1, made their appearance, including HIV-7, the virus that caused the disease known as casually acquired immunodeficiency syndrome (CAIDS), which finally cost young Freddy Jensen-Brandt his life in 2020.

A diabolical virus, HIV-7 was transmitted through the mouth, genitalia, eyes, ears, or even pores of the skin. A common way for young people to acquire the disease was in sporting events, where inadvertent contact with the bodily fluids of a victim could easily occur. Once established in the central nervous system, the virus then emerged from hibernation one to twenty-five years later, devastating its host's immune system.

Both HIV-1 and HIV-2 responded well to drugs created in the mid-1990s, especially to synthetic DNA strands called hybridons that attacked viral genes. A partially effective vaccine came into widespread use after 1998. But the new drugs did nothing to stop HIV-7. Not until the engineering of microbiotic robots using molecular technology in the late 2020s was CAIDS eliminated.

More systemic approaches to disease were gene surgery, performed on embryos conceived outside the womb, and gene therapy, in which copies of healthy genes were inserted by processed retroviruses into the bone marrow cells of postnatal patients with missing or defective

genes. Such techniques proved effective in preventing hereditary diseases, including manic depression, and other diseases such as cancer, arthritis, or atherosclerosis linked to inherited deficiencies in
the body's defense mechanisms.

To be successful, of course, genetic therapists and surgeons had
to know the tasks performed by each normal gene and how specific
health problems were caused genetically. Some of the simplest and
most basic work was done as early as the 1970s, but, as researchers
later discovered, every human cell contains forty-six chromosomes
with a freight of 91,124 genes, each divisible in turn into an average
of thirty-two thousand DNA subunits. Many normal functions and
diseases alike involve the complex, variable, and intermittent inter-
action of several genes or gene segments.

Working with automated DNA sequencing machines introduced
in 1986, molecular biologists needed more than a decade just to map
the human genome, or genetic complex, and much longer still, even
with the help of moltechs and high-speed computers for analysis and
correlation of data, to determine the various functions of each gene
and DNA subunit. As of 2044, the job was still unfinished. But specialists knew enough by the late 1980s to begin systematic gene therapy and, in the early 2000s, gene surgery.

At first physicians applied these techniques chiefly to treat or prevent disease. But the genomic inventory taken by molecular biologists (christened the "biomap" by science writers) bore implications
that transcended medicine. It became possible, screening any boy or
girl's personal biomap, to predict his or her future health in great detail with a relatively high measure of accuracy. Problems that might
surface in later life could be identified, carefully monitored, and given
preventive treatment. So far, you will say, so good.

Unfortunately, these same problems could also be brought to the
attention of anyone who planned to give the person employment or a
position of trust, responsibility, or privilege. Civil libertarians argued
that a man or woman's biomap was a confidential matter, of legitimate concern only to the individual and his or her physician and
genetic counselor, not to be released under any circumstances to
anyone else. By 2010, however, the arguments of civil libertarians
had been shouted down in parliaments, courts, and corporate boardrooms. Biomaps were used freely to help determine their possessors'
fitness for a broad range of jobs and positions of power and influence
in the world system.

Since so many diseases had been entirely or largely overcome, biomaps exposed people to less mischief in the twenty-first century than would have been the case in the twentieth. But mischief was still available, especially if the treatment for a given disease or defect would be costly or, worst of all, did not yet exist.

In the long run, the principal significance of the genomic inventory, as we all know, was not its assistance in fighting disease or its abuse by employers but the avenues it opened to the remaking of *Homo sapiens*. Molecular biologists had been well aware of this possibility from the beginning. Some were loath to inquire into the ethical or political implications, but all recognized the power that knowledge of human genetic endowment would bestow on its possessors. The capacity to repair something abnormal was also the capacity to change something normal for better or worse, or both.

Modest advances along such lines were made early in the twenty-first century without attempting to alter genetic structures. Drugs to improve memory, enhance creativity, sharpen reasoning powers, and speed up thought processes were developed by molecular psychologists trained in the same techniques as the underground researchers who created pop and other illegal addictive psychochemicals. Graduate students regularly swallowed "memory pills" to prepare themselves for comprehensive doctoral examinations, sometimes with spectacular results. Scientists improved their concentration through the use of a class of drugs known as neurone greasers.

But, as the DNA maps took on increasing sophistication and decoded detail, it became embarrassingly clear why some individuals were more intelligent or long lived or attractive or vigorous than others: in the great genetic lottery of life, some people won, and others lost. Desirable and undesirable attributes could be spotted by trained geneticists from conception onward. Conditions in the environment might encourage or discourage their development, but the attributes themselves originated in the roll of the genetic dice. Thus, individual A or individual B literally could not help being clever or stupid, healthy or sickly, slender or obese, beautiful or ugly, industrious or lazy, whatever the case might be.

Ideologues attached to the Old Left deplored this betrayal of their most sacred convictions by science. In the end, however, they made the best of it and rallied to the neomaterialist banner almost as ardently as their conservative opposite numbers. For their part, conservatives went the radicals one better by applying the new genetic lore to a reassessment of racial and gender differences. They cited a rash of studies by anthropologists and molecular psychologists purporting to prove that the yellow (or white) race was superior to all others and that women were, by genetic endowment acquired through ten million years of primate evolution, unsuited for strenuous competitive work in the outside world.

The most influential study, *Gender and Genetics* (1999), by the expatriate Angolan cultural anthropologist Heitor Kimbundu and the Canadian psychologist Frank Lloyd Schwartz, nearly destroyed the reputation of Harvard University Press and was frequently burned by outraged feminists. Yet its evidence was persuasive, at least in an age that doted on materialist explanations of reality. The book became a faintly malodorous classic in the decades that followed.

Happily, arguments about gender did not inspire experiments to alter whatever biological differences separated the sexes. Meanwhile, exhaustive tests with mouse and rat embryos in the 2000s established that gene surgery could improve any mammalian species, a feat that bioengineers working with food plants had demonstrated to the world long before without a breath of criticism. The first crude efforts to engineer superior human types were uniformly unsuccessful, evoking snide references to Mary Shelley's *Frankenstein*.

But, in 2019, at a special closed high-level session in its Zurich world headquarters, the GTC approved a high-priority project to design the "perfect" man and woman. Shielded from public discussion, the GTC directors decided that perfection included not only lofty intelligence but also a ruthless competitive instinct and a dollop of energizing paranoia. Genetic surgeons labored through the years from 2019 to 2024 to meet every criterion, and in 2025 twelve children tailor made by gene surgery were born to GTC executives.

Their experiment did not fail. Although the children were only eighteen or nineteen when the Catastrophe of 2044 intervened, most had already distinguished themselves in various irrefutable ways and would surely have cut impressive figures in the history of the second half of the twenty-first century had they not been killed in the Catastrophe. One, a young woman of barely nineteen, had already clawed her way to the board of directors of General Industries in the spring of 2044. Early death reaped hundreds of other elite children born in the late 2020s and 2030s, bioengineered to similar specifications. Of the eleven known to have survived, two became world-class scientists, two achieved greatness in the arts, and a fifth was Gina Mascagni, founder in 2092 of the Free Trade party, by all accounts the most charismatic (and perverse) political leader of her time.

Yet another frontier of medical research explored vigorously in the last age of capital was prolongevity. Gerontologists toiled on the problems of aging and its reversal throughout the period. They identified most of the biochemical processes involved and generated a few limited solutions, but none that can be termed spectacular. People lived longer mainly because there were fewer diseases to strike them down in early or middle age, not because old age had grown conspicuously less hazardous. Animal bodies, researchers concluded, were simply programmed to undergo a progressive undifferentiation of cell tissue in senescence, along with slower rates of DNA repair and a gradual breakdown of the immune system. In short, the body became entropic, unable to maintain full control over its own processes.

To counter such effects, scientists tried drugs, with moderate success, and genetic engineering, adding gene segments that promoted the repair of DNA molecules and the elimination of carcinogens. As of 2043, one reliable survey reported that persons treated with gerontological drugs and genetic intervention were living 3.3 years longer than persons untreated. It was a beginning, although the discovery of an authentic fountain of youth continued to elude humankind.

The Settlement of Space

The feat of science and engineering in the last age of capital that furnished more vicarious thrills for earthlings than any other was the colonizing of outer space. Most of the outstanding achievements in space colonization date from just thirteen years. In 2020, after two egregious failures, the United Nations (actually a joint effort by Japan, the United States, and the Soviet Union) put a permanent colony on the moon. Its interconnected complex of fifteen cylindrical units housed several hundred residents from six countries.

The next step was the construction of the first entirely man-made space habitat, a colony world build chiefly of lunar raw materials by Hollings-Gray, funded in part by a commission of the GTC. With the invaluable help of moltechs, the colony was established between the earth and the moon in 2023 and was soon the home of more than three thousand people, including a hundred lovable "space kids," whose real and fictional doings dominated the imaginations of earthbound children for two decades.

Then in 2030, again assisted by the microbots of the molecular engineers, Hollings-Gray built a second, even larger habitat in the asteroid belt between Mars and Jupiter. This second world ("Beltworld") was a technological marvel. Powered by direct solar radiation, engineered by AI computers and their robots, exploiting the mineral resources of the moon and the asteroid belt itself, it cost al-most nothing to construct. The prospect of thousands of such self-replicating worlds impressed itself on all who understood what had been done. Half a million people volunteered to live on Beltworld, later named Atlantis, but only 7,250 could be accommodated.

The final heroic stroke of space settlement came in 2033, one year after the beginning of the depression. Under study for most of the century, and preceded by two successful expeditions by American and Soviet astronauts, it was the culmination of everything that space settlers had dreamed of achieving: a permanent and virtually self-sustaining colony on the surface of Mars. The sponsoring body in this instance was the GTC, with generous help from its confederates in the space program of the Soviet Union. Closed biological systems enabled the settlers to grow their own food, generate their own air, recycle their own wastes, and scavenge the crust of Mars for needed raw materials.

But the absurdities of the economic depression on earth soon over-took the settlers. The financially hard-pressed GTC recalled them in 2035, unwilling to commit itself to emergency aid or rescue missions should the colony find itself in trouble. The lunar colony was aban-doned soon after. Six pioneers stayed and tried to keep things going. As we learned later, they did not succeed. The citizens of the two ar-tificial habitats in high-earth orbit and the asteroid belt resourcefully carried on, even after all contact with earth dissolved in 2044.

In retrospect, no one would call the molecular society surprising. For all its great doings, it could have been foreseen by almost anyone aware of the trends of the late twentieth century and capable of ex-trapolating those trends credibly into the future. In many ways it was like the world of the late twentieth century doubled: doubled in popu-lation and wealth, with corporations doubling (and redoubling) their power, with double the inequality, and double the anomie, and double the progress of science and technology, which undeniably made a difference in the lives of everyone but did not change the rules of the social game.

By the late 2030s, of course, humanity had bigger fish to fry than the settlement of space. The world system was disintegrating, long-suppressed national rivalries reemerged, and the threat of financial ruin dulled the adventurousness of the megacorps. The molecular society unraveled as the power of still smaller units of matter—the nuclei of radioactive atoms—came to the fore in the Catastrophe of 2044.

INTERLUDE

What follows is part of a correspondence between your many-times-removed cousin Dina Geijer, a niece of Regine Jensen-Brandt, and the personnel department of Hollings-Gray, the megacorp with heavy investments in chain farming and space settlement. The markers referred to were anomalies, usually added or deleted segments of DNA, found in one DNA strand but not another when comparing paternal and maternal chromosome pairs. Such markers indicated genetic defects, foretelling health problems likely to arise at some point in a person's life even if no problem existed at the time of the survey. Until 2007, employers in the United States were denied access to the biomaps of prospective or current employees, but Congress changed the law that year after conflicting judgments in the federal courts forced a legislative resolution of the issue. At the instigation of the GTC, a uniform global policy on access to biomaps was adopted by 145 countries in 2010.

1222-B Standish Court
908 East Genesee Street
Syracuse, NY 8PL 187-33091
30 August 2028

Office of Personnel
North American Region
Hollings-Gray Corporation
265 West 33d Street
New York, NY 6SL 232-10082

Dear Persons:
I am in receipt of your letter of 29 August, denying me a chance to compete for a position in the Beltworld project. You state that although my educational and professional qualifications place me in the top 1 percent of all applicants for the project, my biomap indicates future medical problems that might render me "unfit for prolonged service in an experimental spaceside environment."
This week I checked with my personal physician, Dr. Ganesa Prasad, who screened my biomap in his laboratory. He finds no reason for your decision. As someone who was persuaded by her cohabitant to abort their son because of the unfavorable results of an embryo gene screen, I

have mixed emotions about the use of biomap data in selecting job applicants. Indeed, I wonder in the light of Dr. Prasad's report whether one of your operatives learned of my ambiguous feelings about the abortion, and whether this might not have been the real reason for your rejection of my application. Nevertheless, I recognize that you had legal authority to access my biomap. All I want to know now is what you found that was wrong with me. Could you have read someone else's biomap by mistake?

I feel entitled to a fuller explanation of your action, and I look forward to receiving it at your earliest convenience.

> Yours truly,
> Dina Geijer

♦

> Office of Personnel
> North American Region
> Hollings-Gray Corporation
> 265 West 33d Street
> New York, NY 6SL 232-10082
> 14 September 2028

Dina Geijer
1222-B Standish Court
908 East Genesee Street
Syracuse, NY 8PL 187-33091

Dear Ms. Geijer:

Thank you for your inquiry of 30 August. It is not corporate policy to release to applicants the results of biomap studies, whether raw genetic data or medical interpretation of data. However, if your physician Dr. Prasad will communicate with our medical department at the address shown on the enclosed form, we will be pleased to advise him of the basis of our decision, and you may apply to him for further information.

Hollings-Gray Corporation hopes that this response will be of assistance to you. Please do not hesitate to contact us again should you have additional questions. Once again, accept our sincerest thanks for your interest in Beltworld, and keep us in mind when you apply for positions in the future.

> Cordially yours,
> Dong Joon Park
> Personnel Associate

♦

1222-B Standish Court
908 East Genesee Street
Syracuse, NY 8PL 187-33091
28 September 2028

Dong Joon Park
Office of Personnel
North American Region
Hollings-Gray Corporation
265 West 33d Street
New York, NY 6SL 232-10082

Dear Ms. or Mr. Park:

With reference to the biomap report that you sent my doctor, Ganesa Prasad, he tells me that the problem you identified was a mental illness, and that there is only a 10 percent chance I will ever experience symptoms of this illness during the rest of my life. He also says that if I do, it can easily be treated by a clinical molecular psychologist. He declined to specify the exact nature of the predicted illness, but assured me that I had nothing to worry about.

May I ask again why you rejected my application out of hand when my "problem" is so insignificant? I could understand if I were a finalist in the competition, and you selected someone else with equally good credentials who had no anticipated problems at all. From what I've heard, you have a thousand applicants for every person who will finally be chosen to live and work on Beltworld. But I really cannot fathom your motives in rejecting me at this early stage. Surely almost every human being alive today has a few defective genes! In fact, according to my doctor, no one has yet been found who is "perfect."

I respectfully request that you give me, or my doctor, a more credible explanation of your company's decision in my case.

Yours truly,
Dina Geijer

◆

Office of Personnel
North American Region
Hollings-Gray Corporation
265 West 33d Street
New York, NY 6SL 232-10082
9 October 2028

Dinu Geijer
1222-B Standish Court
908 East Genesee Street
Syracuse, NY 8PL 187-33091

Dear Ms. Geijer:

Thank you for your inquiry of 28 September. As we advised you in our letter of 14 September, it is corporate policy not to make direct disclosures of the results of biomap readings to applicants for positions at Hollings-Gray. The report sent to your physician by our medical department contained sufficient information to enable him to acquaint you with the nature of your medical problem. However, we do note that Dr. Prasad is not a psychiatrist, geneticist, or specialist in space medicine. It may be that he is not fully aware of the implications of your biomap for work experience in an extraterrestrial habitat.

We suggest, therefore, that you consult a licensed genetic counselor or a space medicine specialist with credentials in psychiatry. The medical department will write you under separate cover, giving you a list of such persons in your area. After you have seen a qualified practitioner, please give him or her the enclosed form for completion and return to our medical department at the address shown. We hope that this procedure will be satisfactory and helpful to you in finding the answers you seek.

Cordially yours,
Dong Joon Park
Personnel Associate

◆

1222-B Standish Court
908 East Genesee Street
Syracuse, NY 8PL 187-33091
1 November 2028

Dong Joon Park
Office of Personnel
North American Region
Hollings-Gray Corporation
265 West 33d Street
New York, NY 6SL 232-10082

Dear Ms. or Mr. Park:

I have now gone through all the red tape you specified in your letter of last month, seen a genetic counselor, given her your form, waited for your medical department to respond, visited my counselor again (this very morning), and guess what? I still don't know why you rejected my application.

The counselor, Marvella Johnson, tells me that in a space habitat so far from earth, under the pressure of having to work with the same small group of people for several years, the "disease" I allegedly have might cause me to suffer emotional distress, even a complete breakdown. But she disputes Dr. Prasad's interpretation of the data, and also that of your medical department, regarding the exact nature of this disease. She says that I don't have the right configuration of defective nucleotides to cause the disease—whatever it is—that you people are worried about. She says I have a few anomalous DNA strands in one gene in chromosome 11, which could trigger a different disease, but a much less serious one, and one that is much less likely to manifest itself, even in a restricted living environment such as Beltworld.

Her conclusion is that you should go back to the drawing board and read my biomap again. Please do so! (Also, would you tell me in your next letter whether you are a woman or a man? I simply don't know which is which in Korean.)

Yours truly,
Dina Geijer

♦

Office of Personnel
North American Region
Hollings-Gray Corporation
265 West 33d Street
New York, NY 6SL 232-10082
12 December 2028

Dina Geijer
1222-B Standish Court
908 East Genesee Street
Syracuse, NY 8PL 187-33091

Dear Ms. Geijer:

Thank you for your inquiry of 1 November, and your calls of 16 and 27 November. I regret the delay in replying. As my secretary may have explained during her conversation with you on the 27th, we fell behind in our correspondence when my colleague Dong Joon Park was transferred to our office in Capetown. The number of applications for the openings on Beltworld has far surpassed our expectations, making it especially difficult for us to respond expeditiously to requests such as yours.

As you know, it is corporate policy not to disclose to applicants for positions at Hollings-Gray the results of their biomap readings. I see from your file that you have complied with our procedures for obtaining further information, but are still not satisfied. I sympathize with you and understand your concern. If you would have Ms. Johnson fill out the enclosed form and send it to our medical department, we will furnish her with a more complete technical report of our findings. Thank you for your patience.

Cordially yours,
Lesley Parnell
Personnel Associate

♦

1222-B Standish Court
908 East Genesee Street
Syracuse, NY 8PL 187-33091
23 December 2028

Lesley Parnell
Office of Personnel
North American Region
Hollings-Gray Corporation
265 West 33d Street
New York, NY 6SL 232-10082

Dear Ms. or Mr. Parnell:

I have to wonder about you people. It's nothing personal, and you may be entirely innocent yourself, Lesley Parnell (man or woman? now I don't know again!), but why is it taking me so long to get to the bottom of this? I read in the paper only yesterday that some megacorp investigative departments know more about people's private lives than the FBI.

All I've wanted to be for as long as I can remember is a teacher of small children on a space colony. Well, I've also wanted to be a mother, but my cohabitant knew how to put a stop to that. Anyway, we're not together any more, for which maybe some of the thanks should go to Hollings-Gray, because I have been pretty lousy company since this whole mess began.

To get to the point, I piled through all your procedures yet again. Marvella saw me yesterday and gave me copies of several printouts your medical department sent her. She checked the data with an associate of hers who works in Rochester, who contacted another counselor in Toronto, and all three of them had a video conference Wednesday afternoon. They compared notes and, Marvella says, they agreed she had made a mistake. I am susceptible to the disease for which you found genetic markers. She wouldn't tell me what it is, because she said just knowing in advance that I had it might get it started. But when I pushed her, she also admitted that persistent treatment with psychochemicals would give me a 95 percent chance of remission or permanent cure. And guess what, Lesley old girl (boy)? She confirmed my hunch that the counseling chain she works for is owned by a subsidiary of Hollings-Gray. Need I say more?

So I think you sold me down the river. And I think that somebody in Hollings-Gray bears a grudge against me and wants me mired here in Syracuse or some other earthside city just because they know it will make me miserable. So I'm going to close this letter with an old Anglo-Saxon expression probably used a lot by my Jutish ancestors that will wreck my chances of ever working for a GTC megacorp but will also give me great personal satisfaction and relief.

Fuck you!

Yours truly (but not really),
Dina Geijer

◆

The disease to which your cousin referred in her letters, as I learned from studying medical records that she later obtained, was a form of schizophrenia (our mental syndrome 119-PR), inherited on chromosomes 11 and 26. Its usual manifestation was a sense of being persecuted, coupled with destructive or self-destructive rage. Dina Geijer tried to kill a Hollings-Gray employee in January 2029, screaming that the corporation was "out to get me." She was treated in a hospital for the criminally insane with the usual agenda of drugs, reconditioned to make her a docile citizen, and spent the rest of her life (meaning, until 2044) happily teaching preschoolers in Boston and then back again in Syracuse. But, from the evidence at hand, Hollings-Gray probably *was* out to get her—although not in the personal way she imagined during the inception of her illness. The megacorps had all-seeing eyes. No human flaw escaped their notice, and no man or woman was beyond their reach.

5

THE CATASTROPHE OF 2044

Containing the Arms Race

In 2044, the lords of capital ran out of luck. They had, from the beginning, made one fatal miscalculation. Even after they seized de facto control of most of the world's affairs in the early 2000s, they did not oust the politicians and set up their own dictatorship. Officially, legally, constitutionally, and sometimes in actual fact, sovereignty remained vested in the various states, which from time to time continued to indulge themselves in struggles for glory and mastery, as they had done in the days of Napoleon Bonaparte, Kaiser Wilhelm II, or Adolf Hitler.

The survival of sovereignty meant that deep within the world system, which was otherwise managed quite rationally, lay a core of irrationality, kept alive and warm by puerile megalomania. As we have seen, capital actually benefited in its earlier days from this division of authority. But in time the division became obsolete and counterproductive. Since the lords of capital had imposed severe limits on the state system but failed to wring its neck, the possibility lingered that one fine day, when the attention of the Global Trade Consortium was occupied elsewhere, the politicians would run amok and plunge the planet into a general war.

Such a war would not have made a vast difference in the scheme of things if the states had not been so awesomely armed. Under the comprehensive arms limitation protocol signed at the Vienna Conference of 1998, they agreed to a formula for containing the arms race. Containment, however, was not the same thing as abolition.

A few facts and figures about the changing makeup of the global population of nuclear warheads will be helpful. In 1987, just before the reductions negotiated at the "summit" meetings of the superpowers in the late 1980s, the armies of the world deployed a grand total of fifty-two thousand warheads. At the time of the Vienna Conference in 1998, they still deployed forty-one thousand, most of them American or Soviet. The third-ranking nuclear power was China, the fourth was France, and the remaining members of the "club" included Great Britain, Israel, India, Pakistan, and South Africa.

Most politicians and generals agreed that, with the exception of short-range tactical weapons intended for use on the battlefield, these missiles and bombs had no value. Or rather they had one value: as a deterrent. Even this was sometimes questioned since experts were not entirely sure that a country already devastated by a nuclear attack would or could retaliate with its surviving warheads.

Just the same, armies continued to develop and acquire nuclear weapons. In 1998, the United States alone had forty-one models of warhead in service (as compared with twenty-five in 1985), ranging from those carried by its largest intercontinental ballistic missiles to shells fired by field artillery. The so-called strategic forces of the nuclear powers included more than 1,300 intercontinental missiles armed with 7,000 warheads, 1,800 submarine-launched missiles armed with 10,500 warheads, and 325 long-range bombers carrying at least 5,500 warheads. All these weapons were designed to bring limitless death and destruction to the homelands of hostile nuclear powers.

The agreements already reached in the 1980s and early 1990s had succeeded in eliminating ground-based intermediate-range missiles as a class and reducing the numbers of intercontinental missiles. But much of this progress was offset by increases in "cruise" missiles— pilotless aircraft that could be launched from naval vessels or aircraft, flying low to avoid enemy surface radar and cloaked by stealth devices to prevent detection from the air. The numbers and varieties of tactical nuclear weapons also rose. In all, the nuclear forces of the world in 1998 included 1,100 cruise missiles and 16,900 tactical weapons.

The comprehensive arms limitation protocol negotiated in Vienna made a difference. The signatories agreed to replace their multiple-warhead intercontinental ballistic missiles with a new generation of mobile single-warhead missiles. Because these missiles were mobile, nested in special high-speed trains or in submarines prowling the deeps, they were difficult to find and hit, which made them ideal second-strike (retaliatory) weapons. Because each missile carried only one warhead, they were also less valuable as first-strike weapons than the multiple-warhead variety. Instead of one missile being able to destroy ten or fifteen enemy missile installations with its ten or fifteen independently targeted warheads, one missile could now destroy only one enemy installation, putting aggressors and defenders on more equal terms.

Within ten years of the first Vienna Conference, the number of warheads in strategic delivery systems deployed by the nine original nuclear powers fell from 24,100 to 3,660 and continued falling, although much more slowly, thereafter. Politicians made it clear that they were intended for deterrence only and did not threaten the peace of the world.

But the politicians seldom commented about their other weapons—especially battlefield weapons, all of which grew in numbers and in versatility as the new century wore on. They came in dozens of models, each designed to suppress certain forms of energy while enhancing others. They could be fired from rocket launchers, field artillery, tanks, tactical aircraft, or even portable mortars issued to infantrymen. Most supplied low yields, by the standards of nuclear weapons—as low as .025 kilotons of explosive force. Some were used primarily to start fires, others to demolish by shock waves, still others (such as the infamous "neutron bomb") to deliver lethal radiation to human targets or disabling radiation to enemy command, control, and communications facilities. The generals liked to emphasize their value as defensive weapons, to blunt an enemy's blitzkrieg. But they could just as readily be used to conduct a blitzkrieg.

A further complication was that, by 2025, five more countries possessed nuclear weapons. After terrific political battles between nuclear pacifists and fanatic nationalists, Japan joined the club in 1999, claiming that it could not play the new role defined in the Vienna accords if its "junior" partner China had nuclear weapons and Japan did not. Australia followed suit in 2008, Sweden in 2012, Switzerland in 2015, South Korea in 2017, and Italy in 2025. For brief periods, several other countries had a small number of battlefield weapons, including Iran, Iraq, Indonesia, Nigeria, Brazil, and Argentina, but as of 2025 all had been relieved of their nuclear arms by the countries in whose zones of domination they belonged.

So, for various reasons, despite the relative success of the comprehensive arms limitation protocol, the world nuclear warhead population (counting battlefield arms) stood on the eve of the Catastrophe of 2044 at about twenty-three thousand, a reduction of only 44 percent from the numbers deployed before the protocol. Politicians rhapsodized over the undeniable fact that the total megatonnage of these weapons was less than one-tenth the megatonnage of the weapons of fifty years earlier, but the difference was illusory. The nuclear arsenals of 2044 needed less explosive force than those of the late twentieth century because they were far more versatile, accurate, and difficult to find and destroy by preemptive attack.

They were also, let us be thankful, "cleaner." In the early 2030s, more than half the conventional nuclear warheads had been replaced by lithium hydride weapons detonated by minute pellets of antimatter instead of fissile materials. As a result, their explosions were relatively free of radioactive fallout. War ministries had ordered the new antimatter bombs primarily so that armies could invade devastated territories without delay, not to save civilian lives or the environment. The motives of the warriors notwithstanding, clean bombs killed fewer people and inflicted less damage on ecosystems.

With so many countries now able to start a nuclear war, many more opportunities arose for mistakes and miscalculations. But the spokespersons of the ruling elites saw matters quite differently. They argued that the proliferation of nuclear arms actually helped stabilize international politics. Most of the countries that had acquired them over the decades, they said, were charged with international "police" responsibilities under the Vienna accords or were states so eminently peaceloving and stable (i.e., affluent) that they would never resort to violence except in self-defense.

Spokespersons further insisted that, the more countries with nuclear arms, the fewer the temptations to engage them or their neighbors, allies, or major trading partners in hostilities. Sweden's nuclear strike force, for example, was widely seen as a guarantee of the continued neutrality and safety of Finland and the two Germanies. Australia's missiles were interpreted as a warning to overzealous expansionists in Japan and China. And so on. "The widespread deployment of nuclear weapons, not just by two but by fourteen nations of our great confederacy," as the director-general of the Confederated States of Earth pronounced in 2031, "is humanity's shield against world war."

On this point the director-general may not have been entirely wrong. At least he had a case. But, when he carried his analogy one step further and declared that "an even stronger shield protects the planet itself from harm, the shield that our member nations have erected in outer space," he was talking manifest nonsense.

The "even stronger shield" to which he referred was yet another system of strategic arms. This reductio ad absurdum of baroque weaponry, a multilayered defensive screen assembled in space and on the ground, resembled the crazy towering constructs of a child's toy building set more than anything; but war ministries of the time invested serious hopes in its capacity to prevent the falling of enemy missiles on home soil.

The vision of such a system was first made popular in the 1980s by the administration of Ronald Reagan in the United States. Picking up the threads of several inconclusive earlier programs (Soviet as well as American), Reagan authorized a massive program of research and development. Once launched, his strategic defense initiative (SDI) gathered too much bureaucratic and corporate momentum for anyone to stop it, although at least two presidents tried. It had its good years and its bad years, but funding continued, results accumulated, the Soviets and later the West Europeans developed their own versions, and, piece by piece, the rival systems were deployed. The American system was deemed fully operational by 2011, the Soviet by 2018, and the West European (with abundant help from Japan) by 2021.

At this distance, the particulars of the screens can have little interest since none of them really worked. All the same, building them was a great labor of adolescent imagination, one of the most enormous enterprises in modern history. After many false starts, the scientists and technicians found that a mix of kinetic-energy and particle-beam weapons mounted on space stations, supplemented by interceptor rockets fired from aircraft or ground facilities, supplied the best protection against incoming ballistic missiles. Specially modified interceptors were also produced to deal with cruise missiles. The computer software to design battle plans and facilitate an immediate defensive "spasm" against attack took more effort to construct than the weapons themselves.

If undisturbed, the American system was capable of preventing at least 90 percent of all incoming missiles from reaching their targets. If undisturbed, it furnished a nearly leak-proof defense of strategic military installations. The rub, from the first, was that no enemy had any intention of leaving it undisturbed, and the engineers never learned how to defend enough of it to make it effective. One of the oldest maxims of warfare was sedulously ignored: an indefensible defense is no defense at all.

Nuclear X-ray lasers, for example, once touted as superweapons for destroying missiles in space, proved too feeble for the task, but quite resourceful as disablers of space stations and communications satellites. Similar uses were found for kinetic-energy weapons. A new generation of robot or manned spaceplanes, capable of operating with equal facility in the atmosphere or in space, emerged to give the defenders further headaches.

To counter the countermeasures, the architects of SDI contrived a variety of shields, armed the space stations and satellites with beam weapons of their own, gave them the capability to dodge and out-maneuver their attackers, and deployed their own fleets of defensive spaceplanes.

But these counter-countermeasures could also be countered. The spiral had no end. In general, the American and West European systems were better designed, and certainly much more fully computerized, than the Soviet system, but the Soviets enjoyed a long lead in ways and means of disabling the SDI installations of their enemies. No side enjoyed a clear advantage. The systems clearly could not survive a general war, and the trillions of dollars spent on them were all—except for several important earthside civilian and military applications—squandered.

Meanwhile, in addition to nuclear and antinuclear weapons, states also outfitted themselves with other trillions of dollars worth of "conventional" arms. Some of these were anything but conventional, including nerve gas, hallucinogenic mists, bioengineered microbial weapons, chemical and gamma-ray lasers, and automated tanks manned only by AI computers. Another arms race, in the oceans, generated a spiral of antisubmarine and anti-antisubmarine weapons that threatened, at one point, to make the submarine obsolete and, at another, to make it invulnerable. In the end, the competing technologies offset one another. Submarines survived but remained mortal.

It goes without saying that, if the nations had manufactured a hundred times more weapons a thousand times more lethal, it would not have mattered if they could have refrained from making war. And why should they have made war? In the last age of capital, the megacorps wielded all the power they required, the rich states had little or nothing to fear from the poor, and the ruling elites were firmly in control.

Yet, as I said earlier, the sovereign states endured. Heeding the flow of policy directives from Zurich, mainstream politicians made little or no use of nuclear weapons as an instrument of state policy. But, even in the highest echelons of power, a few fervent patriots exerted disproportionate influence. The distinctions between Jews and Muslims, Christians and atheists, Marxists and non-Marxists, Russians and Anglo-Saxons, Japanese and Westerners, Catholics and Protestants, Hindus and monotheists, irrelevant as they may seem to you or me, had not dissolved.

In fact there were two political cultures. In ordinary times, the technical and financial superiority of the megacorporate culture prevailed. Founded on exploitation, it nevertheless paid the bills and exuded confidence. But, in less favorable times, the dominant culture lost some of its authority. People doubted and groped for alternatives.

In the 2030s and early 2040s, as the world economy staggered, extremist political movements attained a measure of respectability heretofore beyond their grasp. Some were democratic, like the World party, but not all. Those with the most formidable backing from elements of the ruling elites sought to revive nationalism, racism, and imperialism, in the guise of a people's crusade against what they perceived as a flabby, decadent cosmopolitanism. With colorful exceptions like the Sons and Daughters of Liberty, they functioned inside the established parties, and it was the resuscitators of nationalism within the established order, not the purists on the fringe, who posed the most serious threat to its equilibrium. At various vulnerable spots scattered around the globe, the system of the Vienna accords found itself under attack and unable to forge an effective, concerted response.

The Flash Point

The old powder kegs of Europe were not involved this time. The demilitarization of the two Germanies in 1998 turned out to be the wisest of the Vienna arrangements, effectively removing the heartlands of Europe from meddling by NATO or the Soviet bloc. No part of Europe gave any politician nightmares in the last decades of the age of capital.

The same—with a few reservations—may be said of Latin America, Africa, and East Asia. But, in the Middle East, the major powers were never able to resolve their differences. Nominally, the whole region (with the single exception of Israel) fell into the sphere of domination of the Soviet Union. The other major powers were expected to stand on the sidelines and applaud whatever actions Moscow decreed.

As a rule, this was no problem. When, for example, the Soviets annexed Iran in 2022, no finger was lifted anywhere in the world to restrain or condemn the Soviet Union. "Vienna," as President Remo Romano of the United States commented to newsmen, "is Vienna." In short, a deal was a deal.

But, after the economic debacle of 2032, powerful right-wing dissidents with positions of influence and sometimes even authority in the member states of the CSE began to shed their loyalties to the world community and think again of tribal best interests. Long regarded in sophisticated circles as—irony of ironies—a form of treason, patriotism lost its negative implications and became once again a hallowed prejudice.

The problem of the Middle East was its significance to so many different countries. The Soviet Union insisted on controlling the whole region, under the clear terms of the Vienna accords. The cheap oil of the Arabian peninsula, although running low, still counted for something in the world market. The United States felt a special responsibility to Israel, and Pakistan claimed special fraternal interests in the fate of the Islamic peoples of the Middle East.

What most alarmed politicians and GTC directors was the degradation of the American-Soviet accord on Israel in the early 2040s. The underlying reason was the intensification of the world economic crisis, which strengthened the appeal of narrow national "solutions" not only to the electorate but also to segments of the ruling elites. In the unusually hot summer of 2042, Soviet border guards under instructions from Moscow allowed several bands of Arab terrorists to enter Israel. The resulting mayhem on the West Bank gave Soviet troops a pretext to invade the West Bank to pacify the area, even though Israeli forces were perfectly able to do the job without Soviet assistance. American and Soviet leaders traded insults and threats

of Armageddon for months until the Soviet troops finally withdrew in
October.

A far greater provocation came in December 2043. The Soviet
Union decided to annex Israel and set up a new trusteeship known
as the Autonomous District of the Jordan Valley (ADJOV).

The Soviet decision seemed outrageous to most Americans, but,
from the perspective of the world order that prevailed down to 2044,
ADJOV was a plausible arrangement. When the Vienna conferees had
originally excluded Israel from the Soviet zone, the West Bank territories under Israeli occupation were inhabited by an equal number of
Palestinians and Israeli colonists. But the Vienna accords prohibited
further emigration of Israeli citizens to the West Bank. Between 1998
and 2043, the Arab population of the West Bank territories more than
doubled, while the Jewish population increased by only 15 percent.
As a result, the Arabs once again enjoyed a huge demographic advantage. Agitation for Arab independence grew all through the 2030s.

In 2042, a new Palestinian political formation, the Independent
Front for Freedom in Palestine, replaced the fossilized Palestine Liberation Organization, organizing riots, strikes, and labor slowdowns
throughout the West Bank. Observers from the CSE testified that the
Independent Front was a legitimate indigenous protest movement
and urged the Israelis to recognize and deal with it. They refused. In
October 2043, the Israeli authorities closed every school and business in the Arab portions of the West Bank. On 1 December, Israeli
troops opened fire on a boisterous mob in Nablus. After killing more
than 150 citizens (some of them armed), they were attacked by an
organized detachment of Independent Front freedom fighters. Several dozen Israeli soldiers were killed, reinforcements were called in,
and, in the ensuing massacre, more than five thousand Arabs died.

The news of the disaster spread by word of mouth overnight. By
daybreak on 2 December, the whole Arab population was in arms.
Isolated Israeli settlers were killed or burned out of their homes, Israeli vigilantes responded in kind, and the situation swiftly crumbled
into chaos. As two divisions of Israeli army regulars entered the West
Bank, a mixed force of Russians and Syrians invaded from the north-
east. A full-scale war appeared inevitable.

The Soviet authorities consulted briefly with Washington, but on
7 December, rejecting American warnings, they dispatched an immense army into Israel. Brushing aside the Israeli forces, it occupied

Tel Aviv and Jerusalem. Four days after the invasion began, Soviet authorities in Jerusalem announced the formation of ADJOV, and the *fait* was *accompli*.

From the beginning, ADJOV was an entity wholly dominated by Moscow. Jewish and Arab Communists were put in nominal charge of their respective "provinces," known as Zion and Palestine, but they did not lift a finger without securing the advice and consent of the Soviet military governor, who in turn consulted Moscow on all politically sensitive points. A force of 100,000 Soviet troops occupied the land. Former Israelis who refused to collaborate were summarily shot or whisked to camps or prisons in the Soviet Union.

By the spring of 2044, even the Palestinians decided that they had only exchanged one set of oppressors for another. The Communist mayor of a small West Bank town was murdered in the night by Independent Front irregulars, which gave the Soviets a suitable pretext for outlawing the organization and deporting most of its leaders to Soviet labor camps.

The harshness of Soviet rule in the ADJOV may seem excessive, but it was no worse than the treatment received by most Third World peoples from the core countries entrusted with their management. The two Vienna conferences had set up a system of domination, not charity.

Israel, however, was not a typical Third World nation, indeed not a Third World nation at all. The Jews of Israel lived almost as well and deployed the same advanced technology as the Jews of the United States. In any case, Israel had always been excluded from the zone of legitimate special influence of the Soviet Union. It was technically the ward of the United States, although in practice it behaved more like the fifty-second American state, not an American dependency. When the Soviets erected their new order in the Jordan valley, they had every reason to expect fierce American opposition.

In both countries, domestic considerations counted for more than diplomatic. The Old Bolshevik faction of the ruling party had been looking for many years for a good excuse to seize Israel. Its leaders saw the existence of an American enclave in Southwest Asia as an intolerable thorn in the side of Soviet power and the issue itself as the ideal lever with which to win control of the Kremlin. The Old Bolsheviks argued that, as long as the problem of Palestine went unsolved, Soviet management of its zone would remain (as it had always been) racked with troubles and only barely profitable to Mother Russia. To gain the full cooperation of the Islamic peoples, who made up 35 percent of the population of the Soviet zone, Israel had to go.

Vassily Kravchenko, of course, disagreed; and, while he ruled, the Old Bolsheviks could not force fundamental changes in Soviet policy. When he died late in 2041, they saw their opportunity. Kravchenko's hand-picked successor pursued the same course, but without his disarming guile and political savoir faire. One by one, the inner circle of Kremlin leaders was converted to the Old Bolshevik point of view. The successor was removed from office six months after Kravchenko's death, when he heatedly refused to endorse the plan to test American resolve by "pacifying" the West Bank in the summer of 2042.

In the United States itself, President Mary Chávez faced a quite different situation. Her administration was in trouble with the electorate because of the worsening business depression, which the voters—following centuries of tradition—naturally blamed on the party in power rather than on the lords of capital. The American presidential elections were set for November 2044, and Chávez entertained the desperate hope of winning a second term. With no possibility of a redeeming economic upturn, she had only one clear chance of doing so: by capturing public favor with a sensational victory in foreign affairs. She was further pushed in that direction by the strategy of her Republican opponents in their primary election campaigns. All five stressed the need to restore America's place in the sun and the front-runner called for a "crusade of crusades against the greatest heresy of our times, one-worldism."

Five years earlier, such sentiments would have earned the would-be crusader an anonymous phone call from GTC agents threatening to expose his romance with his best friend's wife, but, in the darker climate of the 2040s, the GTC and its allies decided that firebrands on the far right could be useful and let the man continue unmolested.

It followed that, when Israel was transformed into ADJOV, opinion in the United States reacted with unwonted fury. President Chávez seized the initiative at once, calling for Soviet withdrawal and the full restoration of Israeli sovereignty "by Christmas"—an odd choice of dates. American military forces, which had upgraded their battle readiness after the crisis of the previous summer, were placed on full alert throughout the world.

A thunderbolt struck Washington on 19 December 2043. The

office of the CSE director-general, after several days of uninterrupted mulling, summoned an emergency meeting of the CSE Senate. Composed of one delegate each from the world's forty most prosperous and forty most populous states (which gave several countries two delegates), the Senate met in Stockholm. By a vote of forty-six to twenty-two, with twelve abstentions, it censured the United States for its ultimatum to the Soviet Union and for mobilizing its armed forces, which the Senate branded "a blatantly provocative and irresponsible act." The GTC immediately imposed a worldwide news blackout, but enough people in high places heard enough by word of mouth to get the gist of what was happening and drew the necessary conclusions.

The reasoning of the forty-six senators who voted to censure the United States is not obscure. Although the United States had most of the law on its side, the Soviet Union was considered the more fragile of the two states at this point in time and the more likely to bolt the CSE if worse came to worse.

The next day, as the Senate met again at the request of the United States, President Chávez herself appeared at the rostrum and announced the withdrawal of the United States from the CSE. In her speech, Chávez pointedly compared the action of the Soviets on 7 December to the action of the Japanese at Pearl Harbor on another 7 December in American history. Her Republican opponents sighed and wondered how they could improve on the President's performance. In the end they gave up trying and rallied behind her.

The CSE thereupon hardened its line, ignoring the frantic advice of GTC representatives, and declared a trade quarantine of the United States. We have abundant evidence that GTC agents were trying to manage the crisis and produce a quick negotiated solution, but they misjudged the intensity of the long-stifled passions of nationalism and did not work hard enough.

Christmas came and went without appeasement of the United States by the Soviet regime. In February 2044, the United States broke off diplomatic relations with the Soviet Union. American submarines smuggled thousands of military advisers and tons of supplies into "Zion," where the CIA enjoyed close ties with remnants of the Israeli army operating underground. The American economy was placed on a war footing late in March, as the quarantine took its toll.

Finally, in April, using all their craft, the heads of the GTC applied so much pressure on the CSE that the quarantine was lifted. But the relief came too late. American-Soviet relations continued to worsen. Claiming espionage by the Polish authorities, the United States recalled its ambassador from Warsaw. Days later, Warsaw and Washington severed diplomatic relations as well. All five Republican candidates for president, in an unprecedented display of harmony, aborted their campaigns and backed the reelection of President Chávez. She announced that she would choose as her next running mate the Republican (and Jewish) governor of New York, Nathan Wexler.

The situation brightened briefly in late June. The GTC devised a compromise settlement that might well have done the trick. Under its terms, the Soviets were directed to evacuate all of ADJOV except the West Bank by 15 July, restoring Israel as a sovereign state under American wardship. The West Bank would be added to the Soviet Union's trans-Jordanian trust territories, and the United States would pay a heavy indemnity to the Soviet Union for the expenses of its action as a "surrogate trustee." Operatives of the GTC were instructed to lay their proposals before the Soviet and American governments on 30 June.

The Last Week of the Age of Capital

But once again the GTC had acted too late, still failing to grasp the mindlessness of the process now unfolding. Words, threats, and economic sanctions were no longer enough. On 29 June, a crack detachment of CIA professionals, working intimately with former Israeli army officers and intelligence agents, ignited a rebellion against the Soviet occupation throughout Zion. The Soviet forces were caught off guard, suffering heavy losses in the first two days of the rebellion. Moscow ordered "retaliation without mercy."

On 1 July, the Soviets withdrew their troops from Tel Aviv. They streamed out of the city all morning. Israeli freedom fighters took possession of it at noon, making it their temporary capital. But just after sunset Tel Aviv was obliterated by a pair of twenty-kiloton nuclear bombs left behind by the retiring Soviet forces and detonated by radio signals after their departure. Two hundred seventy-five thousand people died instantly, many in synagogues for sabbath prayers. The Soviet high command promised still greater atrocities if the rebels did not lay down their arms at once.

Some did. Thousands more were killed in house-to-house combat throughout the rest of Zion. Central Intelligence Agency agents on the scene radioed Washington that the Soviets were committing genocide.

On 3 July, Soviet and American leaders remained in almost constant contact by videophone, the president with the chairman, the military chiefs of staff with one another, and both sides with a mélange of official and quasi-official mediators from Western Europe, Japan, China, the CSE, and the GTC. On the surface, everything was calm, orderly, respectful. The leaders avoided inflammatory rhetoric and exchanged (as we know from several tapes that survived) only a few profanities, always in low voices with pale, expressionless faces. The worst recorded epithet was spoken by President Chávez, who called the Soviet foreign minister cerdo (pig) under her breath— whether a reference to his portly figure or his inhumanity, we shall never know.

The fourth of July, a national holiday in the United States, started out much the same. Toward evening, Washington time, it even appeared that the crisis was about to be resolved. The Soviet chairman had floated the idea of a swap, with the United States abandoning its interest in Israel in exchange for Soviet indifference to the fate of Cuba, still a Soviet dependency after more than eighty years. President Chávez, Cuban-American on her mother's side, was tempted.

But she also knew that the Moscow-Havana alliance had been fading since the 2020s, mainly because the Soviets, otherwise excluded from Latin America by the Vienna accords, no longer had any geopolitical use for it. Under the moderate regime of Premier Raúl Santiago, Cuba had meanwhile restored full diplomatic relations with the United States. Sacrificing a still fervently loyal Israel, with its millions of Jewish supporters in the American electorate, for a Cuba destined to fall into America's grasp anyway, seemed a bad bargain.

More to the point, the logic of deals was yielding, resistlessly, to a deeper, more primitive logic, given special authority by the nature of late modern warfare. As experts in strategic thinking had argued for almost a century, the arrival of nuclear weapons profoundly shortened the time available to politicians and commanders for responding to attacks and also multiplied the reasons for launching devastating preemptive attacks of their own. A "graduated" or "measured" response, however prudent it might appear on the surface, actually made very little sense. The Western allies adopted it as their policy, but everyone knew it was absurd. "The NATO doctrine," as the U.S. defense expert Morton Halperin had said many years earlier, "is that we will fight with conventional forces until we are losing, then we will fight with tactical [nuclear] weapons until we are losing, and then we will blow up the world."

This remained, indeed, the official war plan of the Western alliance system down to the early 2000s, although, in case of actual hostilities, it would probably have been scrapped on the first day. But in the twenty-first century, with the demilitarization of Germany and the partition of the globe into zones of special legitimate influence, NATO abandoned even its hypothetical commitment to a doctrine of graduated response. Strategists in all countries agreed that only two options remained to commanders-in-chief if a general war threatened to break out: settlement of the issues at stake by negotiation or a knockout blow lasting no more than forty minutes, aimed at totally disabling the enemy's command, control, and communications network no matter what the cost.

In short, chop off the monster's head before it can act. Never mind its chest or limbs or belly. Decapitate!

For several decades, until the crisis that occupied the summer of 2042, there had been no real danger of a world war. But, having nothing better to do, defense ministries had taken full advantage of the progress of the computer sciences to push the responsiveness of their defensive and offensive weapons systems to the maximum. Systems on all sides were programmed to react to specified attack patterns in milliseconds without human intervention.

President Chávez went to bed early on 4 July with her mind made up. She took a sleeping capsule to ensure that she would be well rested when she arose at 4:00 A.M. In the morning, she mixed an illegal euphoric with her orange juice. Her secretary of defense, David Weiss, briefed her one more time on the current estimated capabilities of American SDI facilities. We do not know what she did next, but at seven she took a copter to the war suite in her Maryland bunker.

At 8:45 A.M. EDT, 5 July 2044, Mary Chávez nodded to David Weiss. He spoke one word into his screen. As the major who lived to tell the tale reported in his memoirs, the word was "Go."

The U.S. war plan, executed without consulting or notifying any other power (to help avoid the leakage of information to Soviet intelligence), appeared to have a reasonable chance of working. Only nine people, including just three civilians, knew the time of the attack, and only nine others, in the military, knew it would occur at all. The Soviets and everyone else were taken by surprise.

Within fifteen minutes of the one-word command by Weiss, 90 percent of the Soviet Union's space-based defenses had been rendered inoperable. Within twenty-five minutes, missiles and beam weapons had eliminated at least 80 percent of its ground-based defenses. Most of its military and naval bases were demolished, together with Moscow, Vladivostok, and several less well-known cities, targeted because of their importance as military command centers. Three-quarters of the missile-bearing Soviet submarines at sea were also sunk or disabled.

The Soviet reply was triggered automatically at 8:45:20 by sensor readings relayed from space. Soviet war-fighting computers correctly interpreted the pattern of the attack and ordered its repulsion, together with a counterstrike aimed at the eyes and brains of the United States and its allies. Even though it was clear that Western Europe had taken no part in the initial American attack, Soviet strategists had programmed their systems to operate on the premise that British, French, and Italian forces not committed in a first strike were held in reserve for retaliatory or "sanitary" second strikes and could not be allowed to survive.

The success of the American strategy depended on neutralizing Soviet defenses massively and swiftly enough to prevent effective Soviet countermeasures. In the result, they were not neutralized massively enough. Computer malfunctions, signal jamming by Soviet counterweapons, and unexpectedly heavy shielding of the most vital Soviet space-based installations conspired to spare the minimum number of weapons needed to decapitate the United States and its allies. Soviet missiles, many of them submarine launched, eliminated the West's principal command centers and disrupted vital segments of its military communications networks.

In short, both sides chopped off the monster's head. By 9:25 A.M. EDT, both sides were blind, deaf, and dumb.

Up to this point, the world system had sustained serious but not irreparable damage. Ten cities had been entirely or mostly wrecked, together with thousands of military installations and nearly every civilian and military facility orbiting the planet in outer space. Including persons still alive whose death was inevitable because they had received fatal doses of radiation or had been burned or crushed beyond hope of recovery, the death toll was approximately eighty million.

Convulsions of a Dead Beast

But what does a headless monster do after it loses its head? Does it collapse in a heap? Or does it run wildly about, thrashing its tail and covering the countryside with geysers of blood?

A real monster would probably collapse in a heap, but a metaphorical monster, such as the decapitated nation-state system, has a wider range of options. If you were the commander of a missile-bearing submarine or a flight of spaceplanes or an armored division or a mobile missile train, and you heard that your country was at war, but minutes later lost contact with your headquarters and every other headquarters, what would you assume had happened? What would you do next?

From the scanty evidence that remains, it is clear that surviving commanders acted in many different ways. Some were paralyzed by the unthinkable nature of the events unfolding and did nothing but sit tight and wait. A few took it for granted that the world, as they knew it, had come to an end and turned over their command to a local government official. Others tried to reach their base or capital city. Some linked up with scattered brother units, and some did or could not.

A small but not insignificant number of commanders elected to continue the war on their own authority. Some of these had armed intercontinental ballistic missiles at their disposal. Some had gamma-ray artillery, or AI tanks, or cruise missiles, or nuclear shells and rockets. Some were stationed in Europe, some on the high seas, some in Asia. At least one hundred spaceplanes survived the first hour of the war while on missions in the upper atmosphere or in space, and many of these were heavily armed.

The one thing available to no commander in the field was a full picture of what had happened to the world on the morning of 5 July, or why, or even who was the "enemy." Authorities in the noncombatant countries, especially Sweden, Germany, Japan, and China, made heroic efforts to contact military personnel everywhere and tell them the war was over, but they were seldom believed. Commanders naturally interpreted such communications as enemy tricks or, worse, evidence of complicity with the enemy. One Russian submarine commander, implored to lay down his arms by clearly authentic Japanese naval officers broadcasting from Yokohama, concluded that Japan was now an ally of the United States, radioed his news to a sister ship nearby, and demolished Yokohama with his last missile. In desperation, Japanese forces engaged the other submarine. Before it sank, it sent a salvo of missiles toward Japan that killed sixty-five million people.

The random ruin of civilization by invertebrate armies went on for weeks. Most of North America and the Soviet Union was destroyed, together with many parts of Western and Eastern Europe, the Middle East, East Asia, and North Africa. A vicious nuclear war between Pakistan and India, started by the Pakistanis as soon as they realized they had nothing to fear from the Soviet Union, devastated most of the Indian subcontinent north of the Tropic of Cancer. China was dragged into the conflict by roving Soviet commanders in Siberia but suffered far less damage in proportion to its numbers than Japan.

I will have more to say about the costs of World War III, and the years of desolation and misery that followed, in another chapter. For now, I have said enough. But please remember that the Catastrophe of 2044, the tragedy of that long, mad, bloody summer, was not the fault of President Chávez, or the Israelis, or the Old Bolsheviks, or the CSE, or any other person or group of persons. Nor was it an accident. If you give several sovereign states the means to eradicate the world many times over, sooner or later the Day of Judgment will arrive. You may avoid it once, you may avoid it twice, you may avoid it a thousand times. But sooner or later it will come. Given the nature of the world system prevailing in the last half of the twentieth century and the first half of the twenty-first, World War III was inevitable. The only oddity was that it did not occur much sooner.

INTERLUDE

These few letters furnish a personal footnote to the unimaginable events of July 2044. My great-grandfather Carl Jensen had two sons. The older, my grandfather, was a lawyer in Washington on business when the Soviet missiles fell. He died there at the age of thirty-seven.

Carl's second son, Harry, was a U.S. Air Force colonel and the commander of a squadron of eight spaceplanes stationed in Greenland at the time of the Catastrophe. Knowing Carl's political views, I am sure he bitterly regretted Harry's choice of careers, but he was not a man to try to run his children's lives. Harry wrote these letters to his wife Olivia.

> *Box Y-2426*
> *APO NY 9ST-22286*
> *10 July 2044*

Dearest Livie,

O God dearest Livie, what can I tell you? What can I say? We showed those bastards, but O my God, I don't know whether you're alive or dead. I just have to write to you and hope that you're okay, and Trish and Steve. I think of you every day and every night, and you're in my dreams darling, I love you so very much.

I'm okay, so far, but you never know what's next, it's just hell. I wish to God everything had turned out different. I know you don't have much news down there. Our base got blasted while we were up, so we found a civilian airport in Reykjavik where we touch down between sorties. The Icelanders are stunned, they just give us fuel and food and let us come and go, but they're in a daze, like us, they don't know what happened.

If you ever read this, please believe I'm okay. The other guys and I have flown three attack flights, taking out Russian supply depots and airstrips along the shores of the Barents Sea and the Kara Sea, above the Arctic Circle. There's not too much smoke and dust in these latitudes, so it's pretty smooth flying.

We can't make any contact with Denver or Washington. No satellite readings, either, but I guess they're all gone, I mean, the cities, the satellites, you name it. Because you're in Oregon, on the coast, I figure you have a chance, if anybody does, thank God. Just keep calm and hold the fort for me darling, I'll be back, as soon as I can, I'll be back. We just have to make sure we haven't left anything these cocksuckers can use.

I'm sorry. I didn't mean it like that, about the Russians. Most of them are ordinary guys like the guys in my squadron. But when they killed all those people in the Holy Lands, they forfeited their right to be treated like human beings. One of my pilots is a Jew, Barney Lipschutz. He's a hell of a brave man, but he broke down and cried like a baby when he heard about the invasion of Israel. We had to do it, Livie. It's a mess, I know. Nothing worked out right. But we had to do it.

I love you darling, pray for me.

Love and kisses,
Harry

♦

Box Y-2426
APO NY 9ST-22286
15 July 2044

Dearest Livie,

I didn't mail my last letter because I don't know how. The base is gone, the post office in Reykjavik won't take letters for outside Iceland, the videophone terminals are all dead.

But I'll save it anyway, and this one, and any others I write, because some day you'll see them. I know that. I know that more than anything. I feel you living, and Trish and Stevie, and everybody in town, I know you're okay. That's what keeps me going.

The best I can make out, this has been the end of civilization, at least in the Northern Hemisphere. We've flown missions all over, trying to find out what happened. You can't see much through the smoke, but the sensors on the planes give us pretty good evidence. The big cities, the bases, everything charred and fried and barbecued, jesus, I don't know. I don't know who won the war, and I don't much care, as long as the Russians lost it. They started this war darling, you have to believe that, they started it, and we finished it, and maybe it finished us, but O God, please not Oregon.

All day I've been giving my plane a lube job and thinking of you, and thinking of Dad. He was in Albuquerque when everything blew, so I'm sure he's dead. I never understood that man. He used to tell me when I was a little kid about the "power structure" and the "system of domination" and I never understood. What I do understand is this darling, and please don't ever forget it. We had the best country in the whole goddam world, we had freedom, we had riches, we had respect, we had the best people, and nobody can tell you anything else. Please believe this, darling. Believe it. We had everything.

It's all ashes and we had everything. I love you and I love Trish and

Steve and I'll be home in a couple more days. We just have to make sure the Russians don't have anything left they can use. You understand. I love you more than ever.

> *Hugs and kisses,*
> *Harry*
> ◆

> Box Y-2426
> APO NY 9ST-22286
> 18 July 2044

Dearest, Dearest, Livie, and Trish and Steve,

I lost five of my planes today. The squadron was attacked by a dozen Russian planes coming out of nowhere, we shot down a couple, but they got Barney and Pedro and Stan, and, well, you don't know the rest of the guys, so it doesn't matter. They're dead. I got clipped in the wing by one of the SOBs, but I'm not hurt. I limped into Reykjavik in one piece.

Before we were hit we found one more Russian town with airfields and troops, swarming like ants. We got 'em with a couple of half-kilo rockets. Turned the sons of bitches to sand.

We have only two planes that will fly now. I'll try to get back to you in one, but we have eight men who all want to go home, and just the two planes. Because I have this bird on my shoulder I have to be the last. You understand. It's like the captain who goes down with his ship. But maybe the ship won't go down.

It's crazy, me writing these letters. I was never much of a letter writer, either. But it helps somehow to talk to you, even if you can't hear or answer.

O my God I want you now!

> *Love, love, and more*
> *Harry*
> ◆

> Box Y-2426
> APO NY 9ST-22286
> 25 July 2044

Dearest Olivia,

Yesterday was the last day of the mission. We had a rocket left, a five-kilo special, so we drew straws to see who would use it. I won. We de-

cided I would take the plane (the other plane conked out) and drop it where it would do the most good. I flew all the way to Riga in Soviet Latvia and let it go nice and easy. There were a lot of people down there, but not any more. I did a second turn over the city after it blew up, and believe me, that baby is gone.

I must sound like a mad dog. You know what? I am. The trouble with this world was, we weren't mad enough. We didn't care for our country like we cared for all our fucking comforts and screwing around. We let the one-worlders (like Dad) be our conscience and we forgot the basic lesson of history, that you have to fight for what you want and stick together, man to man. If we had stuck together, and told the Russians where to shove their fucking screaming bellyaching Arabs five years ago, they wouldn't have marched into the Holy Lands. There wouldn't have been any war.

My dearest wife, and mother of my children, my dearest Livie, I failed you. The whole air force failed you. We weren't good enough to protect you. I don't know if you'll ever forgive us. I don't know if I can forgive myself.

O my God, the world is burnt out. Everything we worked to build, everything we loved and worked to build, is gone. All because we didn't know how to fight any more. Until it was just too damn late.

I'm coming home real soon. We're taking the plane and running a shuttle service. Six of the guys are back home, or as close as they could get. One more trip, to Puerto Rico and Texas, through all the wild colored smoke, and the snow (imagine snow in July, but they predicted it), and then I'll be alone and it's Coos Bay or bust! I know you can't read this, but you will later, and we'll laugh and cry and laugh and make love and say, God bless America.

She's down now, betrayed and bewildered. But maybe some day she'll rise again. For Trish, for Steve, for all of us who bled and died to try to save her.

Closing now with all my love, forever and ever.

Your Harry

◆

Harry Jensen returned to Coos Bay, Oregon, on 27 July. He found his wife and children hacked to pieces by unknown assailants, perhaps a gang of youthful radiation victims from Salem looking for a good time before they died. Such things were not uncommon in the summer of 2044. He left these letters, and a short farewell note, in a safe in the family home before taking off in his spaceplane one more time and crashing it into Mount Hood in northern Oregon the next morning. I do not think he was an evil man, in the sense of deviantly malicious or misanthropic. He was, in fact, a typical man of his time, a good soldier and a loyal American; a simple man; and, through no special fault of his own, a fool.

BOOK THE SECOND
RED EARTH

6

THE COMING OF THE
COMMONWEALTH

Intensive Care

Between 2044 and 2046, the world was like a great hospital, filled to overflowing with gravely and terminally ill patients. Most of them needed intensive care, but the hospital could help only a chosen few. To the outside observer, it might have seemed more like a charnel house than a place of healing.

Occasionally, a few of its wings and corridors would also have resembled fields of battle, as tattered companies of troops from the old war passed through or new wars erupted among contending local chiefs. The collapse of so many national governments made it impossible (or at least pointless) to hold conferences and sign peace treaties and issue orders to demobilize.

But the warring of these years, although sometimes quite vicious and desperate, bore no comparison to what had transpired in the summer of 2044. As armies ran out of munitions, fuel, spare parts, medical supplies, and sometimes even food, they could no longer fight the battles for which they had been trained. One by one, they splintered into brawling guerrilla bands or joined regional constabularies.

The first year, from August 2044 to July 2045, was the worst. I cannot tell you how terrible it was. None of us can imagine. I doubt that even people of the twentieth century could have imagined it. All previous wars had been fought in short bursts in a relatively small number of more or less clearly defined theaters: a pitched battle here, a bombed city there, an exchange of naval fire somewhere else. The First and Second World Wars included many such events, but there were always opportunities for soldiers and civilians alike to regroup, rebuild, and catch their breath.

The war of 2044 was a very different experience. The blows fell heavily, swiftly, universally, and, after the first day, unpredictably, as individual commanders made their individual decisions. The survivors in each country had no sense of what was happening elsewhere. The fabric of society unraveled, leaving families to fend for themselves.

Casualties mounted exponentially. On the first day, eighty million people died or had received injuries soon to be fatal. At the end of the first month, the death toll stood at 700 million. By then, most of the serious war making was over, the missiles, bombs, and shells spent or abandoned. But the dying had just begun. According to the reliable estimates of a team of Australian demographers, two-thirds of the human race was lost in the eleven months after the serious fighting sputtered to a finish in early August 2044. More than five billion people (the whole population of the world as of 1990) died in those eleven months. They died because the earth, transformed and mutilated by war, could no longer support them. Too many vital links had been severed. Too much had been destroyed, too suddenly.

The first year! No, we cannot imagine it. By early August, most of the urban centers of North America, Europe, the Soviet Union, Japan, northern China, and the Indian subcontinent had been devastated, chiefly by nuclear weapons. Fires burning out of control for weeks drove the few able-bodied survivors into the surrounding countryside, which, in the dry late summer weather, often burned as well.

With the cities had gone every major military installation, although many military units, already airborne, seaborne, or in the field, survived. Even installations located underground, such as the great command facilities, were "sterilized," in the hideous jargon of the time, by corkscrew missiles tunneling into their bowels.

Wherever armies used old-fashioned fission bombs instead of the new but costlier antimatter weapons, plumes of fallout (mostly radioactive isotopes of strontium and cesium) spread far downwind from each explosion. The plumes scattered the inhabitants of towns that had escaped direct hits, killing many and threatening every farmer and villager in their path. The loss of life from blast, fire, initial radiation, and fallout, as everyone had predicted, was high.

But not so high as what followed. The denizens of the modern civilized world—including most of the rural population—were slavishly dependent on its centralized technology and services for their day-to-day existence. Deprived of interactive computer networks, telephones and videophones, satellites and electronic media, power grids, water and sewage lines, fossil fuels, public and commercial transport, hospitals, and medical centers, the body social was no longer viable. In many parts of the world, the body social ceased to exist.

A typical post-Catastrophe catastrophe was the unchecked spread of disease. Epidemics of influenza, typhus, cholera, hepatitis, and CAIDS broke loose and killed millions of survivors. In normal times such outbreaks could have been quickly isolated and brought under control, but the bodies of the victims were already weakened by radiation sickness and malnutrition, clean potable water was hard to find, sewage could no longer be treated, medical care and supplies were scarce or nonexistent, and most urban hospitals had been destroyed during the Catastrophe.

A special horror was the problem of the unburied cadavers—of people and also of wild and domesticated animals—that littered the suburbs and the countryside, poisoned the streams, bred disease, and putrefied and stank throughout July. In some communities, bodies were given decent burials or cremated in pyres, but the survivors were not always strong enough or well enough organized to do the job.

The Australian demographic team that toured North America in 2047 reported encountering "bone fields," stretches of open country near incinerated cities where thousands of skeletons still lay, partially covered by thick growths of coarse weeds, telling a story of sick and injured refugees overtaken by brush and woodland fires. In many small towns enough skeletons were discovered to suggest that fallout, or disease, or both, had claimed every inhabitant. Here, at last, the world had heeded the advice of Jesus of Nazareth; the dead were left to bury their own.

Also catastrophic was the change in climate and air quality produced by the nuclear explosions of July. In the mid-1980s, climate modelers had speculated that a nuclear "winter" would seize the planet for months after a full-scale nuclear war. Even a small nuclear war might do the trick, they foresaw, if it resulted in the burning of enough cities and forests. Their views were quickly challenged by other climatologists, leading to so much confusion on the subject that most people, including most politicians, forgot all about it.

The events of July 2044 failed to substantiate fully the warnings of the nuclear Cassandras of the 1980s. As foreseen, the fireball of each explosion lifted into the stratosphere countless tons of dust from the surface of the earth. Shortly thereafter, comparable masses of smoke and soot were pumped into the lower atmosphere by fires. The dust and smoke joined to form a dense pall shrouding most of the earth from the sun. Streaked with bands of dark colors like bruised flesh, the heaviest skies were seen only in northern latitudes, but some of the smoke and dust spread southward. Normal bright sunshine was a rarity until one reached the twenty-fifth parallel—lower Brazil, central Australia, and the Southern African Republic.

But within a month the shroud disintegrated. Nor did surface temperatures in the temperate zone of the Northern Hemisphere plunge to Arctic levels, as once expected. From the few surviving records, it seems likely that temperatures in the Northern Hemisphere dropped by an average of only ten degrees Centigrade and began to rise again slowly as the skies cleared.

All the same, the sudden nuclear autumn crippled agriculture. Yields of wheat, barley, and rice fell steeply. Some areas experienced severe droughts as a direct result of climatic stress. With trade and transport also disrupted, little food was harvested and still less came to market between July and the early months of 2045. Stocks of preserved or durable foods, already depleted by the destruction of urban warehouses and retail centers, disappeared quickly. Although the loss of nearly a billion mouths to feed in the first month of hostilities helped relieve the pressure on available supplies, even this was not enough to make a real difference.

So people starved. They starved by the millions, and then hundreds of millions, and finally thousands of millions. Relief shipments from Southern Hemisphere countries with small quantities of food to spare kept a fortunate few alive along shorelines. Inland, conditions were much worse. Even many farm families starved to death. Africans, long dependent on imported grain, suffered inconceivably.

The real question is how anyone north of twenty-five degrees South remained alive. Those who were not cremated in the nuclear blasts should have been struck down by disease. Those who avoided disease should have starved. Yet, if we can believe the Australian demographers, more than two billion people were still alive in northern and central latitudes in the summer of 2045. How did they manage?

My answer comes in two parts. The larger number of survivors were people who lived in areas not directly involved in the hostilities. In such places, national or at least provincial governments did not fall apart, transportation was not badly disrupted, and tank farms could be built, or existing tank farms expanded, to provide enough nutrients from crops of edible algae to replace at least some of the field crops and livestock destroyed by war and its aftermath.

More than half the people of Mexico, Central America, the Middle East, and Indonesia survived in this way. Southwestern China and most of southern India, including the states of Kerala, Karnataka, and Tamil Nadu, survived. Even in Europe, several countries weathered the Catastrophe, among them Spain, Greece, Poland, and parts of Germany and Scandinavia. None of these countries escaped entirely. Millions of Germans, for example, died from fallout, plagues, and malnutrition, as did virtually the whole population of northernmost Mexico. But the countries themselves pulled through. By the end of 2045 they were already lending tangible assistance to others less fortunate.

Some people also survived in the heart of the war zones. I have given the impression that all was chaos and despair in these zones. By and large, so it was. But occasionally strong regional leaders emerged who succeeded in organizing the remaining human resources of the area, found ways of supplying power to food factories, and improvised transport systems that brought needed supplies to the survivors in their territory. One thinks of latter-day feudal overlords like Orlen Budd, the governor of Oregon in the United States, or Yuliya Dovzhenko, deputy chairwoman of the Communist party in the Ukraine. There was nothing lovable about such people. They soon outlived their usefulness. But clearly they saved millions of lives in the long winter of 2044–45.

The future belonged to others. It belonged to the countries south of the twenty-fifth parallel and, more crucially, to the one international political formation that actually grew and prospered in the aftermath of the Third World War, the World party.

The Ascent of the World Party

At the time of the Catastrophe of 2044, the World party was quite small. Many of its fifty thousand members were in prison. Its founder, Mitchell Greenwald, lived in Christchurch, New Zealand, where he spent his days assisting a repair robot on its daily rounds in a factory that produced fishing gear. It was an ideal cover. In the evenings and on weekends (which at that time normally included Mondays), he kept in touch with party leaders all over the world by coded computer mail and built a cell of party loyalists inside the national government of New Zealand.

Such cells, or "viruses" as they were called, help explain how the World party was able to move so quickly after July. Its program was much too radical and ambitious to appeal to the average voter, but, as the business depression of the 2030s and 2040s worsened and toxic strains of nationalism inflamed world politics, many people in government and the megacorps began to sense that the old technocratic ruling class had lost control of the world system. It was not hard to persuade anyone with eyes to see that a crack-up, perhaps a global disaster, was imminent. Between January 2043 and June 2044, the World party converted more than a thousand highly placed officials in national governments, the megacorps, and the Confederated States of Earth to its program. Banned from taking part in parliamentary politics, it had no choice. But it made the most of its opportunities.

Equally important was the fact that the World party, although small, flourished in every corner of the world. By the spring of 2044 it had viruses in eighty-five governments on every continent, ranging in size from twenty-three World party members in Australian ministries to the cell of only three members securely lodged in the central committee of the Communist party in Moscow. It was particularly strong in India, China, Argentina, Turkey, Mexico, Great Britain, and France. Other viruses operated within the secretariats of the CSE, at Global Trade Consortium headquarters in Zurich, and in all twelve megacorps.

Its program, however radical, appealed to a broad spectrum of people both inside and outside the structures of established power. At one level, as we noticed in an earlier chapter, the World party appeared to defend those structures against reactionary elements. No less heartily than the GTC itself it opposed neonationalism and cries for the restoration of a free market economy. It gave due credit to the megacorps and the CSE for assembling an authentically global political and economic system. But at the center of the program of the World party stood a stern indictment of the existing world order, which it described in one of its well-known underground pamphlets as the handiwork of human wolves. "Our rulers fatten on our flesh, like any wolf pack, but their meat is also their poison."

The unitary world republic called for in party manifestos was to be socialist and democratic. But it would have little in common with earlier "democracies" and "socialisms," which it decried as parodies. The problem with both was the bridgeless gap between law and reality. Giving people jobs and votes, the nominal right to govern themselves and acquire wealth, did not suffice unless they had a self-generated political consciousness and unless they had as much capital (meaning skills, health, property) as any of their fellow workers. In short, there could be no democracy if people were conditioned to behave like sheep, and there could be no equality of wealth if people were denied the chance to acquire and employ every marketable skill. The existence of a manipulative governing class and a hierarchy of work in the present-day world system, which included ostensibly socialist countries, assured that true democratic socialism could not easily, or perhaps ever, emerge within such a system.

Until 2043, the literature of the World party stopped at this point. As Greenwald and others argued tirelessly, it was imperative not to alienate progressive elements in the governing class since their collaboration was essential to any fundamental reconstruction of the system. But, at a party congress held in Melbourne in March 2043, Greenwald and his closest colleagues were persuaded by the relentless march of events to take the inevitable next step: open commitment to a policy of world revolution. Henceforth, viruses planted in the established order, as well as ordinary party members active among workers, were instructed to lay the foundations for an irrevocable rupture with the system. Few members left the party over this issue since almost everyone had believed implicitly in the need for revolution all along. But some found it difficult to adopt the appropriate rhetoric. It came especially hard to members who were lawyers or cabinet ministers.

The World party grew slowly but inexorably in the months that followed. In early 2044, after the United States broke off diplomatic relations with the Soviet Union and the world seemed ready for war, the number of megacorporate executives joining forces with the

World party more than doubled. In June several party operatives inside the GTC convinced their reluctant nonparty colleagues to launch the peace initiatives that could have averted war. But their colleagues took too long to agree. By the time the GTC acted—as we have seen—it was too late.

In the spring (or autumn, depending on one's latitude) of 2045, the World party saw its chance. It had small, enthusiastic cadres with growing worker support in almost all the surviving countries. Its moles remained active in the GTC, whose headquarters were shifted to Capetown in the Southern African Republic, and the CSE, relocated from New York to Buenos Aires. Others enjoyed shares of ministerial or at least bureaucratic power in most of the surviving governments. Vindicated, in a sense, by the Catastrophe, the party was allowed to operate freely in much of the world, although the CSE ban on its activities was not officially lifted until 2047.

Party spokespersons fanned out everywhere bearing a simple and heartfelt message. The Catastrophe was not an accident, they insisted, but something intrinsic to the now-shattered world system; if the system were allowed to regenerate, it would produce another, perhaps terminal catastrophe; the shock it had delivered, and was still delivering, to all its survivors must convince them to form a democratic and socialist world commonwealth without delay. "To the fallen, we must erect a monument," Greenwald told CSE delegates in Buenos Aires, "the monument of a just and peaceful Cosmopolis."

World party leaders did not rely on humanism alone. They appealed as well to a newborn "Southern" regionalist pride that recognized the extent to which the tables had now been turned. For centuries a basically "Northern" world order composed of Northern states and corporations had managed and exploited the Southern Hemisphere. To be sure, a few countries in the core of the world economy, notably Australia, were located in the South. But they had played only a limited and auxiliary role in the grand scheme; in effect the old world system was a Northern system.

Now, and for several more years, the Southern countries had the upper hand. For the South to resurrect the prewar order, said World party activists, would be like suckling the brawny child of a fallen tyrant. In due course the child would grow up and no doubt take its parent's place. The only way to prevent such a calamity was to create a new world order here and now, while the South still had the strength, an order in which the exploitation of any part of the planet by any other was structurally impossible.

Throughout 2047 and 2048 the following of the World party increased prodigiously. It appealed to salient portions of every class, from the lowest to the highest, and managed, although just barely, to escape identification as an ideology of "Northern" or "Caucasian" origins, although most of its founding members had been Caucasians then living in Northern countries.

It also attracted implacable enemies. Many megacorporate executives regarded its plans for the transfer of capital to full public ownership as a sentence of professional death for themselves, which, in fact, it was. Many politicians doubted that they could survive in a truly democratic republic, and the neonationalists among them feared the eventual abolition of national identity and home rule by the global state. The most fervent enemies of all were the leaders of orthodox religious communities, especially in the Muslim world, who saw in the philosophy of the World party a direct challenge to their authority.

I say "philosophy" because the World party did have a philosophy, a set of moral, historical, and even metaphysical beliefs variously known as "integral humanism" (not related to the *humanisme intégral* of the twentieth-century French Catholic philosopher Jacques Maritain) and "the service of being." The latter phrase was the title of a book by Greenwald and his Philippine companion Carolina Ocampo, published in 2042. It became, much to Greenwald's honest indignation, the "bible" of the party. He did what he could to promote alternative texts, a few of which also became popular, but *The Service of Being* remained for decades the clearest exposition of party thinking on the big questions. I will say more about it later.

What matters for now is that the book promoted a resolutely secular, materialist worldview, full of piety for all creation, but finding no place for a creator or a supernature. One critic compared it to the fusion of Marxism and idealism achieved by the early French socialist Jean Jaurès. In any case, *The Service of Being* held no charms for orthodox Muslims or Christians or Jews. They attacked it with all the vehemence at their command. Hindus and Buddhists, by contrast, found it almost palatable, and some Chinese scholars detected strong spiritual affinities with neo-Confucianism.

A complex and difficult political struggle ensued between the

World party, together with several regionally based movements allied to it, and the forces of the old order. In sheer numbers, the forces of the old order held at first an overwhelming advantage. But they were badly divided. The devastation of the countries that had furnished nearly all the global leadership in prewar days created a power vacuum. Javanese vied with South Indians, Arabs with Iranians, Southern Africans with Angolans, Argentineans with Chileans, and Australians (by far the wealthiest of the Southern peoples) with everybody else for preeminence in the contest to preserve the capitalist ancien régime. Despite the breakdown of international trade, even the rump GTC in Capetown aspired to play a leading role in the restoration.

Yet, in each of these areas and in the slowly healing noncombatant countries of the North, the World party had at least some members highly placed in the governing class and, more to the point, a multiplying army of followers in the general population. The spells of the old propaganda, all the old devices of public information management, no longer worked, if only because most of the masters of such black arts had been killed in the Catastrophe. But some credit must be given to the World party as well. Its leaders understood the concerns of working people in the new age. They knew their fears, their hopes for a better life, and their silences: the profound numbness and disillusionment in the face of mass destruction.

Speakers of all political persuasions noted that it was almost impossible to pierce the silence of the people who came to hear them. The people sat and listened. They did not cheer or applaud. Even World party speakers were rarely able to elicit enthusiasm. But they reported one major difference in the response of crowds to their appeals. People nodded. They sat quietly and looked intently at the rostrum. They were hearing new ideas, not justifications and apologia for the old order, and they nodded and gave their quiet assent.

One new idea that crowds initially met with stunned incredulity, but after many repetitions came to believe and approve, was the proposal of World party candidates for a uniform world personal income, known as the "share." Public ownership of capital, the party maintained, was essential, but not enough to assure the achievement of socialism. The capitalist system had thrived on inequalities of status and wealth, which allowed some people to expand their holdings geometrically and sentenced others to lifelong poverty.

By contrast, said the candidates, the coming world commonwealth would limit all working citizens to a single, equal share of the public wealth, regardless of work performed. Those unable to work or to find work would receive a full share, too, and those unwilling to work a half share. Citizens with demonstrable extraordinary needs, for professional or sometimes even personal reasons, would earn a supplementary quarter or half share. In early years the value of a full share would be based on regional income, rising or falling with the fortunes of each region, and in later years on world income, after regional incomes had become more or less equal.

The program for world equalization was especially popular in the countries that lay on the periphery of the capitalist global economic system. But spokespersons for the party pressed the case for equalization with the same fervor in the wealthier countries. Some even argued, perhaps wrongly, that the gulf between rich and poor nations had been a prime cause of the Catastrophe. Other advocates noted the psychological (as opposed to economic) connection of such "structural violence" to the war fever of the 2040s.

In any case, the World party promised to eradicate inequality among nations by the year 2100. "Under capitalism," wrote Greenwald, "the division of the world into a bourgeoisie of rich nations and a proletariat of poor nations was a necessity. For us, it shall be a crime. No commonwealth of nations can endure permanently half rich and half poor."

As it grew stronger, the World party lost its early reticence to move from talk to action. It adopted a strategy of "mundialization," which meant, in simplest terms, winning or seizing power in every country where it had the opportunity and then declaring the country a component province of the nascent world commonwealth. If victory were possible in free parliamentary elections, well and good. If countries had no authentic electoral system, or if the system had been suspended because of the Catastrophe, the party did not hesitate to organize armed revolutions, paralyzing general strikes, or coups d'état. In countries with free elections where the chances of the World party to win power were poor, the party formed an alliance with the least reactionary elements on the political spectrum and worked indefatigably to convert its new allies to the cause.

Not all members of the party countenanced the tough strategies of the late 2040s and early 2050s. A minority of the leadership, nicknamed the "Woolyheads" by their adversaries, approved only nonviolent and open tactics. From their point of view, the majority leaders were unreconstructed Leninists, whose taste for coercion would scar the new body social and eventually breed fresh rounds of war and class struggle.

Led for many years by Beatrix Vandermeer, a Dutch scholar and activist who had been lecturing in the Southern African Republic at the time of the Catastrophe, the Woolyheads seldom mustered enough supporters to control even local formations of the party. But they exerted a restraining influence on the Leninists, casting deciding votes from time to time when the Leninists themselves were unsure what course of action to follow. Without the Woolyheads, the party would have chosen armed force in several situations (notably in the Middle East) when armed force was not needed or would not have availed.

Yet on the whole the strategy of the Leninists proved right. They believed in striking hard, fast, and everywhere, in a political version of blitzkrieg. In remarkably little time they had acquired a momentum that could not be stopped or equaled by any other party or alliance of parties in the decade after the Catastrophe.

Mundializing the Tribes of Earth

By 2049, the World party was prepared to take its first major public action. At a party congress held in Santiago between 27 April and 2 May, it issued the Declaration of Human Sovereignty, certainly the most important political document of the twenty-first century. It summarized the party's global program in radiant prose and called on people of goodwill in every country to deny the authority of their governments and struggle for full mundialization. The articles of incorporation of the GTC and the flags of all nations (including Chile's) were solemnly burned in a great bonfire at high noon on 1 May, the international holiday of working people since 1889. Party workers returned to their homelands full of confidence.

The Chilean national government was the first to fall. Its conservative president outlawed the World party in June. His action prompted a general strike in July, stormy battles between police and World party "defense battalions," and eventually a full-fledged people's revolution led by a World party activist, Consuela Mercedes Castillo, with the backing of portions of the Chilean army and navy. In February 2050, Chile declared herself mundialized, becoming the first country to join the still nonexistent Commonwealth.

Australia, whose government already teemed with known and covert World party members, mundialized in April, quickly followed in August by Uruguay, in September by New Zealand, and in December by Madagascar. All these transitions were peaceful. The biggest prize, the South Indian Confederation, followed suit in 2051. In 2052, Angola, the Southern African Republic, Sri Lanka, Turkey, and Finland mundialized.

By 2056, thirty-five countries had become nominal constituent states of the Commonwealth, six by a combination of civil disobedience and armed struggle, the rest by parliamentary action. They used their voting power, with help from World party viruses, to force the dissolution of the CSE in October 2056. But the life had gone out of the CSE years before.

Early in 2057, the GTC also disbanded, setting up in its place an entity known as the Provisional Trust. The Trust functioned as a caretaking body to oversee the restoration of international trade until the proclamation of the Commonwealth. By this time at least half the directorate of the GTC consisted of World party loyalists. Many corporate executives could at least see the handwriting on the wall, although none of them was prepared at this point to mundialize his or her company.

The final five years of the process were arduous and at times disheartening for World party leaders. Between 2057 and 2062, only eight additional countries mundialized. Two of the original thirty-five abrogated their declarations.

But the new adherents tipped the scales of world politics in favor of the World party. In 2058, both China (in effect the western half of the former People's Republic) and Russia (the Great Russian portion of the former Soviet Union, excluding Siberia) joined. In 2061, Argentina mundialized and, early in 2062, Algeria and Brazil. Although civil and regional wars were raging in parts of North America and Europe, Islamic Southwest Asia was sullen and withdrawn, and the global population stood at only 2.7 billion, the World party proclaimed the Commonwealth on 1 May 2062. It established Melbourne as its temporary capital and called on all governments and peoples to mundialize within one year.

The old struggle between the Leninists and the Woolyheads came to the fore once again over the issue of compulsory mundialization. The Woolyheads argued that, since more than half the human race had freely enlisted in the Commonwealth, the rest could be left alone, to join the Commonwealth whenever they pleased. The Leninists favored the conversion of World party defense battalions into a legitimate world militia and the delivery of the reluctant nations into the fold by force. Waiting until one or more major battle states recovered their former strength, achieved great power status, and armed themselves with superweapons, said the Leninists, was a perfect recipe for World War IV.

Again, the Leninists carried the day. Their position becomes more understandable if one studies a political map of the world in the year 2062. At this point, the only major countries from pre-Catastrophe times still not members of the Commonwealth were Canada and the United States, Japan, half the former Soviet Union, nine countries in Europe, and thirteen in Southwest and South Asia. Except for some of the Asian nations, these were the very countries that had fought the Third World War and had dominated the global economy in the last age of capital. Whatever their present condition, they would someday be in a position to resume their mastery of the planet.

For the time being, many of these countries were not countries at all. The United States, for one, had been so devastated in the war that it broke up during the late 2040s into a hundred statelets, inhabited by fewer than fifteen million people. By 2062, however, the number of American polities had already shrunk to nine, as a result of regional conquests and unions. Three of these claimed to *be* the United States. It was clearly only a matter of time before the republic re-emerged with something like its former boundaries.

The situation in its old adversary, the Soviet Union, was more complex. In the immediate aftermath of the Catastrophe, the forty-five million survivors fragmented along ethnic lines. The Russian Soviet Republic claimed jurisdiction over the whole northern and central area from Leningrad to the Urals. Three other, much smaller Russian republics flourished in Siberia. The rest of the country consisted of forty Baltic, Byelorussian, Ukrainian, Georgian, Armenian, and Central Asian polities agreeing on only one point: that they should never be part of Russia again. But the same centripetal forces that had restored the unity of imperial Russia after the collapses of 1917–19 and 1941–45 would no doubt have triumphed again, sooner or later. The government of the Russian Soviet Republic, which built its new capital near the ruins of Moscow, had every intention of ensuring that they did. As of 2062, it had already managed to annex portions of Byelorussia and was casting a covetous eye on the Ukraine.

In addition, there were, by 2062, five polities in Great Britain, with a combined population of two million; twelve polities in France; three in Germany; several dozen in Italy; and hundreds in what had once been Pakistan, Bangladesh, and the northern half of India. Although Japan remained a single country, only ten million Japanese survived the war and its aftermath.

But, once again, as the Leninists in the World party let no one forget, most of these countries (just like the United States and the Soviet Union) would be staggering to their feet in another generation or two and resuming their familiar places in the arenas of world politics and trade. Throughout the Northern Hemisphere, the birth rate was once more rising after many years of sharp decline, technology was reviving, and the old flags began fluttering again from freshly lathed poles.

Into these convalescent lands World party workers poured by the thousands in the 2030s, joining forces with native members who had survived, preaching their gospel to all who would listen. So many were killed by local authorities or roving guerrillas that in due course the party began providing armed escorts for its political organizers, the so-called defense battalions, which had to fight countless skirmishes. Whenever possible, party representatives also airlifted food, medicine, and other necessities into the areas targeted for conversion. Political rallies took place under big circus tents, culminating in the distribution of first aid kits, clothing, fuel, and food parcels.

The greatest problem encountered by organizers was simply the provincialism of their audiences. Unlike people further south, they had no interest in global issues. They did not care how humankind governed itself or distributed its wealth. For years they had been happy just to stay alive from one day to the next. Party speakers quickly lowered their sights, focusing on local problems. The full message of the World party was seldom heard.

Nevertheless, the party made spectacular gains. It won power in numerous local and regional governments. In 2058 in the United States, its battalions fought and finally defeated the forces of its best organized national rival, the Church of the Purification, which had fielded a ragtag army of more than 100,000 men (styled "Crusaders") in hopes of replacing the old secular federal union with a "Republic of Christ." By 2062, two of the nine American polities (known as New England and Columbia) were virtually ruled by the World party, and party viruses had deeply penetrated three others. The party also enjoyed considerable strength in Japan, northern Europe, and Russia. It performed poorly in several countries that had long been ruled by more powerful neighbors and now relished their independence, such as the Ukraine, Brittany, Basqueland, and Kurdistan.

Whether its hold was weak or strong, the World party failed to mundialize a large portion of the Northern Hemisphere. Its most astute intelligence agents on the scene doubted that more than a few additional fragments of the hemisphere would mundialize of their own accord in the foreseeable future. In some areas, they even noted a dwindling of support. At the beginning of 2063, nearly all agreed that the time for action was ripe, if not overripe.

The decision of the leadership was taken in January and implemented, after careful planning, between June 2063 and November 2068. A skillfully concerted sequence of coups organized by viruses ousted a dozen governments without bloodshed. In the more difficult cases, rapid deployment forces transported by aircraft were generally able to win a prompt victory. Nuclear weapons were not deployed, and no large cities were bombed from the air.

But we must be truthful, as many Commonwealth historians in the early years were not. When the party's defense battalions, conscripted into the newly formed World Militia, engaged local forces in battle, the people did not invariably welcome the troops of the Militia as saviors. Nor were all the victories won by the Militia swift or surgical or painless. Some of the campaigns dragged on for two or three years.

Military records make it clear that at least three million Northern lives were lost, half of them civilian, and that 700,000 Militiamen and Militiawomen died in combat. The fighting in parts of the American South, in the Middle East, the Ukraine, the Pakistani states, and the Sikh republic of Khalistan was especially brutal, with thousands of documented atrocities on both sides.

Finally, in November 2068, the last skirmishes were fought. Humankind found itself at peace under one law for the first time in its history. On 1 May 2070, representatives from all the mundialized countries ratified the Declaration of Human Sovereignty in Melbourne. At the ceremonies, after an hour of speech making by Leninist worthies, the Woolyhead spokeswoman Beatrix Vandermeer reminded the delegates that their triumph had been purchased by blood. "Our Commonwealth, which we founded to bring peace, justice, and equality to the world, spent its first six years killing. Let us never forget what we have done; and let us never kill again."

The ratifying convention sat in silence after she finished, and then, with few exceptions, the delegates rose from their chairs and gave her the most thunderous ovation received by any speaker, even by Mitchell Greenwald himself.

But later, doubts remained in many minds. Had it all been an elaborate and hypocritical charade, to appease conscience and soften grief? Had the Commonwealth been born only to renew humanity's ancient wish for death?

Building the World-City

The architects of the new democratic cosmopolis were by and large a hardheaded group. Without waiting for a constitutional convention or even for elections, they established a "provisional" world regime that, once in place, proved almost impossible to restructure in later years.

Their starting point was an iron resolve to eliminate what they perceived as the three most intolerable evils of the old order: its tribalism (sovereignty of nation or race), its capitalism (production for profit, requiring a society of classes), and its sexism (male hegemony). No compromise was possible with any of the three, said the architects. In order to build the new world-city, tribalism, capitalism, and sexism had to be razed, no matter what the immediate cost.

The Commonwealth dealt ruthlessly with each, but, under the circumstances that prevailed in the 2060s, it was forced to deal most ruthlessly of all with tribalism. It had just two choices. It could accept the existing national groupings but strip them of sovereign power. Or it could dismantle the whole system and begin again. If the ethnic map of the world in 2062 had been more or less identical to the ethnic map of 2044, perhaps even the most intransigent Leninists in the World party would have opted for acceptance. But, above a latitude of twenty-five degrees South, the world's peoples were distributed far more haphazardly than they had been prior to the Catastrophe. In search of food, shelter, and land free of plague and contamination, the survivors had roamed wherever their legs would take them during the early postwar years.

It was an age of *Völkerwanderungen*, like the great mass migrations of the Dark Ages. Areas once exclusively Spanish or Basque were thickly settled by people from France. Italians sought refuge in Austria or Yugoslavia. Americans fled to British Columbia or New Brunswick or Mexico. Brazilians descended in great numbers on Paraguay and Argentina. Vietnamese penetrated deeply into China, Bengalis into Tamil Nadu, Palestinian Jews into Egypt and the Arabian peninsula.

Taking advantage of this new mixing of the races, the Commonwealth abolished national frontiers and more or less arbitrarily carved the planet into one thousand administrative districts known as "departments." Each department was the home of between 2.5 and 3.0 million people, who might be of a single ethnicity or half a dozen. In North America, for example, the Commonwealth established ten departments. One included the former maritime provinces of Canada, half of Quebec, and most of New England. Another joined southern California, Arizona, New Mexico, and western Texas to six former states of Mexico. The southernmost department of the region included not only the Mexican states of Oaxaca, Chiapas, Campeche, and Yucatan but also Guatemala, Belize, and northern Honduras.

The map of the rest of the world was redrawn in much the same way, not even sparing the polities of the Southern Hemisphere that had weathered the Catastrophe with little disruption of their national political life. Thus the six states of Australia, which had a population in 2063 of sixty million people, were reorganized into twenty-three departments, and the old Australian federal government vanished. The former Northern Territory was incorporated into another department that included New Guinea and the eastern islands of Indonesia. New Zealand and the island groups of the South Pacific were divided among three departments.

Essentially, the one thousand departments of the Commonwealth wielded no greater powers than the ninety-five departments of the former French Republic and were, in many respects, modeled after them. Each had a governor, appointed by the Commonwealth, and a consultative assembly elected by the people of the department, but no legislative authority, no independent judiciary, and no army or militia.

All real power was vested in the world government. Its capital city remained Melbourne until 2085, after which it dispensed with a capital altogether, except on rare ceremonial occasions. The privilege of hosting these was rotated among the cities of the world. But the real governing of humankind took place electronically, with little need for the physical presence of officials or representatives in any one place at any one time.

The central institution of the Commonwealth, the People's Congress, consisted of two popularly elected delegates from each department. The Congress made the laws and appointed the Executive Council, a body of fifty senior ministers, all of whom served at the pleasure of the Congress and could be removed by a simple majority vote of the Congress. Heading the Executive Council was a president, selected by the Council itself from its own membership. The president had the power to dismiss any minister but not to appoint the fallen minister's successor, which remained a prerogative of the People's Congress. There was also a system of world courts of original jurisdiction and appeal. Its judges were chosen for life by the president with the consent of the Congress, and they in turn appointed the judges of the departmental courts, which tried local civil disputes or criminal cases.

To enforce the laws and policies of the Commonwealth, the World Militia was granted a monopoly of armed force, except for lightly armed departmental police units. After the troubles of the 2060s, it shrank to a permanent body of about one million men and women, equipped with a wide variety of the most advanced weapons, including tactical nuclear and beam weapons. Token forces of the World Militia were stationed in every department, and at least half a million troops were kept in battle readiness at all times in three large Commonwealth military facilities, located in the territory of the former countries of Mexico, Italy, and Sri Lanka.

Until the widespread disturbances of the period after 2127, the Militia was seldom needed to engage in actual fighting. But the Congress more than once authorized its dispatch to departments threatened with insurrection or civil war. A typical example of its value came in 2075, when a force of Islamic guerrillas in a department of Southwest Asia was dissuaded from taking military action by the sudden descent into their midst of 100,000 airborne Militia troops. The guerrillas were disarmed with only a few dozen casualties and their leaders imprisoned.

Was the Commonwealth a true democracy or a stage-managed dictatorship of the World party? Was the People's Congress a facade for the despotic rule of the Executive Council? Critics note that

World party candidates won 1,565 of the 2,000 seats in the first Congress, in part because many of their opponents boycotted the elections. Of the fifty ministers in the first Council, thirty-seven were World party members and five others were fellow travelers closely allied to the party apparatus. Every president until 2098 was a member.

Nevertheless, the party enjoyed vast public support. It did allow authentic opposition parties to flourish and campaign for office, as long as they refrained from preaching violence. And throughout the twenty-first century it was a party—this much cannot be questioned—of ideologues, not powermongers.

As ideologues, the leaders of the World party persuaded the first Congress to legislate virtually the whole social program of the party. The formula of the equal share for workers was adopted, along with a somewhat more complicated system of supplementary fractional shares for people with special "needs," which in practice amounted to incentive pay for high achievement. Temporary exemptions from the formula were also provided to encourage the rebuilding of the war-mangled global economy in certain key industries.

Three ministries were assigned the task of eradicating regional economic inequality. With timely infusions of public capital, transfers of technology, educational reforms, and the reorganization of world trade, they did their jobs.

Inspired by several keen analysts of late capital, such as Harry Braverman in the twentieth century and Hashimoto Shunsho in the early twenty-first, the party was committed as well to a policy of ensuring that work hierarchies did not revive under socialism. Beyond equality of incomes, workers needed to acquire a range of skills that would earn them equality of status in the workplace and the body politic.

In monopoly capital or in the self-styled socialist countries before the Catastrophe, most people were poured at an early age into an educational and vocational "stream" from which escape was at best arduous and at worst impossible. Each stream had its own characteristic subculture. Access to higher streams was limited to the offspring of elites or to those fortunate enough to develop, while still children, proficiency in certain specially valued behaviors and talents, such as command of the speech patterns of the hegemonic class.

The Commonwealth dedicated itself to building a socialism that, by contrast, would enable individuals to master a variety of skills, giving every worker entry into many "streams." Some workers, be-

cause of disabilities in nature or nurture, might require more training, more encouragement, or more patience than others, but, in the
end, no one would be banished to permanent oblivion in the lower
depths of society; and the whole concept of "depths" and "heights"—
in short, of work hierarchies—would eventually fade from public
consciousness. Achieving this goal demanded, among other things, a
drastic reconstruction of public education and the introduction of a
system of participatory management in the workplace.

The result, soon noted, was the rapid progress not only of social
equality but also of democracy, as people exercised their full responsibilities as workers, citizens, and electors and took a livelier interest
in public issues. Decades were needed, but the class system of the
last age of capital did finally erode and disappear.

At the same time, the Commonwealth carried out the promise of
the World party to end private ownership of capital and production
for profit. The megacorps were consolidated into democratically
controlled state corporations founded on the principle of production
for use and need. Smaller businesses were transformed into cooperatives, where people with a flair for enterprise had a chance to exercise their skills, without also earning the opportunity to exploit or
degrade their fellow men and women.

Take note: fellow men *and* women. The People's Congress enacted
legislation to require, from the outset, that all workplaces, including
government bureaus, state corporations, schools, and cooperatives,
employ roughly equal numbers of men and women. The maximum
allowable ratio of either sex to the other was set at three to two. The
ratio applied not only to the workplace as a whole but also to the
skill groups within each workplace, to protect women (or, sometimes, men) from segregation.

Many specialists in management grumbled. A few filed angry suits
in the world courts to overturn the gender laws. But the urgent social demand for skilled women workers soon revolutionized the expectations of both sexes. By the close of the twenty-first century,
gender-ratio laws were no longer needed, and the Congress uncere-
moniously repealed them all.

The close of the twenty-first century was a time of happy account-
ing in many other respects. It marked the end of the "Great Housecleaning" program, which I will describe later, the program that
restored the biosphere to good health. It marked the arrival of what
the development ministries termed a "two-to-one global economy,"

in which no department in the world had a net annual income more than twice as high as any other. The ultimate goal of a "one-to-one" economy still eluded planners, but it was well within reach by the year 2100.

The close of the century also marked the achievement, in fact as well as in theory, of a two-to-one domestic economy, in which no citizen earned more than twice as much as any other in his or her department. The exemptions smuggled by the Congress into its own legislation had badly compromised the principle of "one worker, one share," but the last exemptions expired in 2093. Although it was still possible for a worker to earn an extra quarter or half share in exceptional circumstances, the multiple shares common in the 2070s and 2080s were no longer available. At the same time, the minimum income, given to anyone unemployed by choice, was raised from a half share to three-quarters.

Looking backward, the architects of the Commonwealth could take legitimate satisfaction in its performance down to 2100. They had constructed a unified, democratic, and socialist world order. They had abolished poverty, economic inequality, and war.

But the Commonwealth was not the Millennium. Its unitary world political system brought with it a unitary postmodern world culture that strove to homogenize humankind. The all-pervasive power of the world state and its educational networks severely curtailed the exercise, if not the legal possession, of fundamental civil rights and liberties. Local cultures had to fight relentlessly for bare survival. Worse still, the laws of the Commonwealth required such a vast machinery of bureaucratic regulation to ensure compliance that the system became as topheavy, in many respects, as the technocratic world order of the last age of capital.

All the same, something like the Commonwealth was more or less inevitable. It had to come, to make possible a collective future for humankind. Perhaps its methods were too draconian. All things considered, no doubt they were. But, as Greenwald reminisced in his last appearance before a World party congress in 2089, "We were in the business of slaying dinosaurs. In the end the World party was the only force available to do the job. We may have regrets, but we apologize for nothing."

One year later the old man died in a floater crash that also took the life of his beloved colleague and companion Carolina Ocampo. In a private ceremony, in a garden near the former world capital buildings in Melbourne, their ashes were scattered among the roses. A thousand old friends came to say goodbye and watered the rich earth with their tears.

INTERLUDE

I offer you this time a single letter, written by my Aunt Lucinda, a niece of the Harry Jensen who commanded the U.S. spaceplane squadron in 2044. Captain Lucinda Jensen was a Militiawoman in charge of communications for a brigade of troops sent to subdue partisans in the western Ukraine in 2068, one of the last and bloodiest combat missions of the century. Aunt Lucinda's correspondent, the political scientist Nikos Tangopoulos, had been her academic adviser during her student years at Tutu University in Capetown.

WMFS 119-2349-GX
27 June 2068

Dear Nikos:

I have a few hours to myself before I go on duty again, so I thought I'd invade your mind. Is that all right? If not, just turn off your monitor. I know it's been three years since you last heard from me and I know you never wanted me to join the Militia in the first place, but I hope we're still friends. You didn't answer the letter I sent you in 2065. Maybe I was getting too personal.

I won't be personal now. What made me want to write to you is our mutual interest (I flatter myself, don't I?) in politics. The class you used to teach (still teach?) in neonationalism was my favorite of yours, and I still carry around a disc of your book.

But that was all theoretical. As it should have been. What I'm doing now is a practicum in neonationalism, right out in the field. Oh, quite literally! Until you've experienced the mud of the Ukraine at this time of year, you don't know mud.

And until you've seen how passionately these people cling to their mud, and their religion, and their language, and their pathetic history, forgive me, but you don't know neonationalism! I mean, not from the inside, not the way it feels.

I realize you grew up on Cyprus, but the problem with Turkey had long since been settled when you lived there. And the blacks had been ruling the Southern African Republic for ten years before you emigrated to Cape-town, so that doesn't count, either, except for echoes and aftershocks.

Nikos, what am I doing in this place? Who am I to tell the Ukrainians they can't have a country? Yes, I understand. I'm flirting with treason. Nevertheless I'm deadly serious (wasn't I always?).

It's not what I do personally. My job is simply to keep our units in touch with each other and our operations HQ in the Crimea. But after a month of killing and killing and killing, I don't believe in myself any more. Maybe you were right. Maybe I shouldn't have joined the Militia. There was no way to imagine it would be anything remotely like this.

Let me give you a few examples. Three days ago our people found evidence in a village that the people were supplying food to a detachment of partisans. We didn't shoot anybody. We just spirited most of the villagers away in trucks and waited for nightfall. When the partisans arrived to pick up their food, we sent out a young girl to bring them to a barn. She was thirteen, scared white, but she did what we told her because we had her parents and her kid brother.

When the partisans entered the barn, we surrounded the place. They sensed a trap, broke out, and started shooting. By the time it was all over, the girl was dead, all four partisans were dead, seven of our men were dead, and because our colonel thought the girl had tipped off the partisans, he executed her parents on the spot. For attempting to escape. But I heard him on the radio. They didn't try to escape. They were hog-tied. They couldn't move.

Or last week. The partisans captured a whole town, the town of Ko-lomyja. They came down out of their bases in the Carpathians and took the town. We lost our garrison, forty-five people. They raised the Free Ukranian flag from the town hall and radioed the news in all directions. They even designated Kolomyja as the official capital of the Free Ukrai-nian Democratic Republic. They shot down two of our planes with anti-aircraft missiles stolen from us months ago. So we collected data from remote sensors, pinpointed their barracks, and vaporized the whole force. Col. Hamdoun bragged that the strike was so "clean" it killed only a few hundred civilians in Kolomyja. I think he was telling the truth. When we recaptured the town, three-quarters of it was still standing.

You left out the Ukraine in your book, but I suppose you know most of its history. Ruled for centuries by Lithuanians, then Poles, then Rus-sians. Half independent for two years after the defeat of Russia by the

Central Powers in the First World War, then vacuumed into the Soviet Union in 1922. Its first real taste of freedom (wrong word?) came after the Catastrophe. Not many Ukrainians survived, but those who did made the most of it. Two Ukrainian republics were formed, one in the west, one in the east, and in 2055 they came together as the Free Ukrainian Democratic Republic. The people of the FUDR were the happiest Ukrainians in history. Or so you'd think, interrogating their fighters. I've sent dozens of interviews to Melbourne for the archives. They ring true.

But the Ukraine isn't really what I want to ask you about. I tap into dispatches from our troops in a lot of places. I'm not stupid. When I joined the World party, in '61, right after graduation, I did it because I thought it was our only chance for peace, and because I was—and still am—a dedicated socialist. It was that Book Red Earth by Helga Ritter (you loaned it to me, remember?) that really won me over. One world, where countries and classes no longer mattered, where people could simply be people, instead of Jews or women or Chinese or doctors or any of the other masks we wear to hide our identities. But I tap into the dispatches, and I read the Militia newsdiscs, and what I read is something different.

Nikos, there are millions of people in this world who don't think as we do. They're saying, the World party is for majorities. It's for all the big countries, the ones that have always called the shots, only now they've decided to join forces instead of fighting one another. Why? Because they figure it's a safer way to keep on ruling the world.

I don't know if I believe that. But it's plausible. Perhaps what we call "the service of being" is simply the service of a homogenized, dominant, majoritarian world culture that will turn into the greatest tyranny the human race has ever known. When you're in the majority, you don't even think you have a special culture of your own, you think you represent "universal values." You want to crush everything that isn't "universal," that could ever be a threat to your power.

The twentieth century called it genocide. The only difference is that, instead of trying to kill the people who are different from us, we kill their cultures. We dismember their societies, burn their flags, erase their memories. If they resist, we kill their fighters, too. But our true objective is to destroy their image of themselves, the kind of people they want to be.

And it isn't just what we've done to the little countries. It's the whole style of the party now that it's really building a world state. We don't consult the people we're supposed to represent. We lecture them. We say, we're going to do this, and we're going to do that, and we do it, and that's

the end of the story. No one can tell me the so-called provisional consti-
tution of the Commonwealth will ever be replaced when we finally stop
killing the people who don't choose to join us.

Where does all this lead, Nikos? Are we gods? Do we always know
best?

I can hear you saying, "But Cindy, listen, isn't the new government
what you always wanted? Isn't it socialist? Isn't it democratic? Isn't it
color-blind, gender-blind, classless, and free? Doesn't it mean the end
of war?"

And I stammer out something, and you say, "Besides, was there any
other way? Can you imagine what the world would be like if we hadn't
taken charge? Can you imagine the mystical magical spontaneous inte-
gration of two and a half billion people from five hundred countries?
Don't be a fool!"

No, I can't imagine. I don't know any of the answers. I only know our
red earth is red with blood.

That's all. Write to me. Please.

As ever,
Cindy

◆

Aunt Lucinda's letter to Nikos Tangopoulos was intercepted by Militia intelligence. She received an honorable discharge after a brief
hearing and returned to her adopted hometown in Africa. She married a black aerospace engineer. Later she received a certification in
law at Tutu Upper School (her old university, renamed) and spent
fifty years as a defense counsel for political dissenters. I never met a
more loving woman.

7

THE GREAT HOUSECLEANING

Red Is also Green

Students of the history of the World party, like historians of every-thing else, cannot resist the urge to find "precursors" of their chosen topic in earlier times. They have pointed to the three great socialist Internationals of the nineteenth and early twentieth centuries, to evangelizing world faiths such as Islam and Baha'i, to the peace movements of the late modern era, even to the Global Trade Consortium, which, for all its rapacity, did construct a highly integrated world order.

In *Icons and Ironies,* the critic Molly Warner of Cardiff notes the peculiar affinity of the World party in its "classical" or "heroic" age with the long-forgotten party of the Greens in late twentieth-century West Germany. The Greens were primarily a German phenomenon, although they inspired the formation of similar groups in other European countries. Composed of pacifists, socialists, feminists, and environmentalists, the party found itself pulled in several directions at the same time as each faction struggled to elevate its own special cause to paramountcy, meanwhile taking shrewd advantage of every lurch or stumble of the old order to steal votes away from the conventional parties. How the factions managed to collaborate for even a year is still not clear. When an East German Communist dissident, Rudolf Bahro, fled to the West and joined the Greens, he spoke with passion of his transition "from Red to Green," as if the two colors were incompatible.

In fact they were not. What gave the Greens their unique strength was the intimate bond that formed between the leftists and the ecologists in the party, each recognizing that the other had something vital to contribute. The leftists came to acknowledge that the biosphere was in mortal danger, and the ecologists came to acknowledge that the chief reason for the danger was the hubris of capital, whether managed from corporate boardrooms or state ministries.

The World party, too, was both Red and Green. In the 2060s, its attention centered on the elimination of the nation-state system and the capitalist structure of the world economy. But after 2070 its chief concern was to make the planet fit once more for human habitation.

The reclamation of the biosphere was not something that could have been achieved on a local or regional basis. The biosphere was a sphere, as round as the earth itself. Its winds and waters flowed wherever the laws of physics decreed. No country could hold them prisoner. Their riches and their poisons flowed with them, indifferent to the angular boundaries contrived by men and women. Restoring the biosphere to good health required rigorous planning by a central world agency that could marshal all the human and technical resources needed for the task.

After several false starts, the Congress created the Planetary Restoration Authority (PRA) in the summer of 2073. By the time the PRA started its work, some of the most serious problems had solved themselves, or nearly so. Radioactive contaminants from the nuclear explosions had decayed and lost their toxicity. No longer drained by overpopulated cities or agribusiness, major aquifers regained twentieth-century water levels. Largely stripped away by the blasts, the ozone layer over the Northern Hemisphere returned in fewer than ten years. While the ozone was depleted, ultraviolet radiation struck the unprotected surface of the earth in massive doses, damaging plant life, causing skin cancer, and injuring eyes, but by 2052 the amount of hard solar radiation slicing through the atmosphere had returned to prewar values. Most important of all, the decline of world industrial production by over 90 percent in the first two decades after the Catastrophe sharply reduced the consumption of fossil fuels, which in turn slowed the progress of the greenhouse effect.

To prevent a recurrence of the woes of modern industrialism, the PRA recommended, and Congress legislated, a phased worldwide ban on the combustion of fossil fuels. A variety of alternative energy technologies, some new, some old, were available. For the most part, the transition occurred effortlessly, although energy costs did rise by as much as 50 percent in some parts of the world.

The highest priority of the PRA was reforestation. Prewar developers had already eliminated most of the earth's tropical rain forests. The synergy of sunlight, air, and bare soil leached of its minerals by heavy rains transformed many deforested areas in the tropics into "hard" deserts, with surfaces like brick, from which only the scrubbiest plants could wring sustenance. The temperate forests of the Northern Hemisphere had suffered losses almost equally severe, compounded by the raging fires of the Catastrophe, which destroyed millions of hectares of woodland.

The PRA fielded an army of foresters and went to work. Years of intensive land reclamation were followed by years of seeding and transplanting. Tropical plants grown from specimens found in greenhouses and botanical gardens in the Southern Hemisphere replaced many of the species wiped out by prewar developers. Hardy new varieties of trees created by plant geneticists also helped in the rebuilding of both tropical and temperate forests. It took thirty years, but, by 2105, the world had as much forested land as it did in 2000, and not a single tree was under attack from acid rain.

The PRA set as its next target the restoration of the forests and wetlands lost between 1900 and 2000, which it achieved in still another thirty years. The most devastated areas of the Northern temperate zone were transformed into permanent wilderness areas, reserved for wildlife and recreation. In some ways a visitor from the nineteenth century would have felt more at home in the early twenty-second century than in the early twenty-first. In 2135, for example, at the close of the PRA's second Thirty-Year Project, the population of the former United States stood at only forty million. No city had more than 250,000 inhabitants, and the ratio of agricultural land and wilderness to "developed" land was approximately what it had been in 1880.

Another major task of the PRA was the recovery of shores and lowlands lost to rising sea levels in the middle decades of the twenty-first century. The destruction of so many trees and phytoplankton (which metabolize carbon dioxide and exhale oxygen), combined with the injection of large quantities of carbon and nitrogen oxides into the atmosphere during the war itself, acted to keep ambient temperatures quite high throughout the rest of the twenty-first century. They began a slow descent in the 2080s, but, as late as 2100, the world was still measurably hotter than it had been at any time in the twentieth century, and sea levels had dropped by only one meter.

Adapting techniques once used by Dutch engineers to build polders in the Zuider Zee, the PRA first reclaimed most of the flooded areas of Florida, a task completed in 2079. Work continued in other parts of the world for many years, ending with the draining and full restoration of the rich delta lands of the former Bangladesh in 2091.

Other PRA teams restocked the new tropical rain forests with fauna bred from zoo animals, dredged the bottoms of lakes to remove billions of tons of pollutants, and, in war-devastated areas not converted to wilderness, constructed deep concrete landfill systems to entomb the wastes and rubble of the Catastrophe.

A favorable report on the progress of the PRA by a panel of independent scientists appointed by the Congress was made public on 15 September 2099. It found the earth clean, green, and safe at last. Forests, oceans, and lakes were in excellent health. Air quality was higher and freshwater supplies purer than they had been since the dawn of industrialism. Concentrations of all the major greenhouse gases were falling steadily. Desertification had been arrested worldwide, the fertility of topsoils had been renewed, and every useful square meter of land lost to rising seas had been reclaimed. Congress commemorated the occasion by declaring 15 September a world holiday, popularly known as Earth Festival Day, which we have celebrated ever since.

The Demographic Transition

Restoring the biosphere to harmony and equilibrium would have been pointless had the Commonwealth not also taken steps to regulate population growth.

Was "growth" really a problem in the second half of the twenty-first century? Nearly six billion people died between July 2044 and July 2045. Birth rates in the Northern Hemisphere and in tropical countries fell precipitously, not regaining prewar levels until the 2060s. For years survivors were reluctant to bring children into their ruined world. Even when they did, infant mortality was abnormally high because of inadequate medical care and the diminished immunity to disease of both mother and child. It might appear that what the world needed in the early decades of the Commonwealth was un-restricted reproduction.

The world needed nothing of the sort. Measured by the carrying capacity of the prewar environment, most of the countries that had fought in the Third World War were now underpopulated, to be sure. But the prewar environment no longer existed. In the 2050s and early 2060s, these countries all had too many survivors to care for. As they recovered, birth rates began climbing faster than the pro-duction of basic goods and services. Other, less affected parts of the Northern Hemisphere, such as Mexico or southern India, were also overextended, as refugees entered them from war zones, agriculture was slow to revive, and birth rates did not fall enough to compensate.

Even some of the relatively unaffected countries of the Southern Hemisphere had demographic problems. The rich ones, like Aus-tralia, had long since reached zero population growth, but the less affluent, like Chile, Namibia, and Madagascar, were as desperately crowded as before the war.

It made sense, therefore, to curtail population growth as much as possible in the last third of the century. The Commonwealth en-couraged and rewarded one-child families in all departments, and in some, as late as 2090, parents with more than two offspring were heavily fined. The world population growth rate, estimated at 1.2 per-cent per year in the first decade of the Commonwealth, dropped to .5 percent per year in the third. As incomes tended toward equality and as parents in previously undeveloped economies became less dependent on the labor of their children, families grew smaller by choice.

The worldwide demographic transition to zero growth was com-pleted in 2110, by which time there were 3.7 billion people on earth. Of these, 4 percent lived in North America, 10 percent in Central and South America, 18 percent in Europe, and 14 percent in Africa. Asia and Australasia accounted for the remaining 54 percent, with 7 per-cent in the Middle East, 19 percent in South Asia, 26 percent in East Asia, and 2 percent in Australasia. Curiously, these figures resemble those of the year 1970, except that the share of North America (in-cluding the former Mexico) had been cut in half, Africa had grown at the expense of Asia, and the share of the lower Southern Hemisphere had increased fourfold.

At first, several Congresspeople from areas once affluent and densely populated, such as the former coastal states of the United States or the former southern counties of Great Britain, argued that their departments should be exempt from demographic regulation until population levels had reached "normal prewar levels." This notion was promptly challenged by World party leaders, who saw in it a veiled neonationalist attempt to regain lost power and privilege. Why, they asked, should people from North America be allowed to procreate freely but not people from such other war-depleted areas as northern India or eastern China? In the new world economy, the old gap between rich and poor countries no longer existed. People everywhere had the same rights and responsibilities.

Nor did policymakers see any point in multiplication for the mere sake of multiplying. Even if the planet could be forced to support ten times 3.7 billion people, or one hundred times 3.7, it would grow increasingly difficult to guarantee the quality of life in such a world. Humankind needed space for privacy, for wilderness, for rest and quiet. Too many people still alive remembered too well the frantic noise and bustle of the last age of capital. Every bill to exempt one or another department from demographic regulation was soundly defeated in the Congress. Representatives of the smaller political factions often joined forces with the World party bloc in opposing such bills.

The only concession to lingering neonationalist sentiment was legislation to subsidize the resettlement of refugee families in the departments where they lived before the Catastrophe, if they wished to return. Enough of them accepted the offer to compel the redrawing of departmental boundaries in several parts of the world in 2079 and again in 2083. But Congress insisted on limiting the number of departments to one thousand and on keeping their populations roughly equal.

Another incentive to maintain zero growth became apparent early in the twenty-second century, as the progress of medicine enabled everyone to live longer lives. After 2123, the death rate began dropping faster than the birth rate, resulting in a small temporary increase in the world's population and public campaigns (without coercive legislation) to glamorize childlessness and promote emigration to extraterrestrial colonies. The campaigns were greeted with considerable derision, but they—or something—must have worked. The population, which rose to 3.78 billion in 2125, fell back to 3.72 billion in 2130 and continued to hover between those values for the next four decades.

The New Global Economy

If multiplication for the sake of multiplying seemed absurd in the new climate of world opinion, so did production for the sake of producing, or, what amounts to the same thing, for the sake of producing profits. Many statistics once dear to economists, such as the annual growth rate, lost all meaning and were no longer computed.

But the Executive Council included twenty-two ministries devoted entirely to management of the global economy and one so-called superministry of planning that coordinated the efforts of all the others. Their single mandate was to ensure that every citizen could buy what he or she needed at the lowest possible price, with every purchase worth every "Commoncent" (the unit of world credit) paid. Foods were grown to nourish, durable goods were made to last, and nothing was produced merely to "sell." A ministry of consumer research kept in close touch with the wishes of consumers through polls, interviews, and careful analysis of sales figures. A ministry of consumer protection warranted the safety and reliability of all marketed goods and services.

The reality was seldom equal to the theory. Production managers often had little real interest in hearing what the public wanted and pulled wires to make forecasts of consumer demand correspond to what they were already geared to produce. Attempts to inform consumers about new products or services, essential as the postwar technological revival unfolded, sometimes degenerated into advertising crassly designed to mold consumer preferences. Quality standards in many areas were difficult or prohibitively costly to establish and even more difficult to enforce. When production managers did make serious efforts to turn out goods of the highest class, they were often frustrated by arbitrary ceilings on allowable costs decreed by officials in the ministry of planning. A special grievance of shoppers was the long waiting line or waiting list for scarce merchandise, the bane of the prewar Soviet economy.

But, on the whole, the new global economy served the needs of the average citizen more efficiently and more democratically than its predecessor. It began functioning even better toward the end of the century as older workers, accustomed to capitalist incentives, retired and were replaced by a new generation with revised priorities.

Of course not all the goods and services generated by the new economy bore a price tag. Many were furnished in limited or un-limited quantities by the Commonwealth without charge. All medical care, all prescribed drugs and prostheses, all schooling, all electric power, all broadcast and informational services, and all local public transport were unconditionally free, financed by the difference be-tween the price of goods and services sold by state corporations and their production costs as well as by a tax on the income of coopera-tives. But there was no need for a welfare system since all adult citi-zens earned at least a three-quarter share of the standard personal income whether they worked or not.

In some instances public services were available only in fixed amounts. Citizens not on public business who wished to journey outside their district of residence, for example, were issued an an-nual travel card entitling them to ten thousand free kilometers. If they chose to go further, they were required to pay a surcharge of so many Commoncents per kilometer.

The transport system illustrates quite well the difference between the regime of capital and the economic policies of the Common-wealth. In the last age of capital, the most significant status symbol and index of personal wealth was the large private automobile or floater car, which spent most of its days sitting, unused, in garages or parking lots. The waste of resources defies calculation.

Worse yet, the system fed on itself since every citizen so equipped was one less citizen likely to make extensive use of public transport. As a result, public transport atrophied, forcing more and more citi-zens to buy private vehicles. The growing fleets of such vehicles meant fat profits for their manufacturers and for those who supplied the fuel, kept the vehicles in repair, and built the ever more elaborate and expensive roadways on which they scurried back and forth.

In the Commonwealth, personal vehicles were made available by transport cooperatives for rental, but the sale of anything larger than a battery-powered cart big enough to seat two persons was pro-hibited by law. Almost all travel, local or otherwise, took place on state-operated urban rail systems, supersonic magnetic floater trains, or air and spacecraft. Public transport networks were so dense that a traveler could reach any chosen destination, no matter how near or far, at no matter what hour, without inconvenience or delay.

The unavailability of personally owned means of rapid transport also helped reinforce the public philosophy of the Commonwealth, which valued use above possession. Capitalism had cultivated in consumers an insatiable hunger for personal ownership of whatever they could afford to buy, and more. Those who acquired one private vehicle wanted two. Those who had two wanted three. It was impossible to have too many. "Collectors" gloried in the hoarding of vast numbers of books or paintings or clothes or houses or guns, whatever caught their fancy. "Shoppers" took an almost sexual pleasure in browsing through displays of merchandise and buying as much as they could carry home. Men and women sought identity, respect, and status not in what they did but in what they owned.

In the days of the Commonwealth, such behavior was diagnosed as sociopathic. It soon disappeared almost entirely. Increasingly, people opted for collective ownership of many kinds of durable goods. Neighborhoods established "goods pools," in which five or ten families joined to purchase appliances, cameras, tools, recreational equipment, and the like. Another popular institution was the consumers' cooperative, which functioned along similar lines and made it possible for members to have the use of many more goods than ever before at far less cost to each individual household.

But in one respect the new economy and the economy of late capital resembled one another closely: both were world systems, the new even more so than the old. The government of the Commonwealth established a global division of labor more thoroughgoing than any in world history. Each department, and each of the districts within departments, specialized in the production of certain goods and services and imported the rest. In the last age of capital, the volume of international trade at its highest point totaled only 30 percent of the gross world product, whereas by the year 2100 interdepartmental trade accounted for 75 percent of the world product.

Since the Commonwealth had one thousand departments and the United Nations (later the Confederated States of Earth) only two hundred sovereign nations, these figures are not really comparable. But in 2112 the Indian economist S. N. Bhandarkar published a comparative history of world trade that showed that the territories once occupied by the nations of the CSE were exporting 52 percent of their goods and services to the territories of other former nations by the end of the twenty-first century. By this measurement, the global economy of the Commonwealth was nearly twice as interdependent as the global economy of late capital.

If one may believe Commonwealth ministerial reports, the chief beneficiaries of the new interdependence were the people themselves. Because regions were highly specialized, because each produced what the training of its people, its raw materials, and its soil and climate suited that region to produce best, everyone benefited. Prices were lower, the productivity of labor and technology was higher, and the variety of goods and services available to the consumer was substantially greater than under any previous economic system.

The only problem with such reports is the small word *best*. The experts at the ministry of planning who decided what each region should produce were not infallible. Even when their assessment of a region's potential was sound from a purely economic perspective, it was often wrong because it failed to take into full account the wishes and values of the people who actually lived there.

The representatives of many districts accused the planners of perpetuating economic stereotypes and creating a new planetary hierarchy of skills. Central American districts that wanted to sell information services, for example, resented having to grow tropical fruits. Middle Eastern districts offering to produce medical supplies resented being assigned the recovery of oil for the manufacture of plastics. In theory such things could not happen since the planners were enjoined by law to respect local preferences in reaching their decisions. In practice such things did happen, more often than the People's Congress ever knew.

But, if one can excuse the poor judgment of individual planners and overlook the authoritarian tendencies inherent in the system, the new global economy did surely represent the most comprehensive experiment of all time in exploiting the advantages of regional specialization in world trade. Our own economic "order" seems, by contrast, like pure undifferentiated chaos.

In the end, what made the new economy work as well as it did, apart from the genuine egalitarianism and not wholly ineffective democracy of the Commonwealth itself, was the swift revival of technology. The same wizardry that had so often saved the lords of capi-

tal came to the aid of the planners of world socialism. Thanks to the
survival of several technologically advanced countries, notably Australia, the Southern African Republic, and Argentina, it took less than
a decade, from the mid-2050s to the early 2060s, to bring the level of
world technical competence to the point at which progress in many
fields had stopped in 2044. Southern engineers collaborated with
their surviving counterparts in the North to train a new generation
of skilled specialists. By 2063, engineers were applying this freshly
retrieved competence to the construction of factories, mines, information networks, and research laboratories throughout the Northern Hemisphere.

Their most outstanding early accomplishment was recorded in
the field of energy. The banning of fossil fuels by the People's Congress removed any temptation to turn again in that direction. Fusion
generators were built in large numbers in the 2070s, as a stopgap
measure, but continued to deliver far less energy than anyone had
foreseen prior to the publication of the Grushkov-Pula equations.
Another line of attack, also mounted in the 2070s, was the solar energy farm. Many such farms had been constructed during the last age
of capital. Engineers now discovered an ingenious technique for collecting solar radiation in deserts. By surrounding wastelands with
huge curved mirrors, they captured three times as much sunlight per
Commoncent as any earlier collection system. Environmentalists
complained that the mirrors desecrated the landscape, but the few
legal judgments in their favor were overturned on appeal by the
world courts. As of 2079, the first year in which no fossil fuels were
burned, humankind took 37 percent of its energy from nuclear fusion, 31 percent from solar and wind farms, 10 percent from hydrogen, and the rest from dams, geothermal sources, and biomass.

The success of the new solar farms launched a further round of research. Scientists had long toyed with the idea of stationing solar cells
in high synchronous orbit around the earth and transmitting the energy to the surface in the form of microwaves. Unfiltered by the atmosphere, direct solar radiation dwarfed any other energy source
and could never be exhausted. The Soviet Union had almost decided
to build such a system in 2009 but was deterred by the apparent success of fusion generators. In 2081, Commonwealth engineers submitted plans for a gigantic program of solar power satellites that
would cost 140 trillion Commoncents but would pay for itself in a

decade and generate five hundred quads of energy per year, more than the whole world currently used. The ministry of energy ap proved their plans, Congress voted enough funds to build and launch ten trial satellites, and the race was on.

The initial results were disappointing. Costs exceeded estimates by 300 percent. But, by the late 2080s, the technical problems had been solved, expenses were pared, and the system became fully operational (at a price of 210 trillion Commoncents) in August 2090. Enthusiasm ran so high that Congress added another world holiday to the calendar. It declared 22 August Energy Day, in tribute to the designers of the system, five ethnic Russian engineers. We no longer celebrate Energy Day, as we celebrate Earth Festival Day, but we can still admire the zeal, industry, and genius of the men and women whose work it honored.

Upward Bound

By the year 2100, the solar power satellite system, known in the media as the Sun Ring, supplied humankind with 65 percent of its energy. The attention of the wizards turned next to deep space, which had been neglected for many years.

Neglected, but not forgotten. By now a whole new civilization had established itself far from earth. The colony in high orbit around the earth ("Moontown") and the much larger habitat in the asteroid belt ("Atlantis") were not evacuated before the Catastrophe and carried on without terrestrial help. Breaking off contact during the Catastrophe with Hollings-Gray, the megacorp that had built them, the colonies reorganized as self-governing cooperatives. The two worlds kept in touch with each other and with survivors on earth by radio.

While earthbound humanity was struggling to stay alive in the late 2040s, the moltechs of Atlantis constructed a sister habitat, called Lemuria, which by 2065 had as many inhabitants as Atlantis. The one spaceship in dock in Atlantis at the time of the Catastrophe supplied the model for a dozen others, enabling the colonists to roam freely through the belt, exploiting its abundant mineral resources. Less adventurous, the smaller group of settlers in Moontown were at first content to stay put. But in the 2060s a ship from Atlantis brought them the equipment that they needed to build their own spacecraft and replicating systems. In just a few decades they had fabricated nine more colony worlds. They formed a loose-knit federation with each other and with the beltworlds known as the League of Space Cooperatives.

On Energy Day 2091, as a speaker in the Congress ruefully pointed out, more than forty-four thousand pioneers were living in twelve distant space colonies, getting along quite well without their ancestors, and performing feats of derring-do every day that (except for the engineering of the Sun Ring) terrestrials no longer even attempted.

Three months later the ancestors and their far-flung progeny finally met face to face. Two ships from Moontown, carrying two original earth-born settlers and twenty of their descendants, arrived at one of the Sun Ring space stations. Shuttlecraft ferried them down to the planet for a tumultuous reception in Chongqing, the current ceremonial capital of the Commonwealth. From the outset, the "spacers" made clear that they had no intention of being engulfed in the Commonwealth, whose penchant for large-scale projects and centralized systems they distrusted.

Still, the encounter went reasonably well. The president of the Executive Council assured his visitors that the colonies had earned their independence. The head of the spacer delegation, the Australian-born biotechnician John Fletcher, issued a public statement commending the people of earth for their swift recovery from the Catastrophe and hoping for cordial relations between the Commonwealth and the League.

Some hard-line World party ministers in the Council were uneasy about the existence of an organized independent polity not under the jurisdiction of the Commonwealth. Would the spacers eventually become rivals of earthlings and start a new cycle of wars? Would neonationalists take advantage of the formal recognition of spacer independence to demand the same recognition for their own people?

The objections of the hard-liners were debated seriously but, in the end, voted down. At the same time, the Council did agree to use the expertise regained in building the Sun Ring to launch an ambitious space program of its own in the twenty-second century. Such an effort would bring the Commonwealth into close contact and collaboration with the League worlds. In the process, many thought, the League worlds would grow much closer to the mother planet and eventually see the wisdom of joining the Commonwealth.

The Commonwealth space ministry set as its first goal the reopening of the lunar station built by the United Nations in 2020 and subsequently abandoned in 2036. A large expedition transported in three spaceships landed on the site of the moonbase in 2105. It began its work by disinterring the bodies of the six obstinate men who had chosen to stay behind in 2036 and sealing them in a small mausoleum built on the site from lunar materials. The bodies had already been found and given appropriate burials by a team of scavengers from Moontown, but the ministry ordered the reinterment as a tribute from earth to earth's own "heroes" and as a way of reasserting earth's claim to lunar soil.

By this time, the soil of the moon had already been deeply scored by Moontowners and their colleagues from the other high-orbit communities, who mined its minerals and shipped them back to their home worlds by electromagnetic mass-drivers. They had also helped themselves to equipment from the abandoned lunar station itself, but they had never bothered to establish permanent living quarters on the moon. Within ten years, the United Nations lunar station had been completely rebuilt and expanded to house a thousand full-time residents. A second settlement grew up in the Moscow Sea on the far side of the moon, with room for three hundred people. League representatives signed a pact with the commander of the stations to facilitate cooperation between station personnel and visiting miners. Friction was not unknown, but in general the treaty worked satisfactorily.

In 2109, another expedition was launched from the Sun Ring, this time to Mars. The crew stayed only a few weeks, ascertaining that the facilities of the deserted GTC colony could be refurbished with little effort. In 2111, a full-scale expedition landed at the site, which returned to vigorous life almost overnight. A disastrous chemical fire destroyed most of it in 2115, but there were plenty of volunteers to rebuild and repopulate the colony.

By 2140, Mars had twenty thousand inhabitants, most of them scientists and engineers. Scientific stations flourished on five of the least inhospitable moons of Jupiter and Saturn. Also by 2140 the space ministry had placed several hundred space habitats in lunar, terrestrial, and Martian orbits and several hundred more in the asteroid belt, with a total population of more than five million. The League built new worlds, too, although not nearly so many. As foreseen by the Council, the affairs of the League worlds became inextricably entangled with those of the Commonwealth. Trade and tourism thrived. But the League refused to surrender its sovereignty. The spunk and tenacity of its citizens had a subtly subversive effect on the populations of Commonwealth habitats and helped prepare them for the years of dissent and transformation that followed.

Meanwhile, in 2116, scientists commissioned by the space ministry succeeded, at last, in perfecting a continuous-boost fission-to-fusion drive that would enable spacecraft to travel at speeds approaching six thousand kilometers per second. Up to this point, most ships had still been propelled by liquid fuel rockets, as in the twentieth century, or by mass-drivers. The new engine revolutionized far-space navigation, bringing most of the solar system within weeks of earth. It went into regular service for flights to Mars, the asteroid belt, and the outer planets and their moons in 2120.

Also in 2120, another team of Commonwealth scientists and engineers tested the first workable laser-pulsed fusion engine in space, a drive that enabled spacecraft to reach speeds almost four times greater than the hybrid model. Originally developed by one of the megacorps in the 2030s and then shelved because of the depression, it was less cost efficient but found an immediate use in powering a small fleet of drone ships sent out to explore neighboring star systems. The first drone left the Sun Ring bound for Alpha Centauri in 2129, with others following in 2131, 2134, and 2135. They took various routes, with the object of visiting seven stars in all. Since they attained a peak velocity of only 7.5 percent of the speed of light and the stars in Alpha Centauri are 4.3 light years from earth, we shall not receive the signals sent back by the first drone until 2258.

After the fall of the Commonwealth, as you know, we learned how to make faster journeys. When the telemetry from those ancient drones is finally received, in 2258 and thereafter, it will tell us nothing we have not already learned long ago for ourselves.

Closer to home, the trustworthy fission-to-fusion vessels continued to perform well, bringing the most remote habitats and stations within easy reach of the mother planet. By the middle of the twenty-second century, the human race lived happily in many parts of the solar system. We look back on the days of the Commonwealth with a mixture of grudging admiration and profound sorrow, but there is little to regret about the exploits of the space ministry. In some ways it was the most seditious agency in the Commonwealth because it held up for all earthlings to see the infinite variety of life in the cosmos.

INTERLUDE

Our pages of family history continue with an exchange between two brothers, Arne and Knud Brandt, grandsons of Regine Jensen-Brandt. Arne was born in 2058 and emigrated to Hightown, one of the Moontown replica colonies, in 2094. Only a handful of earthlings, all with special gifts, were granted citizenship in League worlds. The spacers recruited Arne because of his proficiency in AI systems analysis. Knud, his younger brother, was a physical therapist, illustrator, and sculptor. Returning from North America to the land of his ancestors while still in his twenties, Knud made his home in the department of the Commonwealth that included the former southern counties of Jutland in Denmark and the former state of Schleswig-Holstein in Germany.

> *Hightown*
> *DF-Net 12(5/6)*
> *1 August 2096*

Dear Knud,

Hello from afar. You may be surprised to receive this. I don't think we've corresponded since I was a grad student and you were still a kid. But Father says you're not too pleased with me. He thinks I should "explain" myself to you because he's given up trying to make you understand my point of view. Is it really that bad?

Poor Father. It's obvious he never inherited any of Grandma Regine's imagination. First his younger son trots off to Europe and strikes down roots in the native sod. Then his older son flies away to live in a star. He doesn't fathom either of us, does he? He's such a steady man, so precise and predictable and uncomplicated. We must disappoint him.

I am sorry for one thing. Now that we're so far apart, I don't know you any more, not really, or how you live, or the men you sleep with, and I've lost all serious touch with Father and Mother, too, in spite of the letters we send back and forth.

Maybe letters won't help you and me, either. But I'd like to try.

I gather the main problem is that you can't imagine why I would want to live and work outside the Commonwealth and pledge my allegiance to a "foreign" government. For years most of us hardly knew what the word "foreign" meant. When I was growing up, the only time I saw it outside a textbook was in the communiqués of some of the wilder neo-nationalist dissident organizations. They always referred to Militiamen as foreigners.

As you remember, the meeting with the League people in Chongqing changed everything. Earthlings found themselves negotiating with an alien power. Your reaction was to draw back, narrow your eyes, grit your teeth. Mine was very different. We stopped talking about it in 2092 or 2093, but you had to know I was already considering emigration.

Father thinks I've been starstruck. The romance of deep space. He doesn't pretend to understand such things himself, but it makes a nice clean uncontroversial story to tell friends and relatives. Mother, bless her black heart, said I just wanted to be a big fish in a little pond. She's at least 15 percent right. I'm sure being a big fish entered into my calculations at some level. Father may be 15 percent right, too. I do like the idea of frolicking up here in this gorgeous revolving doughnut. It has its romantic side.

Of course. Just as the life of a neo-Viking appeals to the romantic in you. By the way, if you're such a bona fide unreconstructed World party man, why did you bother to return to that little corner of the Great Unified Oneness where the Brandts and the Jensens started out? Did the Oneness get to you, too? (I had to ask!)

Anyway, no, wanderlust and egomania are not the full answer. Just between us, if it were only a question of geography, I'd rather live on earth. Hightown is the most beautiful place I've ever seen, but you can explore the whole doughnut in a week. It's no substitute for those glorious wide open spaces of earth.

So why am I here? I'll tell you. I can't handle the regimenting and standardizing and equalizing and God-awful smugness of life on earth. Most of you don't even see it. Things were bad enough in the '70s, but at least we had a sense of going somewhere, overcoming odds, making the earth a decent place to live. Since about 2085, the Commonwealth has turned into an enormous spice grinder. The bureaucrats dump all the peppercorns and nutmegs and cinnamon sticks and stigmas of saffron into the hopper and grind and grind and, behold, out comes a uniform brown dust.

Brother Knud, it may be fair, it may be equal, but it's not life any more. Have you honestly found anything in Jutland that you couldn't have found just as easily in the valley of the Mississippi or the mountains of Tibet? Wherever you live on earth, it's always the same regulations, the same ideology, the same deadly sameness.

Well, I didn't mean this to become an indictment of your life. In fact that's not my point at all. My point is, you should feel free to live in one place and I should feel free to live in another. It's nobody's damned business how or why, just the same as it's okay for you to love men and for me to love women. We got over that little problem years ago.

So, please, be happy in the old country. But let's not homogenize the whole solar system!

Jeanne sends her love. There's a big population boom here, with all the new worlds to fill, so we're hoping to spawn. I'll let you know when you achieve unclehood.

Fondly,
Arne
♦

Esbjerg
DDES 221-8008-CK
14 August 2096

Dear Arne,

Surprised to hear from you. But it was a treat. You're the same old earnest Arne!

I can't reply in kind. No, I didn't moan to Father about your desertion. No, I'm not a Viking. No, I don't give my heart and soul to the World party. Father always exaggerates because he confuses theater with truth. I'm just a showman at heart, you know that!

I came to Esbjerg to speak Danish. That's all, no more, no less. Truth this time, not theater. You like stars, I like the sound of Danish.

Tell me what it's really like up there. You talk about whizzing around in all that variety, after the sameness of Terra Firma. But I thought each

Moontown colony was an exact replica of Moontown itself, manufac-
tured by microbots? Tell me I'm wrong! Help, help! Save this poor boy
from delusion!
   P.S.: I do miss you.

                              Love,
                              Knud
                              ♦

                              Hightown
                              DF-Net 12(5/6)
                              17 August 2096

Dear Knud,
   Many thanks for the letter. I was afraid you wouldn't get around to
answering, but I apologize for my fears, also for misconstruing Father, if
that's what I did. Or should I say I was crazy not to realize that Father
was misconstruing you? You have to be literal with Father, Knud! When
will you learn?
   Okay, you have a point about the replication process. Hightown was
built in the '80s by a combination of microbots and man-sized robots and
macrobots as big as the statue that stood in the harbor of New York City
before the Catastrophe. It's almost identical to Moontown, physically. It
looks the same. But it doesn't feel the same.
   Take Moontown. I've been there a couple of times, also to three of the
others. It's a kind of Fourierist phalanstery. People receive shares of
stock for their work. The stock earns interest, and you can save the
earnings and buy more stock, if you're frugal. The interest rate goes
down for each additional share you own, so nobody gets obscenely rich,
but by earth standards, Moontowners are capitalists.
   Hightown is entirely different. The community was set up by a single
family, the Yamashita family. They jointly own and manage the whole
place. All the rest of us are hired help, so to speak. We sign on for re-
newable five-year contracts. Everyone gets an apartment, ration cards
for food and clothing, and free unlimited use of all the community ser-
vices and facilities.
   But the Yamashitas aren't feudal overlords. All of Hightown is just an
experiment, designed by a couple of Moontown sociologists, and char-
tered and capitalized by the Moontown Common Council. Each of the

other new colonies has its own social system, no two alike. After twenty-five years, we'll compare our results with everyone else's and see what we've learned.

So what is life really like up here? Well, for starters, life is comfortable, clean, practical. Hightown keeps reminding me of that cruise we took with Father and Mother when I was sixteen and you were eleven. Remember the ship, how we loved running up and down the decks and exploring all the salons and the playground and the club room for teenagers and the swimming pool and the barber shop? Remember the "snacketeria," where you could get anything you wanted, any time of the day? It was the best vacation we ever took. I don't even want to think what sacrifices Father and Mother had to make to pay for that cruise. It lasted only seven days, but in my memory we sailed for years and years.

Hightown is like a cruise ship, only much bigger. It rotates once a minute, which creates a gravitational effect at the rim equal to earth's. Most of the town is a thick circular tube, 8.5 kilometers around. In the center sits a smaller tube wrapped around a central sphere. The inner structures, where the gravity ranges from low to nil, are connected to the rim by a dozen hollow spokes. We use eight of the spokes for jogging and cycling and swimming. The other four serve as transport corridors equipped with moving roadways joined to others in the inner ring, so that residents can reach any point in town in almost no time.

The inner ring is reserved for workshops, laboratories, and gymnasia. We live and raise our food in the outer one. When you're strolling around there, you have the feel of being out of doors, it's so big. We've got miniature parks, with trees and gardens and ponds, and there's a sunshield above the colony that gives us fourteen hours of gently filtered light and ten hours of darkness every day. All our electricity comes from an array of solar panels on the outside. It's free and it's inexhaustible.

Jeanne and I live in a terraced apartment house made of lacquered moonbrick. The rooms are small, but efficient, with retractable furnishings. You can eat either at home or in any of six dining halls, if you make a reservation. We usually prefer to go out because there's more variety available in the dining halls. The menus change every day, and, for better or worse (I'm still not sure which), when you eat there, you know almost everybody you see. At the moment there are 2,158 of us. We have space for at least 1,200 more. Hence the green light for babies. But before the replication began, when it was just Moontown, you had to wait sometimes five years to get a "child license."

Of course we grow all our own food. Grains, vegetables, fruits, fish, in astonishing variety. I've toured the farms. Most of the agriculture is dry, in air or sand. One of the other colonies, Starshine, keeps dairy cattle and poultry, but we manage quite well without either.

Is this what you wanted to know? I realize it's a jumble. Most of it is probably common knowledge on earth by now, but maybe you'll believe it since it comes from your older and wiser brother. In fact I saw an earthside holocamera team here only a month ago, shooting a documentary. If you watch it, don't expect to find me. I kept well out of their way. Hightown has a grand total of eight earthlings, all of whom I know, and five were interviewed for the program.

You didn't say anything about your work. Are you still in geriatric fitness training? Have you exhibited recently? My job here is basically the same as on earth, except that I do more troubleshooting. They have adequate general purpose systems, but the brains need a lot of redesigning to handle specific tasks.

Take care of yourself. Jeanne says hello.

As ever,

Arne

◆

Esbjerg
DDES 221-8008-CK
9 September 2096

Dear Arne,

Wow! Double wow! The Hightown Chamber of Commerce presents "Capitalism on Parade"! Are you really serious? You live like a rat in a gilded cage acting out a script written by "a couple of Moontown sociologists," and you're a happy boy.

Okay, I asked for it. I opened up your sluice gates. A thousand pardons. But I thought you remembered me a little better. It almost hurts. And we said Father was the guy with the literal mind!

No, I meant something different. I know they feed you and keep you breathing. I even know about how they recycle the air and the water and the piss and the dung. It's marrrrrrvelous!

But come clean, O wise one. You could find a nice shiny laboratory to inhabit right here on Terra Firma. In fact the Congress just voted funds to set up one thousand volunteers in a simulated space colony in South

America. They plan to lock 'em up and throw away the key and see what happens after two years.

It's all part of a program to send up colonies of our own next century. One of these days you'll have neighbors. But leaving the planet to find freedom? Is your own intelligence artificial?

Obviously you never figured it out. We're free down here because we're anonymous. The bigger the government, the more distance between Us and Them, the more hidey-holes. Should I repeat that? Bigness equals anonymity equals freedom.

But look at life in Hightown. You have 2,156 fellow mortals watching every move you make. You go to the dining hall and 231 friends and neighbors turn out to monitor what you're eating and with whom and how long you chew your cabbage.

Not for this boy, thank you very much. Esbjerg has 85,000 people. The Department of South Jutland and Schleswig has 2.9 million people. I'm proud to say I don't know 99.8 percent of them. I'm even prouder to say the same percentage doesn't know me!

Any time I get tired of being what you call a neo-Viking, I can zip off to Bangkok and become a neo-Thai or rattle on down to Hobart and become a neo-Tasmanian. My income won't change much, but I can speak a different language and look at different scenery.

Nobody will care. I can be a complete stranger and nobody will care. Nobody will know me. Maybe I don't want to be known!

Enough already. I'm transmitting the reviews of my latest sculpture show. It didn't go too well, but what the hell! It was a show, and I loved it.

> *More love,*
> *Knud*
> ♦

Hightown
DF-Net 12(5/6)
16 September 2096

Dear Knud,

It makes no sense for us to quarrel just because we don't understand why the other guy is satisfied with his life. If I can believe Father, if I can believe what you write, I think my little brother is okay. I know I am. So let's leave it there. We should be grateful we discovered how to be happy long before the biotechs ran out of ways of keeping us alive.

But your letter set me to wondering why I really emigrated. Variety?

Freedom? I guess not, in any ordinary sense of the words. I may have been fooling myself. So let me try again.

The nub of my distress on earth was something more fundamental even than my feeling of confinement. Or rather, it underlay that feeling.

You're right about the advantages of bigness. What draws me to Hightown is not that it's small. I already confessed to you that I'd rather live on a big ball like earth than inside a hollow tube the size of Hightown. Sometimes, at least, I'd rather be anonymous, too.

So I've been thinking. The best I can come up with is this. The Commonwealth may be an improvement over the old world of the nation-states and the megacorps, but it has one towering overwhelming fault. It's why I suffocated there, and why I breathe so easily up here, even without the shield of anonymity.

Can you guess? The nub of my distress on earth, Brother Knud, was simply that the Commonwealth suffers from a terminal case of messianic megalomania. The founding mothers and fathers needed to be megalomaniacs because they had to save us all from ourselves, immediately, ruthlessly, categorically. But megalomaniacs can't ever quit. They go on saving people, long after they've already been saved.

The result is englobement. The Commonwealth wants to englobe you and me and Jutland and Europe and the earth and why not the colonies and the solar system and the galaxy and the whole roaring cosmos?

It reaches out its loving arms and takes us all in. The World party, the world state, the world culture, the world mind, the world soul. Its philosophy is, Leave nothing outside. Incorporate everything. Swallow reality whole.

In the end the Commonwealth turns out to be just another variation on the ancient theme of man's exploitation of man. Another feeding time for Moloch. Another rite of spring.

But number me among the missing. I don't want to watch it happening again. And if the Commonwealth ever decides to englobe Hightown, we'll just open our windows and let the winds of space rush in. There are some things, little brother, worse than absolute zero.

As ever,
Arne

◆

Hightown
DF-Net 12(5/6)
11 October 2096

Dear Knud,

I haven't heard from you in a while. Yesterday I happened to re-read the letter I sent you last month. Maybe that's why you didn't reply. Look, I apologize for the apocalypticism. You didn't need or deserve it, although, as I said before, it was your own letter that shook me up enough to put me in the mood. I really hadn't figured out why I left earth until then. Maybe I should have kept it to myself.

Jeanne heard some good news last week. She's pregnant. In fact twice over. She's carrying twin boys. Do you think I ought to name them Arne and Knud?

Take care, Uncle. And forgive me.

Fondly,
Arne

♦

Esbjerg
DDES 221-8008-CK
29 October 2096

Dear Arne,

Don't torture yourself! You can't offend Uncle Knud. Not with political diatribes anyway. I just got involved with a new man, and your letter slipped my overheated mind.

It's beautiful news about the twins, but for the love of englobement, please give them more amusing names than Arne and Knud! How about Castor and Pollux? I suppose that's what everyone names their twins, up your way.

Well, as I say, stop worrying. You moonmen worry me, though, when I don't have anything better to do. I'm sure all the earnest patriots in the bad old days felt just as you feel. They never wanted to be englobed, either. So they each built their own little world with their own little army and before they knew it, boom, Boom, BOOM!

I like it peaceful, myself. Safe for Castor and Pollux. Safe for people and dogs and trees. I can take a lot of englobement if it means I'll be safe. Does that make me a coward? Or does it make you a monster?

*Don't answer that! Regards to Jeanne, and give the little guys a pat on
their embryonic noggins for old Uncle Knud.*

Love,
Knud

♦

The correspondence between Arne and Knud went on for many years,
but they never again discussed politics. The twins, named Carl and
Otto for their great-grandmother Regine's father and uncle, became
noted interstellar explorers. I hope you have a chance to meet them
some day.

8

WE, THE PEOPLE

The New Working Class

In the last age of capital, politicians delighted in broadcasting appeals to that great amorphous collectivity, the "people." Even demagogues and dictators doted on the people. For fascists it was the "folk," for communists the "masses," for bourgeois democrats the "electorate." Seldom more dangerous in premodern times than driven cattle, the people had grown into a coherent, articulate force that the governing class ignored at its peril. As we have seen, the politicians and their partners in the megacorps found ways of engineering compliance and even loyalty, but the efforts they expended were both strenuous and costly.

In the Commonwealth, the people at last came of age. A new society emerged, a postmodern, postcapitalist society without classes or significant differences in wealth and status. Or so the leaders of the World party professed to believe. In this chapter I want to examine whether the revolutionary changes in the world order wrought by the Commonwealth were translated into an authentically democratic society and culture.

Most scholars nowadays would argue that, despite the benevolent intentions of many party leaders, the attempt to forge a true democracy was ineffective and premature. It took a century and a half, including two world wars, to dispose of the European aristocracy after the French Revolution had already "disposed" of it. Was it not absurd to expect the bourgeoisie to disappear just because the World

Revolution declared it illegal? In the first half of the twentieth century, the Russians and Chinese dismantled their privileged classes and were then compelled to create new ones to take their place. Why should the World party have done any better?

These are the questions that most of us nowadays raise. But perhaps most of us are wrong. In my own view, which may also be wrong, the Commonwealth *did* succeed in summoning a democratic society out of the ashes of capital. We today are the proof of it. We today are its children, however vehemently we may deny our pedigrees.

Clearly, the social order assembled by the early leaders of the Commonwealth was not the work of the people. It was the work of a small number of willful men and women who gained popular support with many of the same techniques used by their capitalist and Communist predecessors. But, when they implemented their program of equality of income and equality of skills, they produced a new worldwide working class capable of standing on its own feet and thinking for itself. Thanks to the progress of medicine and, later, the eugenics program of the Commonwealth, the leadership even managed to remove most of the inequalities inflicted on humankind by the blind forces of nature. The circumstances that led to the downfall of the Commonwealth were, in part, circumstances for which the Commonwealth deserves our heartfelt thanks and warm approval. In this sense, it did its job too well.

The "new worldwide working class" was, of course, not a class at all. Everyone belonged to it, except those few sociopaths who refused employment, a group that never rose above 10 percent of the population in any department of the Commonwealth. By the harsh standards of Karl Marx's time, it was also only marginally a class that worked.

Even in the last several decades of the age of capital, labor had become significantly less onerous, and the workday and workweek had been shortened, as a result of major advances in computerization and robotics. In the days of the Commonwealth, further refinements in automation virtually eliminated routine labor, both manual and mental. Citizens were encouraged to acquire training in at least two and preferably three or four skills. Your cousin Knud Brandt, for example, earned certificates of competence in geriatric fitness therapy, illustration, and sculpture. His brother Arne was an AI systems analyst but also, although he fails to mention it in the letters we sampled, a writer of fiction. Typically, a person worked in one field for about five years, returned to school for retraining, found employment in a second field for several years, and then worked in both alternately, while learning a third skill in his or her spare time.

For the most part, workers avoided tenured posts in favor of consultancies and contract jobs that allowed them to move from assignment to assignment and take the fullest advantage of their various skills. The usual commission required about twenty hours of service a week. In the year 2095, 3 percent of the work performed was in agriculture, 6 percent in factory and mine supervision, 15 percent in technical consulting, 5 percent in managerial consulting, 11 percent in health and medicine, 21 percent in public services, 7 percent in personal services, 5 percent in arts and letters, 8 percent in scientific and technical research, and 19 percent in education.

That was 2095. Eight years later, the ministry of labor reclassified students as workers, in keeping with the long-standing policy of paying adult students in certified educational programs the same full income received by other working citizens. When adult students were added to the ranks of teachers and school administrators, the share of work performed in education rose from 19 to 37 percent.

The change in the classification system of the ministry of labor, which may seem like a tedious bureaucratic detail, was symbolic of one of the most remarkable achievements of the Commonwealth in the eighty-five years of its effective rule. It signaled the arrival of a new definition of work. Previously, *work* was an economic term, denoting labor performed with an assignable market value in a system of social relations of production for profit or use. Even the work of students might be labeled productive labor if one conceived of it as vocational training, essential to the performance of tasks in the marketplace.

But, under the new definition established by the ministry of labor in 2103, all adult students were workers, whether their studies were undertaken to satisfy a market demand or not. Work had come to include the enlargement of the self, on the premise that every increase in personal capacity achieved without exploitation of the labor of others represented a net gain for the whole society of associated selves. Today we think of such premises as embarrassing truisms, mindless demonstrations of elementary social arithmetic, but this was not the case at the turn of the last century. Men and women had to struggle fiercely to give them currency, against deep-seated preconceptions inherited from an earlier age; in the end the struggle was won.

In the same period, the People's Congress, after stormy debates, passed the Sabbatical Law, which took effect in 2109, granting to all workers twelve months of fully reimbursed personal study every seventh year of their adult lives. Mechanics tried their hand at the fine arts. Artists learned physics. Mathematicians dabbled in poetry, computer scientists took instruction in nursing, kindergarten teachers studied industrial management.

Counting both sabbatical leaves and vocational instruction, the ministry of labor was able, by the year 2129, to report that adult citizens were now devoting 53 percent of their work time to education. Some officials predicted that the figure would soon rise to 75 percent or even 85 percent, but it stalled at this point and remained there until the Commonwealth disintegrated later in the century. What it would be today, if we had the bureaucrats to keep track of such things, I can only guess.

In any event, the educational establishment grew prodigiously after 2070. A uniform global system of lower, middle, and upper schools was developed in the 2070s, accompanied by legislation requiring attendance at each level for several years, the exact number depending on individual proficiency and progress. Slower learners spent a little more time in lower and middle schools, faster learners a little less. Entrance to upper schools (formerly known as universities) occurred for most persons at the age of fourteen or fifteen. After earning certification in at least one vocational skill, students chose their first work opportunity, normally at the age of sixteen or seventeen. They returned to upper school for further training in their mid-twenties and, again, at various intervals, throughout life. Initial exposure to upper school was deliberately limited to two or at most three years, on the plausible theory that young people are seldom highly motivated to pursue advanced study until they have spent some time in the working world outside the classroom.

For nearly all children, formal education began at the age of four. Lower school (for ages four to nine) and middle school (for ages ten to fourteen) bore only a faint resemblance to the elementary and secondary schools of the last age of capital. Instead of herding two or three dozen students into a classroom and drilling them throughout the day in the same narrow range of simpleminded subjects year after year, schools offered personalized instruction, tailored to the abilities and interests of each student. The ratio of faculty to students in lower and middle schools was fixed by the ministry of education in 2083 at five to one; in some departments it fell even lower. Routine learning was expedited by interactive computerized teaching machines.

The curriculum consisted of a formidable array of basic skills and a comprehensive program of what were known as "world studies." Students acquired fluency in at least three languages (including their own), mastered the rudiments of arithmetic and higher mathematics (including calculus), learned drawing and music, and received elementary training in computer science and robotics.

The liberal education furnished by the program in world studies was designed to stretch the child's mind as far as it could reach. World studies introduced pupils to anthropology, philosophy, sociology, economics, world history and culture, prognostics (once known as future studies), and the fundamental natural sciences, from astrophysics to paleontology.

In the beginning, some of these subjects were withheld until middle school years, but, by the 2090s, preparatory versions of each were taught even in lower school. What healthy, well-fed child of six would not be more interested in stars and dinosaurs and feudal chivalry than in the educational pablum fed to the schoolboys and schoolgirls in the last age of capital? What healthy, well-fed child of six cannot learn foreign languages more swiftly and with less embarrassment than any adolescent or adult?

Upper schools, too, were quite different from their counterparts in the last age of capital. Throughout the world in the twentieth century and the early twenty-first, universities provided tests of endurance rather than programs of instruction. Students flocked by the hundreds into lecture halls where teachers of minor competence declaimed potted outlines of knowledge found just as easily in any number of textbooks. The shrewder students did not even bother to attend, which mattered very little as long as they passed their examinations, no great challenge for anyone with a modicum of intelligence who had skimmed the approved texts.

In the upper schools of the Commonwealth, the emphasis fell on learning how to do something well. Instead of degree programs, the upper schools offered learning programs. The typical program lasted for two or three months, requiring the student to devote all his or her time to the mastery of a single discipline or skill, under the tutelage of one or more instructors certified in that discipline or skill After completing one program, the student took a well-earned holiday of two or three weeks and then returned, fresh, to enter another. The largest classes were seminars, studios, or laboratories enrolling up to ten students, but most instruction was given privately. The ministry of education fixed the faculty-student ratio in all upper schools at three to one.

Comprehensive upper schools employing thousands of tutors were located in every sizable town and rural district of every department. These schools soon became the chief centers not only of learning but of higher culture generally in their region, filling the role once played in medieval times by churches and cathedrals. The exhibitions and performances abundantly available on campus attracted thousands of visitors from the surrounding community, who were always welcome. In addition, many professional artists, musicians, creative writers, scientists, philosophers, and other such folk lived and worked (and taught, if they wished) on or near the school campus.

The curse of formal education in the Commonwealth, according to its most trenchant critics, was the certification system. Students who finished a learning program in upper school, for which they had to pass grueling proficiency examinations, received a "certificate of competence" entitling them to enter a vocation that utilized the skill in question. A good many vocations required more than one such certificate. Anyone who wished to teach the same skill was obligated to enroll in upper-school learning programs specifically designed for prospective tutors, from which they earned a "certificate of teaching competence."

From this distance, it all seems straightforward enough, given the penchant of the Commonwealth for highly centralized and standardized systems; but the regulations defining skills, vocations, learning programs, teacher programs, and the educational requirements of vocations soon became immensely complicated. In many instances they were also arbitrary, decreed more for the sake of bureaucratic logic and symmetry than for sound professional reasons. By the third decade of the twenty-second century, the vitality of the upper schools, in particular, had been sapped. Growing numbers of students began to seek instruction at "free learning centers" staffed by uncertified teachers.

With hindsight, we may see the rise of the free learning centers as a great turning point in the whole history of the Commonwealth. The system was breaking down, although at first scarcely anyone in the educational establishment, even the much-vaunted prognosticians who trained students to chart and weigh alternative futures, had the slightest inkling of it. Revolution boiled under their noses, but for years they smelled nothing.

Homes and Families

It is perhaps significant that we began exploring the social history of the Commonwealth by discussing work. On the whole, work life was more fulfilling in the years of the Commonwealth than home life. Or, let us say, more fulfilling than family life. A man or woman's home is wherever he or she happens to sleep at the moment, and anything can serve. The meanest room can change into a warm nest if the person chooses to make it so. Homes are not places but states of mind.

The traditional modern family, however, did not adjust well to the social environment created by the Commonwealth. Social commentators kept their eyes peeled for the emergence of a new, representative type of postmodern family, and from time to time claimed to have spied it, but all that really happened was a further deterioration of the modern family unit, a process that had begun in the twentieth century, if not before. For this deterioration, the social policies of the Commonwealth must take most of the responsibility.

For example, the war on sexism declared by the Commonwealth brought women fully into the work world, and not just as adjuncts or junior partners of their husbands. In itself, this was a step forward, but it did not strengthen family bonds. On the contrary: free choice of vocation and schooling throughout adult life kept husbands and wives apart much of the time. Another result was the common decision to defer parenting until the fourth and fifth decades of life and to raise at most two children, more often only one or none. The demographic policies of the Commonwealth and the disappearance of child labor reinforced such decisions. Even when children did join the family, most (and sometimes virtually all) of their care was provided by professional children's centers.

Not all couples found the new order of things inimical to wedded bliss. Divorce rates were quite high throughout the period, but surveys made by the ministry of children and family life also disclosed the existence of millions of tolerably happy childless marriages and equally happy marriages with one or two children boarded much of the time in care centers. Partners not infrequently reported that long separations from one another increased passion and reduced connubial friction. Nor did the children themselves suffer demonstrably from parental neglect. Their needs were met by skilled professionals with advanced training and an inborn predilection for their tasks. Often the children received far better treatment from the professionals than they could ever have expected from their bumbling natural parents.

The real issue was the utility of the family as a social unit. Did it any longer serve much purpose? Apparently not. As the divorce rate climbed, the marriage rate dropped. By the year 2100, 45 percent of all persons living with a member of the opposite sex did so without benefit of a marriage contract, spending an average of only three years in the relationship. Twenty percent had opted for various legalized alternatives such as the five-year marriage (renewable on demand) and the group marriage, for three or more persons, with escape clauses to allow easy egress from the group.

Even more telling was the revelation of the world census of 2100 that a majority of the adult population lived alone most of the time. To the question, "Have you shared a habitation for more than seven consecutive days with a spouse or sexual partner during the past six months?" 55 percent replied in the negative. Sexual liaisons remained a large part of life, inside or outside marriage, but literal cohabitation diminished steadily and, with it, much of the old sense of family.

Some prognosticians studying the census returns foresaw the extinction of marriage as an institution by the year 2150. Without large families, without property to pass on to descendants, without full-time responsibility for the care of children, without husband and wife regularly living under the same roof, without taboos against those venerable biblical sins of fornication, adultery, and divorce, the interest of society in the married state dwindled almost to zero. One Congresswoman from northern Europe, Sigrid Thorvaldsen, introduced legislation in 2104 to abolish marriage forthwith. Her bill eventually reached the floor of the Congress and was defeated by a vote of 1,734 to 212, but the fact that she had 211 supporters was not lost on anyone. A later, similar attempt in 2122 garnered the support of nearly four hundred Congresspersons.

At the same time, no institution offered itself as a viable alternative to the old nuclear family. Group marriages worked in a few scattered instances but more often dissolved within a few years.

In the main, therefore, Commonwealth men and women did one thing best: living alone. They found themselves enjoying their own company more than experts had anticipated, and their children suffered only a little, when they suffered at all. Yet many people complained that life had become too cool and detached. They cast a nostalgic look back to the Dickensian warmth of homes and families in times gone by (a warmth exposed by social historians of the Commonwealth as largely mythical) and sighed for lost domestic joys.

Perfectly Human

How healthy were these increasingly single men and women of the new age? As we have seen, the progress of medicine during the last age of capital had liberated humankind from most diseases, lengthened the average life span, and raised the possibility of improving the human species itself. The physicians and medical engineers of the Commonwealth carried this earlier work much further and made its blessings available to everyone. In no other area of life did the Commonwealth achieve more, and in no other area did its accomplishments arouse such bitter controversy.

One of the first ministers of health, Qian Gundi—a tough-minded, dour physician from Hangzhou who served in that office for an unprecedented twenty-five years—issued a statement of goals in 2071 that defined the agenda of the government in the broadest possible terms. "We propose," she said in her preamble, "to allow every man and woman on earth to live a full life, and we propose to make every life perfectly human."

In short, the ministry promised the eradication of disease, the removal of disability, and the bioengineering of a higher race. Qian was warned by the president to cloak her programs in more ambiguous language, but she never retracted her remarks, and they were tacitly, and later openly, endorsed by subsequent presidents of the Council.

The least difficult of the three paramount tasks of the ministry of health was the conquest of infectious and degenerative disease. Most of the fundamental work had already been done in the early twenty-first century, although ground was lost during the plague years that followed the Catastrophe. Health offices throughout the Northern Hemisphere were forced to devote most of their efforts in the 2060s and 2070s to the rebuilding of hospitals and the restoration of prewar standards of public hygiene and preventive medicine. Epidemics, malnutrition, exposure to nuclear and ultraviolet radiation, and bad or nonexistent medical care had produced a diseased and crippled generation, prey to many ills. Bringing the survivors back to good health, whenever possible, was the most urgent business at hand.

But by 2080 the lost ground had been recovered. Antibiotics, vaccines, bioengineered antibodies, gene therapy, and immune system stimulants reasserted humankind's control of disease. Even the most resistant viruses were defeated by all-purpose programmable microbiotic virucides, first developed in 2028–29 by molecular biotechnologists and improved in the early 2070s. The last known victim of an immunodeficiency disease caused by viral infection was an infant boy who died in 2078 in central Africa, where the HIV-1 and HIV-2 viruses had originated. The disease came full circle and then vanished, a century after its rampage began.

The ministry of health targeted the 2080s as the decade for freeing humankind from both inherited and acquired disabilities. Prenatal gene therapy or surgery to correct inherited disabilities, available to the children of elites in the last age of capital, became a standard obstetrical procedure before the end of the century. Nuclear-powered prosthetic limbs and hearts were generally obtainable much sooner, as well as artificial kidneys, blood vessels, joints, and bones, adapted from prototypes developed in the late twentieth and early twenty-first centuries. Electronic converters enabled the blind and deaf to interpret visual and auditory stimuli.

All these techniques had already been well known before the Catastrophe. The Commonwealth reduced their cost and distributed them to the rank and file of the disabled. More innovative was its program of growing replacement limbs and organs and, ultimately, whole bodies from cells donated by patients. Experiments completed before 2044 had already demonstrated the feasibility of cloning human beings in artificial wombs. Further research on regulating the expression and repression of genes had suggested that even parts of the body could be grown under laboratory conditions.

The biotechnology of gene regulation was perfected in the late 2070s, and the first successful transplant of a cloned heart took place in Brisbane in 2081. Eyes, inner ears, livers, lungs, kidneys, legs, and hands followed shortly. But fierce opposition in the Congress forced the cancellation of projects to clone whole human beings.

The most ambitious, and by far most controversial, project of the ministry was the Genetic Initiative. Detractors nicknamed it the "*Übermensch* Program," after the German philosopher Friedrich Nietzsche's vision of the Superman. Briefly put, the Genetic Initiative proposed to redesign the human race, raising it to the highest physical and intellectual standards that could be set by science with popular consent.

The key to the project was the completion of the genomic inventory already begun in the late twentieth century and still not finished at the time of the Catastrophe. If, said the geneticists, it were possible to learn the precise function of every gene and genetic subunit, separately and in combination with others, it would also be possible to remake, and perfect, *Homo sapiens*. The mistakes and shortcomings of nature could be rectified. By microsurgery outside the womb, the genes of embryos in the first days of life could be altered and returned to their mothers for the usual nine months. Their descendants, if they mated only with other descendants, would inherit all their enhanced qualities. Persons of anything but the highest physical and mental capacity would never be born again, once the new race had fully replaced the old.

In 2086, after years of intensive work by scientists in many parts of the world, the human biomap was complete. Over three billion separate genetic functions had been identified, some involving scores of interacting genes. Procedures were proposed to improve the human anatomy, lengthen life, and enhance cerebral functions. None could be tested on human subjects, but the Congress authorized preliminary research with laboratory animals, fully recognizing the limitations of such an approach.

Plans for anatomical modifications met with the least resistance. Gene surgeons suggested operations to sharpen night vision, strengthen the spine, shorten the intestinal tract, remove the appendix, improve dentition, and bring the mammary glands and genitalia into closer congruence with the dimensions celebrated in erotic fantasy. No one projected surgery to reshape facial bone structure or make people taller or change their skin color. The specter of a race of long-boned blond Apollos, invoked by critics of the Genetic Initiative, had no foundation in the surgical designs actually submitted to the ministry of health.

Another set of modifications was developed to extend the average life span. Gerontologists discovered that in senescence a single gene sequence orders the release of chemicals that interfere with the manufacture of fresh DNA, thereby inhibiting further cell reproduction. Nature's way of killing off dead wood and making room for the new generation, the chemicals might at one time have been invaluable to the survival of the species. They could now be dispensed with. Biotechnologists argued that excision of the offending segment would delay the onset of "natural" old age for decades. Coupled with genetic and hormonal therapies to facilitate DNA repair and retard cell damage, the new procedure was expected to give human beings the longevity of giant tortoises, and perhaps much more. Although the clinical evidence was not conclusive, hopes ran high.

Cerebral enhancement, the last portion of the Genetic Initiative, was deeply controversial. The scientists who mapped the location and sequenced the DNA of the genes responsible for directing the manufacture of the human brain had ascertained, in collaboration with brain physiologists, the genes and genetic subunits that determine the various competencies known collectively as intelligence. They had also charted the genetic structures that produce the aesthetic, creative, and moral faculties of humankind. Comparisons of the DNA of individuals of all types unveiled critical differences in genetic endowment that condemned some people to dull or sociopathic lives and gave others entrance to lives of high achievement.

On the assumption that everyone would like as much raw intelligence as possible and would wish for various other gifts and talents as well, researchers presented plans for redesigning the DNA of human embryos so that each embryo would possess the faculties of the most intellectually and creatively superior persons known to genetic science. They would also receive genetic modifications to render them more sensitive, caring, altruistic, sociable, and honest.

The howls of protest and derision that met the report of the Commission on the Genetic Initiative when it was first made public in 2093 led to two years of bitter debate in half a dozen committees of the People's Congress. Opponents objected on many grounds: the danger of unforeseen genetic damage to unborn children, the chance that a new species of uniformly superior individuals would lack variety and challenge, the risk of future racial conflict between "old" and "new" humanities, the curtailment of free choice, and the impossibility of deciding objectively who or what is "superior."

Supporters of the commission's report, which included most of the

World party Congresspersons and their ministers in the Executive Council, dismissed each argument in turn. The critics, they charged, sought to replace the socialist ethic of the new society with a reactionary gospel reviving Herbert Spencer's "survival of the fittest."

Late in 2094, Qian Gundi herself wrote one of the most widely published replies to the opponents of the Genetic Initiative. She admitted all the hazards and uncertainties. But the alternative was to abandon the whole project and refuse to seize democratic control of human evolution. Far from creating a uniform race and culture, the Initiative would only raise the human average to a higher plateau, from which further interventions or random mutations would raise it still higher in the course of time. Moreover, uniform abilities did not mean uniform performance. Mozart had felt no compulsion to ape Bach, just because nature gave him comparable gifts. Shakespeare and Goethe were evenly matched, but they did not write interchangeable verse. "Equality of genius," she wrote, "ensures only the possibility of works and lives of equal greatness. Can the human race ever have too much greatness?"

As a loyal World party member from girlhood, Qian bristled at the indictment of the Initiative for its allegedly undemocratic and neoracist tendencies. How, she asked, could there be a truly egalitarian society if people differed widely in intelligence, imagination, and altruism? What could guarantee, except the Genetic Initiative, that new elites of power and privilege would not arise to exploit the less able or less fortunate in times to come? "Socialism," she concluded, "opposes superior classes, not superiority."

Between 2093 and 2095, the debate proceeded. By a vote of 1117 to 876, with only seven members abstaining or not voting, the People's Congress passed the bill authorizing the full program of the Genetic Initiative in December 2095. A small number of embryos volunteered by natural parents were genetically modified and implanted in their mother's wombs. After thorough review of the clinical evidence, prompting several major changes in the surgical program, a second, much larger batch of randomly selected embryos received the treatment ten years later. In 2123, the Congress voted to make the surgery, further refined and improved, available at no cost to all prospective parents anywhere on earth or in deep space.

With what results? Down to the end of the days of the Commonwealth, only certain values could be measured with any precision. By the battery of tests that Commonwealth psychologists had devised to evaluate the varieties of intelligence, the first members of the higher race, *Homo sapiens altior*, were all in the upper .5 percent of the population. Half were in the upper .1 percent. Their general health was better, they compiled exemplary records as citizens and workers, and unmistakable signs appeared that they were destined for long lives. A report published in 2146 revealed that, of the twelve thousand persons treated between 2097 and 2107, only 5 percent showed any decline in coronary efficiency, breathing capacity, or basal metabolic rate, all of which—in *Homo sapiens*—fall irreversibly after age thirty or thirty-five. By then, millions of new subjects had received the same treatment. Early indications were entirely favorable in almost every case.

The Service of Being

The discipline and esprit de corps of the World party deserve most of the credit for the passage of the bills establishing the Genetic Initiative in the People's Congress. But the party had powerful support from the dominant worldview of the late twenty-first and early twenty-second centuries. Even several leaders of the opposition, who had everything to gain from the defeat of measures identified so closely with the World party, could not bring themselves to vote against them. In their heart of hearts they believed (and most of their constituents believed) in the soundness of the government's bills. This was particularly true of members of the Free Trade party founded in 2092, a movement that challenged the economic policies of the World party but split into several squabbling factions on issues of health, education, and culture.

Seen from a great distance, the worldview of the Commonwealth bears a strong superficial resemblance to the neomaterialism of the last age of capital. Perhaps more than superficial. In a sense, it represented a recrudescence of neomaterialism. Its most typical manifestation in philosophy was the "substantialism" of Helmut Rheinlander, Claudia Lazzeri, and Ivo Hristić, which combined an assertion of the irreducible reality of matter and energy with the argument that in human consciousness the primeval substance of the universe had "leaped to trans-being," an event equaled only by the self-creation of matter and energy themselves.

Substantialism was, in effect, a conversion into the language of professional philosophers of the views of Mitchell Greenwald and

Carolina Ocampo in *The Service of Being* (2042), the "bible" of the World party. Retaining a materialist view of the knowable cosmos, it upheld an absolute qualitative distinction between preconscious and conscious substance. Substantialists concluded that, although humankind was the unconditionally determined product of matter and energy, it also had the filial responsibility to re-create itself. To quote Hristić's *Preface to Substance* (2088), "It is the task of trans-being [human consciousness] to serve being [material nature] by the negation of the will of being [laws of physics]." Only when humankind was in full command of its own evolution could it discharge its obligation to its creators, just as matter and energy had been obliged by "the will of being" to create themselves from nothingness.

Substantialism, clearly, lent its entire weight to the Genetic Initiative, which could be viewed as a practical application of the new philosophy. It also supplied strong arguments for continuing the exploration and colonization of deep space and for preserving the unity of humankind in a single socialist commonwealth since "trans-being" was itself a single entity, collectively and indivisibly real.

In the period just before and after the Catastrophe, a time of painful self-reappraisal for all modern culture, the dominant intellectual paradigm had shifted from the neomaterialism we explored in an earlier chapter to a frantic nihilism reminiscent of, but much wilder than, the irrationalism of the twentieth century. Philosophers and artists had surpassed even the most outrageous iconoclasts and deconstructionists of late capitalist culture. They reached their apogee in the performance art of Louis-Philippe Leroy de Rien ("King of Nothing," pseudonym of the Belgian artist Louis-Philippe Boulanger), whose final work was his own flayed skin, tattooed from forehead to foot with an obscenely garbled version of the *Discourse on Method* of René Descartes. Exhibited by his mistress Sophie at the Show of Horrors in Grenoble in 2058, it marked the end of a short, ugly, ferocious age and the decline and fall of the meagerest of worldviews in the long history of ideas.

As substantialism emerged from its academic sources in the 2060s, it helped inspire—or explain?—comparable movements in the arts and in literature. Artists and writers blended meticulous realism with a reawakened sense of moral possibility. By contrast with earlier periods, the high culture of the Commonwealth may have seemed naive, even gullible and unsophisticated. It made heroes and heroines out of common folk, with its characteristically substantialist stress on the duality of humankind, half matter, half spirit striving to abolish matter. Critics occasionally drew unkind comparisons between substantialist art and the "socialist realism" decreed by Joseph Stalin and Andrei Zhdanov in twentieth-century Soviet Russia. But the truly creative minds went well beyond anything imagined in the sterile diatribes of these long-dead comrades.

The question that lingers after reviewing samples and anthologies of the high culture of the Commonwealth is whether, in fact, it had a "high" culture at all. By its own lights it did not. The ministry of arts and letters, from the 2080s onward, struggled for a new socialist and democratic definition of culture. In 2092, in the now celebrated Preamble to its annual report to Congress of that year, the officials in the ministry reached the conclusion that distinctions between levels of cultural achievement (high/low, serious/popular, avant-garde/traditional) were antidemocratic, except when applied to the art and literature of earlier times.

Cultural achievement, said the Preamble, was the expression in symbolic form of the values of a society. It belonged to everyone, like the society itself, and everyone alive had the capacity, with qualified training, both to create and to enjoy appropriate symbols of all sorts. For critics to establish a pecking order ranking the works of artists, and the artists themselves, was to institute in the world of arts and letters a nobility or privileged class. For exhibitors, theater directors, concert managers, and publishers to award public exposure to only a small group of highly touted "popular" or "major" or "trend-setting" artists was to foster a new elitism that deprived artists and their public alike.

It was the duty of the ministry, the Preamble continued, to fight cultural monopolies. In the Commonwealth, where education was free and unlimited, where incomes were equal, where everyone was able to take a full and active part in the cultural life of the society, why should the wealth of the many be diverted to the promotion of the egos and careers of a few? "From today," the Preamble concluded, "the avant-garde is abolished. We no longer need one. Today we are all artists, and all of us who create deserve equal access to the consciousness of humankind."

In practical terms, as the body of the report went on to specify, abolishing the avant-garde meant requiring all officials in charge of authorizing worldwide publication, exhibition, or performance to grant no more than one "opportunity" to an artist or writer in any given ten-year period, with a sliding scale of comparable limitations at the departmental and district level. An opportunity, as defined by the ministry, varied from field to field but included such obvious examples as the publication of a novel, an exhibition or a reproduction of a suite of photographs, and the live or recorded performance of an opera.

Opponents of the ruling noted that it violated the equally important principle of free democratic choice by consumers. If the world's people liked one opera so much that they clamored for another by the same composer, was it not tyrannous to block the worldwide distribution of the second opera? But, said ministry spokespersons, avant-gardes were still more tyrannous. In any event, the clamor for celebrities was only a residue of the last age of capital, when media merchandisers and their clients made fortunes exploiting the cravings of an immature and bedazzled public for synthetic heroes. Today's public knew better, or soon would.

Many artists and writers agreed. The majority of professional critics, who made their living by the scrupulous (or unscrupulous) evaluation of creative work, disagreed heatedly. Criticism as an art, craft, or science in its own right became almost extinct in the later years of the Commonwealth. In this one area the ministry of arts and letters stood its ground obdurately. It would not be moved. The result was the atrophy of a vital tradition and, some would say, the mediocritization of culture.

Yet it is surely true that never before in history had so many people taken so vigorous a part in so many facets of creative life. Local and regional arts fairs, festivals of film and photography, dance tournaments, musicales, poetry readings, and cyberconcerts took place in joyful profusion all over the world. One person in nine was a professional artist or writer during at least some part of his or her adult life.

Science, philosophy, and scholarship thrived with equal exuberance in the days of the Commonwealth. Apart from criticism, the one traditional cultural enterprise that did not was religion. The World party actively opposed all forms of religion as opiates in the blind or knowing service of class domination. The secular pieties of substantialism in many ways took the place of religious feeling. Absorbed in the myriad tasks of postwar reconstruction and social transformation, most people deserted the old faiths. Only in the last years of the Commonwealth, when the historic world religions joined forces with other oppositional movements in the society, did they regain something of their old appeal.

In the main, the closing decades of the twenty-first century and the opening decades of the twenty-second were a happy and busy time for the human race. The new abundance, coming so soon after the Catastrophe, raised spirits throughout the world. The new equality fostered pride and self-confidence in hundreds of millions of "ordinary" people who, only a short time ago, had looked forward to nothing. When the substantialists proclaimed that it was time for humankind to become more than human, to break the bonds of suffering and death forged by nature, they responded with eager hearts. Their enthusiasm, kindled by the policies of the Commonwealth itself, assured its ultimate negation.

INTERLUDE

My father Poul Jensen was surely the most important person in my life. Born in 2041 in Flagstaff in the former North American state of Arizona, he spent the bitter years after the Catastrophe with his mother and sister Lucinda (later Captain Lucinda Jensen of the World Militia), scratching out a miserable existence near the north rim of the Grand Canyon. A little brother, remembered only as "Rags," died in 2046 of typhoid fever at the age of three. The family later moved to Capetown, but Poul stayed behind, earning certification of teaching competence in history at the University of Arizona, which had transferred its main campus to Flagstaff. Like his sister, he joined the World party at an early age. Unlike Aunt Lucinda, whose loyalty was shattered by her experiences in the Ukraine, my father never wavered in his support of the party and its philosophy. He went on to become a historian, a statistician, and, in later life, the chief counselor of the Service of Being Fellowship in Phoenix. The Fellowship was a worldwide auxiliary of the World party, where members and friends could socialize, receive informal lay counseling on personal problems, and hold conferences and seminars on public issues. From my father's advice column in the *Phoenix World Citizen,* a weekly newsdisc, I have culled a few examples of his work as a counselor.

30 April 2127

Client L-0011.

Case. *Client is a supervising engineer in a satellite power receiving station, on extended holiday with friends in Canyon District, Saguaro Department. She has a troilist marriage with two men in her home department in South America. The relationship is stable. The men are also lovers. She states, "I want this marriage to last, but my husbands are threatening to apply for divorce if I persist in sexual liaisons on the outside. Since our marriage began [in 2125], I have had affairs with eleven other men, mostly on my initiative. These people mean very little to me, but I need the reinforcement."*

In interactive counseling, client was asked about her girlhood. She states, "No, I was not popular with boys. I was overweight and withdrawn, having only one or two close female friends. My mother and father were separated, and I lived with her. In fact I never saw my father again after I was thirteen." Client was asked about the pattern of her extramarital affairs. She states, "They peak early. Most of the men I've seduced are cool and distant. I have to work on them. My biggest satisfaction, it's almost like an orgasm, comes when the man is sexually aroused in spite of himself. I break down his reserve, keep him at bay for a while, and then go to bed with him. After that, the man usually becomes infatuated with me, which is nice at first, but I lose my fever, and the affair slowly winds down."

Advice and Conclusion. *Most likely the root of your problem is inadequate self-esteem in childhood. You were unpopular, coming from a broken home, deserted by your father. There is nothing you can do about any of that now, except to recognize that your insecurities may originate in experiences beyond your control.*

After you've recognized that much, take yourself off the hook. Forgive yourself. Forgive your father. Press delete. Clear the screen.

Then examine your present-day life. What happened to these eleven men you had affairs with? It sounds to me like serial murder. You migrated from man to man, proved your power, and left their corpses behind you.

At the Fellowship, where I counsel many people every week, we would say that your crime is irreverence. What you've done is to treat being as if it were not-being. Confusing yourself with not-being, you imagine that others are not-being, too.

Does this sound like gibberish? Let me explain. What I call "being" is another word for reality, which we experience in three forms of ascending specificity: universe, humankind, self. Humankind is expressed from the being of the universe by the chemical bonding of molecules. Selves are expressed from the being of humankind by the union of parents. As living selves, we are therefore the children of all being.

But the self-encapsulated self tries to live as if this were not true. It denies the being of others, just as, in the final analysis, it denies its own being. It says, "These others are not real. They are my fantasies, my toys, my objects. I can play with them as I please, because I, too, am just an illusion, a mere temporary slithering of protoplasm."

So we call this irreverence. Instead of revering the being in which we are all conjoined, you put it to use. You treat it as if it had no existence of its own. This applies to your relationship with your husbands and to your relationship with other men. Forgive yourself. At once! Do it today! And start again, in a spirit of piety and love for being.

I do not mean that you should stop having sexual affairs; but if your marriage contract excludes such affairs, and cannot be rewritten, then you must leave the marriage. It is as simple as that. In marriage, the partners may always give one another freedom to enjoy their bodies and minds outside the bond, but their gift, like all gifts exchanged by equals, must be free.

If you do leave your marriage, remember that in the future, when you initiate a relationship, it must be for piety and love, not for use and profit. In the Commonwealth, we are all equal under the law and in the face of cosmic being. No one is worth more than another, and no one is another's instrument. Look at the man you desire. See him not as a lump of clay but as a living vessel of being. Revere one another. Be to one another all that is possible.

◆

14 May 2127

Client L-0112.

Case. Client is depressed and frustrated. His Pentatonic Sonata for Cyberhorn and Moonflute was rejected for performance by the Saguaro Departmental Chamber Players because an earlier work of his had been *performed by the same group in 2119. Client states, "My [earlier work, title deleted to protect client] was almost nominated by the music jury for world performance. The sonata is infinitely better. The district jury may pick it, but that's as far as I can go, unless I wait to submit the piece in 2129 when I'm eligible again. By then I may have stopped composing. It becomes more and more difficult to care."*

Client is active in local musicales, has a second vocation as a music commentator on Phoenix Holovision, and a third as a designer of women's clothing. His compositions show great verve and originality. A still earlier work received worldwide and deep-space performance in 2108. Recordings of it remain in production. Client was asked how he thinks of himself. He states, "I think of myself as pretty damned special. I listen to some of the fornicating noise nowadays in Phoenix Hall, and it fills me with rage that juries bury my music so tone-deaf people like [names deleted, to protect client] can bruise the ears of the unsuspecting public." In reply to a question about his need for counseling, client states, "I don't need counseling at all. I need compassion. I need attention. I need a prescription for psychotropes to keep me from going crazy."

Advice and Conclusion. *Not a few creative people feel as you do, especially those who have enjoyed favorable notice early in their careers and who are now at the peak of their creative impulse. The love and applause of fellow creatures is always welcome, especially if we can tell ourselves, and others agree, that it is well deserved. To find such notice abruptly withheld may be painful, even in a good cause.*

But there is a distinction between the innocent pleasure taken in applause and a craving for honors that becomes an end in itself. In the days of the megacorps, when all of us were conditioned to live like ravenous sharks, even the greatest artists devoted half their energies to the pursuit of awards, royalties, and mass adoration. It was a cliché of criticism that the greatest artists nursed the greatest egos.

Today we have a new society. Even in the year 2127, it still seems blindingly new to me. Many older artists and nearly all our younger ones, born in the high noon of the Commonwealth, have learned new priorities. In their consciousness, art is self-expression, not self-aggrandizement. It furnishes its own rewards, in fulfillment that needs no confirming roar of the crowd, no niche in a pantheon.

You give yourself away when you say, "I need attention." This is the cry of an infant. I refuse to believe that you really do (in some forlorn desperate sense) need attention, although it matters that you think so.

You are too fine a workman. You have forgotten yourself too often in the heat of creative fervor to play the mewling infant. Live here and now in the honest service of the being-in-you. The place you may or may not have in world history is beyond your power to know or change.

But there is something all of us do need. We do need a productive relationship through work to fellow men and women. I am told there are 2,768 certified composers in Saguaro Department. Each deserves a little time in the sun, which your sacrifice helps them receive. Take pleasure in what you have lost, for their sake.

Nor have you lost everything. You still have your music. When a work of yours is played in a friend's home, in a neighborhood park, at a campus fair, and five or six people listen, have you not found attention? Has some part of your being not entered into theirs? If your Sonata were heard by six million people instead of six, would it make so much difference? How would it change the music? How would it change you? Could you see the faces of six million people or answer their questions or understand how your work touched their lives?

You have a call to write music. Never falter or turn away. Serve being as you were meant to serve, and it will serve you.

◆

24 December 2127

Client M-0004.

Case. Client is a Lutheran minister, born in 2090, daughter of a Lutheran minister who survived the Catastrophe. Her father is a man of fierce and flinty faith, not unkind, but unyielding in his religious convictions. Asked how she felt about her father, client stated, "I love this man more than anyone I know, but I think he is slightly mad." Her own faith is much more tentative. In recent years it has begun to fade out altogether. Client feels she can no longer serve in the ministry but reports that she is unable to leave "because it would kill my father. He's so proud of me. I just don't have the heart to break his."

Client was pressed to define her own beliefs. She states: "I have prayed on my knees for hours, as the young Martin Luther prayed. But the Holy Spirit is always silent. Papa says to speak directly to Jesus. He says I must let Jesus come into my heart. But Jesus, too, is always silent. I love Jesus, I really do, I love this man who suffered so much to free us all from death. But Jesus says nothing. I keep thinking, I have my own life to live, but I can't get it started." She admits that, if her father were dead, she would leave the ministry and become a teacher.

Advice and Conclusion. All the evidence suggests that you are a rational, well-integrated young woman. Your love and respect for your father is understandable, but, like so many people I counsel, you have not quite found your own identity. You are not responsible to your father, nor has he any right to form you in his image.

Leave the ministry. Tell your father why, and pray for his patience and acceptance. If he cannot be proud of someone who goes her own way and serves being as her conscience demands, then he is no better than the jealous Jehovah you no longer worship. But his shortcomings are his own. Not yours.

You say you love the man Jesus, but he does not answer your prayers. As any child knows, a man who died thousands of years ago is in no position to answer prayers. It is not even certain that Jesus ever lived, although I am reasonably sure he did. The gospels paint the picture of an effective preacher and moralist who left a powerful, if somewhat ambiguous, impression on his followers. So be it. Nevertheless, he died. He died, it would seem, because he made the authorities of his time uncomfortable. In any event, he died.

You may say, "But he lives! Look around you and see how many people feel his presence!"

Jesus is indeed a presence, even in death. He is one of the great metaphors in world literature. He is a metaphor for the triune nature of being: at one and the same time, the mortal self, a carpenter from Palestine; the messiah and prince of humankind; and the son of God, the emissary of all being.

How poor would all of us be, without such metaphors! You did well to love Jesus. Love him as you love Muhammad as you love Buddha as you love Krishna as you love the Tao of Heaven.

In the words of the poet, "All being cries to us, / Shouts above our deafness." Serve being!

♦

My father died the next year, at the age of eighty-seven. He was still a man in middle years, by the medical standards of the time, but he had missed a few checkups, and his heart stopped. I remember him as almost preternaturally wise, yet with a simple, trusting, solemn mind. It has been so long now, so many years, since I touched his hand and looked into his bright gray eyes. After he died, my mother sat by him for hours. "Kiss your father goodbye," she said to me, when I arrived, too late, at his bedside. I bent and kissed his cool forehead. The fire had gone from him, but I kissed him again and again.

9

VESTED INTERESTS

The Injustice of Liberty

To be honest, the story in this chapter is one I wish I did not have to tell. Those with responsibility for the common business of human-kind today take a certain wry pleasure in chronicling the collapse of the Commonwealth, as no doubt they have earned the right to do. I share their values, but I am too old and as a historian of modern civilization, too conscious of the vast difference between life under capital and life under the Commonwealth to share their views of the world-socialist era. Its shortcomings are clear. But it was not an evil time, not a time of frustration and anguish, as you may have learned in school. I was a young man in its heyday. I know better.

Nevertheless, the Commonwealth could not be all things to all people. Its central dilemma was scrutinized in a book by the sociologist Khader Barakat of Al-Khalil, *The Injustice of Liberty,* first published in 2113. The World party had instituted a regime of unity, equality, democracy, and liberty, wrote Barakat, but "liberty came last on its list, almost as an afterthought." More to the point, there was no way, and would never be a way, of reconciling the first three principles with the fourth. Unity excluded liberty of secession, equality excluded liberty of enterprise, and democracy excluded liberty of self-determination for minorities. "The only liberty left to us is the right to mourn the loss of liberty."

It goes without saying that Barakat overstated his case. But in a sense he was not far from the mark. Whenever liberty threatened (or appeared to threaten) unity, equality, and democracy, liberty suffered. By the same token, the Commonwealth was more egalitarian than democratic and more unitarian than egalitarian. All regimes must have priorities; all regimes must make choices. The Commonwealth was no exception.

From the first, the leaders of the World party struggled to avoid the mistakes of the various "socialist" dictatorships of the twentieth and early twenty-first centuries. They were well coached by Greenwald and others on the perils of political paranoia. They recognized that a complex postmodern social democracy could not survive, with the best intentions or the worst, if its citizens passed their lives in fear and trembling.

The leadership also understood, or claimed to understand, that the deliberate manipulation of opinion by data controllers and media experts was futile in a society that had access to alternative sources of information. The credibility of public authority would be fatally compromised.

Early in its history, the People's Congress enacted a Code of Civil Liberties. Freedom of expression and worship, freedom of movement, freedom of choice of livelihood, freedom of association, freedom of consenting sexual behavior, freedom of marriage and divorce, the right of legal due process, the right to control one's own reproduction, and the right to die were all defined in abundant detail and placed under public protection. Discrimination on the basis of gender, race, sexual preference, or religious affiliation was prohibited. The right to form economic cooperatives was reserved to any registered group of three or more adult persons.

But so disproportionate was the power of the Commonwealth and its global structures to the power of the private citizen that in 2078 the Congress felt it necessary to establish a new branch of government, known as the tribunate. The citizens of each department were empowered every five years to elect a board of independent tribunes, which heard and investigated charges of violation of the civil liberties of individuals or co-ops by public authorities. If the board found sufficient evidence of a violation, it interceded directly with the officials involved and also, if necessary, represented the plaintiffs in court. The departmental boards in turn sent one representative each to a worldwide electoral college, which chose a World Chamber of

Tribunes. The World Chamber heard cases only on referral from departmental boards, in situations requiring tribunal intervention at the highest levels of government.

The tribunal system was often accused of collusion with the authorities and in many instances did not serve citizens honorably. Composed largely of members of the World party, the typical board was reluctant to restrain or prosecute colleagues in public service.

But sometimes it did. In one well-publicized case in 2102–3, a board in Africa accused the district police of torture and blackmail. The plaintiff was an unsavory man with a long criminal record who had once worked for a gang of neocapitalist smugglers. But the tribunes found merit in his charges. When the police refused to launch a serious investigation, the board passed the matter on to the World Chamber. The Chamber interceded with the Commonwealth ministry of justice. After inquiries, the ministry ordered the arrest of more than a hundred officials in the plaintiff's department. Several went to rehabilitation clinics, and the plaintiff himself received an official apology.

If such things did not happen every day, they were also not rare. In a single year, chosen at random (the year 2110), the departmental boards received 3.2 million complaints, acted on 1.3 million, won local relief for almost 800,000 citizens, and referred the cases of 66,750 others to the World Chamber. The Chamber also had the power to conduct independent audits of the records and budgets of ministries and even to introduce legislation into the People's Congress. The Congress, in its turn, had the power to impeach tribunes accused of malfeasance. During the history of the Commonwealth, the Code of Civil Liberties was amended or supplemented several hundred times as a result of bills introduced into the Congress by the World Chamber; and two world tribunes were impeached by the Congress and removed from office by the high court for intergovernmental suits.

All the same, as Khader Barakat insisted in *The Injustice of Liberty,* the liberties guaranteed by law were not the liberties enjoyed from day to day by most of the world's people. For every case brought into the courts or boards of tribunes, a thousand wrongs may have gone unreported or unseen by the victims themselves.

One focal point of criticism, perhaps not wholly deserved, was the Commonwealth ministry of public safety and its analogues in every department and district. The ministry conducted surveillance operations against innumerable persons and groups suspected of anti-Commonwealth activities. It maintained a data bank even more sophisticated than the GTC International Data Storage Center. Although not as ruthless as its predecessors, such as the American CIA or the Soviet KGB, it did exist. Its knowledge was prodigious, its authority extensive, and its capacity for covert mischief terrifying.

Yet, like all security agencies since the beginning of civilization, the ministry of public safety was merely in the business of law enforcement. Reflecting deeply held convictions of the World party leadership, the laws themselves often posed a far greater threat to civil liberty.

The laws regulating publication and performance, for example, not only equalized cultural opportunity: they also prevented the appearance of many works of art and literature that might have undermined public confidence in the Commonwealth. Censorship as such was rarely practiced, but routine enforcement of the regulations ensured that, once a writer or artist hostile to the new society captured worldwide attention, he or she would have no opportunity to exploit the advantage with a second work for at least ten years.

A comparable policy thwarted scholars critical of the Commonwealth. The ministry of science and scholarship imposed no formal limitations on publication. But the number of works submitted to research juries appointed by the ministry was so vast that, although brief technical reports in the sciences appeared without delay, authorization to publish books and articles was often deferred for many years. Toward the end of the Commonwealth, oppositional movements resorted more and more often to self-publishing (once known in the Soviet Union as "samizdat").

The regulation of culture and scholarship is merely one illustration of how the laws of the Commonwealth curtailed fundamental civil liberties. The global educational system, with its standardized curricula dictated by the ministry of education, had an undeniably chilling effect on religious freedom, not to mention political dissent. Children were exposed in their schooling to a variety of ideologies, beliefs, and values, but within a conceptual framework determined by the dominant world outlook. The media, too, were more or less fair-minded and not overtly hostile to oppositional views, but, again, within a conceptual framework established by the Commonwealth, which operated all broadcasting services.

More crucial still were the laws of the Commonwealth restricting the freedom of citizens to pass from religious or political belief to relevant action in the society. Then as now, many religions and ideologies demanded application of their tenets in the everyday world. Then as now, some demanded social reconstruction.

Consider Islam. The *shari'a,* the body of Koranic law, specifies not only forms of worship and faith but also a particular organization of society, from governance and economic life to the relations between the sexes. Belief in the *shari'a* is not consistent with life in a secularized social order, and no orthodox Muslim can accept the prevalence of such an order in a Muslim land. He or she may have no choice, thanks to the force majeure of invading infidels or traitorous heretics, but the duty of every faithful Muslim is to resist unbelief and restore God's *shari'a* as soon as possible.

Under the Commonwealth, however, the departments of Asia and Africa where Islam held sway received no special consideration. Even in areas such as the Arabian peninsula or the shorelands of the eastern Mediterranean, sacred to Islam, officials faithfully enforced the laws of the Commonwealth. Much of the indigenous population consisted of secularized, well-educated unbelievers weary of Islamic authoritarianism and no less loyal to the Commonwealth than citizens elsewhere. A substantial minority adhered to a reform movement, variously known as Contemporary Islam or Islamic Democracy, that sought to fuse elements of the Islamic tradition with the dominant values of the Commonwealth. But as many as half the people in some departments were orthodox Muslims, for whom the *shari'a* was absolute and inalterable. For them, the guarantee of religious freedom in the Code of Civil Liberties meant little. No one interfered with their daily ablutions and prayers, but they were not free to build an Islamic civilization.

The same restrictions applied to fundamentalist Jews, Christians, Hindus, Buddhists, Sikhs, and many others. Against supporters of neonationalist or neoracist ideologies, the Commonwealth took even stronger measures. Attempts to form neonationalist social clubs, cultural centers, and political parties were ruthlessly prosecuted by the ministry of justice. Although several neonationalist factions did, in fact, flourish in the People's Congress, they were elaborately disguised as something else in order to survive. It would have amused scholars from the last age of capital to study the desperate marriages of convenience arranged by Turkish and Armenian neonationalists, or by Poles and Ukrainians, or by the Ibo and the Hausa, once mortal enemies, to advance their respective causes.

When all is said, however, the Commonwealth never resorted to the infamous abuse of civil liberty practiced daily by the fascist and Stalinist regimes of the twentieth century. It was even more liberal, on the whole, than the bourgeois democracies at their best. Still better, by safeguarding the right of the people to elect their own representatives and maintain an alternative economy, it laid the groundwork for its eventual peaceful supersession. The possibility of the nonviolent passage to a new order lurked in the laws and policies of the world state from the time of its inception.

A Mighty Maze

If one reads the novels, stage and holovision plays, and multimedia superscripts of the Commonwealth era, the negative vibrations one picks up seldom concern the outright denial of civil liberties by the almighty state, but something—in its own singular fashion—ultimately more corrosive and perilous. What appears to have most disturbed writers critical of the regime was its sheer bulk and the crushing weight of its bureaucracies. "To help people," says the cynical comic villain in Stella Stitham's classic tale, Castle Chip, "you must first wrap them in meters and meters of red tape, like May Day mummies."

Bureaucratism was the real inner horror of life under the Commonwealth and the source of most of its deepest frustrations. It got out of control almost at once and then grew steadily worse. With the highest of motives, I should add. Few officials enlarged their empires for the sake of personal gain or to make work available to cronies. There was always plenty of work to do in the Commonwealth, and incomes could not be multiplied by abusing public trust. The difficulty, already familiar from the experience of governments in the most advanced countries during the last age of capital, was not so much corruption as the logic of the postmodern welfare polity.

According to that logic, laws, regulations, and codes of procedure are written to be enforced. They are to be enforced strictly, comprehensively, and without detours or shortcuts. To ensure full compliance, every operation must be checked and double-checked, and the work of every checker and double-checker must be audited by outside agencies. Nothing must be taken for granted or left to chance or informal agreement. Otherwise, how can one be fair or just?

Under the Commonwealth, officials were instilled from the first day of their training with the conviction that every person and every district and department on earth or in space had to receive the same treatment as every other. Favoritism was anathema. Favoritism would lead, trainees were told over and over again, to a restoration of private capital, privilege, and the class system. Hence, enforce every law, every regulation, every procedure of every code. At all costs. The government of the Commonwealth was a government of laws, not of men and women. So it was, and so it would always be.

The single most arduous task entrusted to the bureaucrats, no doubt, was the implementation of the laws securing equality of income. We have already examined them, in another context. But let me review them once more. The basic income was known as a "share," a percentage of the gross income of the citizen's home department, paid out to every adult worker or person unable to work. Those who refused employment received a three-quarter share, and those with demonstrable special needs earned a quarter or a half supplementary share. In addition, the ministries of development toiled throughout the years of the Commonwealth to redistribute material resources and technology worldwide with the goal of equalizing the incomes of all departments. As we saw, by the close of the twenty-first century, the richest departments earned no more than twice the income of the poorest, a great leap forward from conditions in the last age of capital. By the 2140s, the two to one ratio had been improved to a three to two ratio.

Such transformations did not happen easily or without a price. In the days of the Commonwealth, citizens did not have equal abilities, and departments did not have the same human or natural resources. Differences of nurture, culture, and geology could not be wiped out by bureaucratic regulations. But much could be, and was, done.

When the historian peers into the records of the ministries of the Commonwealth, just how much *was* done becomes readily, and frighteningly, apparent. He or she can read the proceedings of literally millions of hearings held to determine if a person was able or unable to work. Other millions, hundreds of millions, were conducted to determine eligibility for supplementary fractional shares. Each action taken involved the completion of countless forms. Difficult cases required approval by higher authority or intervention by tribunes or courts, or all three.

The same complexities hounded the program to equalize departmental incomes. The transfer of resources out of a given department into another demanded enormous amounts of discwork by the development ministries themselves and was then subject to a lengthy process of challenge and appeal by affected citizens or cooperatives. Auditing the accounts of cooperatives to determine how much income tax they should pay, holding jury hearings to schedule publication and performance of creative works, and coordinating global environmental projects such as reforestation with local authorities are three additional examples, among many, of tasks of the global bureaucracy that devoured time in the pursuit of fairness and equality. Even the tribune system, created to protect civil liberties, often consumed more bureaucratic energy than it was worth. Litigious citizens abused the system, and almost everyone who resorted to it found the discwork daunting.

In the People's Congress debates frequently turned on proposals to rationalize the bureaucracy, but such efforts usually led nowhere. Or, rather, they led to still more crusts and strata of bureaucratic regulation. Reformers devised remedies as labyrinthine as the procedures they were charged to simplify. Critics cried for more "standardization," failing to see that the impulse to standardize lay at the heart of the problem.

When a new ministry of official procedures was set up in 2119, it promulgated a code of standardizing regulations that succeeded only in making matters significantly worse. Bureaucrats everywhere scrambled to comply. Old tried-and-true methods were junked in favor of "simpler" ones that required endless adjustment, requests for clarification, and explanation to affected citizens. Many public servants spent as much time filling out questionnaires documenting their compliance with the code as in performing their usual duties. Yet, if you examine the new code, you will see for yourself that it was a marvelous piece of social engineering fairly bristling with logic and symmetry. Its only defect was that it did not work.

The English poet Alexander Pope once described "this scene of man" as "a mighty maze! but not without a plan." So it was with the bureaucracy of the Commonwealth. The maze of officialdom had its master plan, its rationale, its reason for being. It converted law and policy into social reality for billions of human beings. Since a planet could not be governed as a single community by rules of thumb or guesswork, the only viable alternative to bureaucratism was not to have a world state at all.

But the exasperation that people felt was also real. The toll exacted by the system was as tangible as anything in their lives and caused more strain and suffering than all the supposedly nefarious machinations of the ministries of justice and public safety combined. By the second quarter of the twenty-second century, the system, never robust, was essentially lifeless and sterile. It had nowhere to go but down, and out, forever.

Raised Voices

The time has arrived to examine the structured political opposition to the World party, and ultimately to the Commonwealth itself, that arose late in the twenty-first century.

World party leaders always insisted that they could coexist happily with other parties committed to dissenting ideologies. Nothing in the Commonwealth, they said, was more essential to the continued health of their party than a candid opposition voicing the legitimate concerns of the people. But did they mean what they said? Were they comfortable with the prospect of an opposition large enough someday to dislodge them from office? As Gina Mascagni, founder of the Free Trade party, scornfully addressed her political enemies in her maiden speech to the People's Congress, "You need us to prove your tolerance and benevolence; your smiling mask is moulded from our flesh."

In the first Congress, 78 percent of the members belonged to the World party and another 11 percent to local offshoots of the party that generally supported its policies. Five percent were independent. The remaining members represented more than thirty small parties and political movements of all kinds.

By the time of the fourth Congress, elected in 2092, the number of seats held by the World party and its local allies had been cut to 71 percent, and the 580 opposition members included 222 independents and the representatives of only twelve parties, of which the strongest was the Free Trade party. Five other parties were covertly neonationalist formations, and three spoke for religious communities (Roman Catholics, Sunni Muslims, Shi'a Muslims).

The Free Trade party had its roots in oppositional societies trace-able to the first days of the Commonwealth and composed largely of former businesspeople and their families who had lost their fortunes and enterprises in the conversion of the world economy to socialism. For years these societies thrived on rancor and disgruntlement, but in the 2080s they were brought together in a working quasi-political alliance by Gina Mascagni, whom we met in our fourth chapter. One of the few products of the GTC experiments in human genetic engineering who outlived the Catastrophe, she was by all accounts the most brilliant woman of her generation.

Mascagni was born in 2033, the daughter of a wealthy Italian industrialist. When the war broke out, she was vacationing in the South Pacific on her father's yacht. The Mascagni family sought and found asylum in Chile, where they prospered for the next five years, until the confiscation of their wealth in 2050 by the newly mundialized Chilean republic. Alfredo Mascagni, the girl's father, committed suicide, and she and the rest of her family, including her mother and two sisters, fled to Argentina. She was a young and proud woman of twenty-eight when Argentina also mundialized, leaving the family once again "penniless."

Up to this point, Gina had taken only intermittent interest in politics, preferring to apply her phenomenal intellect to mathematics and econometrics. But the traumatic events of 2061 in Argentina transformed her into a feral political animal. She spent the rest of her long life harassing the socialist global state and all its works.

Mascagni was shrewd enough to realize that popular support for a new age of megacorporate capitalism would never be great enough to bring it back again. But numerous citizens of the Commonwealth did resent the restrictions placed on their earning capacity and on their entrepreneurial and creative talents by an increasingly leaden bureaucracy. They were easy prey for a woman of Mascagni's abilities. She opposed the Commonwealth in the People's Congress for more than seventy-five years. Cold, strident, and sarcastic, with piercing black eyes and a corona of tousled white hair, never married and never bested in debate, she lingers in memory as the Commonwealth's most formidable antagonist.

Fortunately for the leadership of the World party, the appeal of her political program failed to equal the intensity or brilliance of her persona. The Free Trade party garnered 11 percent of the vote in its first attempt to win congressional seats, largely on the strength of a razzle-dazzle campaign orchestrated by Mascagni and the many free trade societies she had brought together in the 2080s. Its strength rose to 13 percent in the elections to the fifth Congress but fell slowly thereafter, as other, more attractive movements emerged to compete for the same constituents.

The program of the Free Trade party included just three basic points: reform of the personal income laws to permit double, triple, and even higher shares as in the earliest days of the Commonwealth; the legitimation of global marketing cooperatives, together with a ban on further transfers of wealth to less affluent departments; and the introduction of what Mascagni called "personal enterprise." Her scheme for personal enterprise would have allowed individuals to form tax-free joint stock companies, with all profits paid out to stockholders (up to their personal income limit) and the balance invested in capital expansion. She was accused of economic legerdemain, elitism, and racism. She was pilloried in the media for her "consecration of selfishness." Her party never elected a single congressperson from Africa or South Asia, the chief beneficiaries of worldwide income redistribution. But, in parts of the Americas and in Europe, Mascagni enjoyed a wide following.

In the first and second decades of the twenty-second century, oppositional movements marked time, with fluctuating support. Parties with more radical programs, including the Democratic Rally for Neocapitalism, drew off voters from the Free Trade party. There were also a Dignity party, which attracted citizens in the poorer departments; several new religious parties (Sikh, Hindu, Animist, Baptist, Pentecostal, Mormon, Hinayana Buddhist, and Sufi); the True Communist party, preaching a return to unalloyed dialectical materialism; the Natural Life party, which fought the Genetic Initiative with ferocity; and several small ethnicist parties left over from the previous century, which made no public declarations of their goals but consisted exclusively of the members of a single historical ethnic group and canvassed only in districts thickly settled by their compatriots.

None of these movements caught the imagination of enough voters to overcome the strength of the World party in the People's Congress. Until 2121, the World party never held fewer than 1,133 seats (56.6 percent) in the Congress. But opposition slowly grew. Although the genius displayed in some of the party's early programs, from the Great Housecleaning and the Genetic Initiative to the colonization of deep space, had earned widespread respect, in the eyes of many thoughtful citizens in the 2120s that genius was now spent and burned out.

The time approached for a fresh political initiative representing the visions of younger people. In 2117, in what was once India, a group of men and women in their twenties and thirties formed a movement that later became the Small party. Inspired in part by the ideas of the twentieth-century decentralist economist E. F. Schumacher, in part by the teachings of Rabindranath Tagore and Mohandas K. Gandhi, in part by the mid-twenty-first-century mystical feminism of Pola Persichetti, Liisa Jylhä, and Sunita Coomaraswamy, the Smalls ran their first candidates in the congressional elections of 2121, winning forty-eight seats. The World party had its worst showing ever, electing only 987 members, which forced it into a coalition with the True Communists and the Dignity party.

Limited at first to South Asia, the Small party quickly gained support all over the world. When elections were called again in 2124 after the True Communists left the ruling coalition, the Smalls reluctantly entered into partnership with the Free Trade party. Campaigning as the "Free-Small alliance," the two parties won 31 percent of the vote and sent 640 representatives to the next People's Congress, 457 of them members of the Small party. The Smalls had become a force to reckon with.

As the Small party evolved, it gradually took on the contours more familiar to us in recent times. But at first it was not only the party of heterogeneity: it was extraordinarily heterogeneous itself, almost to the point of chaos. What held it together, and gave it so much enduring appeal, was the simple belief that humankind had reached the point in its history when its communities no longer needed the carapace of a global polity. The Smalls likened the Commonwealth to a huge tortoise, slow of foot and heavy of shell, carrying the human race on its back. "The tortoise," said a spokesperson, "has labored long beyond its time. It deserves a decent and honorable retirement."

But when pressed to specify the shape of their preferred future, the Smalls typically replied that it would have no shape at all. They agreed with their temporary allies in the Free Trade party that citizens should have the option to form personal enterprises and earn whatever they earned. But economic issues did not consume them. Their battle cry was heterogeneity. If observant Muslims wished to set up a society governed by the *shari'a*, then they should be free to do so. If Hindus living among them objected, then the Hindus should be free to leave and form their own societies. If one community wanted to live under capitalism, another under socialism, and another under anarcho-syndicalism, their choices should be respected, just as colony worlds with different social orders thrived in peace in the League of Space Cooperatives.

The result would be, said the Smalls, "a various world," part one thing, part another, part something else again, as each group of men and women styling itself a community designed its own future. In place of standardization would come multiplicity, in place of conformity free expression of personal and collective values. As a popular Small party slogan ran, all that humankind could expect of its communities in return was the commitment "not to harm others, as you care for yourselves; not to deny others choice, as you choose for yourselves."

World party publicists scoffed at the mottos of the Smalls, pointing to the very name of the party as evidence of its bondage to a narrow, parochial, unfree vision. "We call ourselves the World party," wrote one such spokesperson, "because we try to know and advance the best interests of all the world. The Smalls are known as the Smalls because they want our species to parcel itself up into a million wrangling microcosms, each going its own way." The "various world" of Small propaganda was a euphemism for a uniform world of antediluvian villages, "powered by windmills and populated by neobarbarians who cannot lift their eyes above their own picket fences."

The publicist had a point. The Small party's formula for universal freedom was in fact a prescription for smallness, for the miniaturization of society. Although Small politicians in the final decades of the Commonwealth never argued that all communities were obliged to choose a decentralized way of life, they rarely spoke of anything else. By urging that every community choose its own future, they virtually excluded the possibility that humankind would choose to remain under the common laws and regulations of a global commonwealth.

In any event, what did the Smalls mean by a "community"? The concept was often illustrated by Small party speakers but never clearly defined. Neonationalists assumed that "community" was more or less the same thing as "ethnicity," which led some of them to throw their support (ignorantly and unwisely) behind the Smalls in the Congress. At one time or another, several Small politicians did speak with approval of "ethnic communities."

But to judge from the full range of party literature in the period between 2121 and 2147, the only common denominator in the Small vision of community was smallness—or, rather, smallness and voluntarism. Communities were small groups of individuals and families living together voluntarily as self-sufficient and self-governing states. In such a context, *small* meant "small enough that the affairs of state may be conducted by all the people acting as a body voicing their general will." Jean Jacques Rousseau had expressed the same view 350 years before.

In practice, *small* meant communities of one, five, ten, or twenty thousand people—at most, twenty. Living as we do today, we may not find this so very strange, but, in the context of the times, it was a vision that bordered on the fantastic. Some World party members laughed at it; others paled with rage and indignation.

The lines were thus drawn for a long and increasingly bitter struggle, which only one side could win. The worldviews of the two parties were almost diametrically opposed. The World party adhered to a substantialist philosophy, the Smalls (for the most part) to one or another school of ecomysticism. As social scientists, the members of the World party were descendants of Comte and Marx; the Smalls sprang from Rousseau, Fourier, and Proudhon. The World party believed with a passion in the world state, seeing all separatist movements as invitations to a renewal of the discord and violence that had plagued humankind since the dawn of civilization. The Smalls denounced the world state as obsolete. For members of the World party, the study of history revealed the steady growth of centripetal forces, climaxing in the integration of all humanity. The Smalls compared the flow of history to a wave, rolling landward, cresting, and breaking against a rocky shore, leaving behind a thousand foam-topped pools sparkling in the noonday sun.

Between the two visions of life and futurity, no compromise was imaginable. None was ever tried.

Lowering the Flag

The elections of 2124, we now see, marked the beginning of the end of the Commonwealth. No one in the World party thought so at the time because the party rebounded from its humiliating showing in 2121 and captured 1,093 seats, enabling it to govern without help from its former allies. The rocket-like rise in the fortunes of the Small party (from 48 seats to 457) was regarded as alarming but offset by the continuing downward drift of the others.

One trend that went almost unnoticed in 2124 was the election of four congresspersons from a once insignificant party of Tamil-speaking Hindus and five others representing Sunni Muslims in the Middle East. The religious parties as a whole had fared poorly in the elections of 2124, but the success of the Hindus and Muslims furnished evidence of a major flaring of separatist sentiment in Asia.

Separatism erupted into violence early in 2125. Protesting the secular bias of the Commonwealth's public schools, the newly elected Hindu congresspersons mobilized campaigns of public protest and civil disobedience in their respective departments. Students, even the youngest, refused to attend classes or participate at home by interactive holovision. At about the same time, the five new congress-persons from the Sunni Muslim departments threatened to lead se-cession movements unless their constituents were permitted to live under Koranic law.

Negotiations in both regions soon collapsed. When the governor of one of the Middle Eastern departments proclaimed its indepen-dence, World Militia troops were flown from Colombo to depose the governor and dissolve the departmental assembly. They encountered ragged but stubborn resistance from local police forces. Over a hun-dred lives were lost in twenty-four hours of heavy fighting. A second Middle Eastern department seceded the next day, quickly followed by another in the Indian subcontinent.

With the full backing of the Executive Council, the president of the Commonwealth now made a serious strategic blunder. Hoping to smother the rebellions quickly, he ordered troops from the Colombo garrison to occupy police and government facilities in all three de-partments and arrest more than a thousand persons identified by intelligence sources as ringleaders.

The troops carried out their missions with laudable efficiency and few casualties. But citizens throughout the invaded depart-ments responded by calling general strikes. The Hindus prayed and fasted. The Muslims locked their doors and barred their win-dows. Telecommunications systems were sabotaged or unplugged. The standoff lasted three months. After secession movements gained strength in several adjoining departments, the president finally re-called his troops. As many as five thousand people had died during the emergency.

An intergovernmental colloquium convened in 2126 did finally resolve most of the issues in dispute. Concessions made by the Commonwealth mollified local opinion, for the time being. But the Smalls saw their chance. In the Congress, in the media, in political rallies throughout the world, they exploited the government's handling of the crises in Asia as prime examples of how its dull, obdurate passion for a standardized planetary culture had drained the world order of all life and all honor. Small party leaders urged citizens everywhere to emulate the brave burghers of Damascus, Amman, and Madras. They called for strikes, boycotts, mass protests, and waves of civil disobedience to force the resignation of the president and his whole Council.

The year 2127 was a time of troubles without precedent since the 2060s. Heeding the Small party agitators, citizens in communities scattered around the world participated in programs of passive resistance, with varying degrees of effectiveness. Several cities in North America, eastern Europe, and Africa, and many others in the Middle East and the Indian subcontinent, were nearly immobilized. Finally, in June, the president—Nnamdi Awolowo, a frail, elderly West African politician from the Dignity party—resigned without further delay and was replaced by the only Muslim on the Council, the minister of communications, a black woman from the suburbs of New Chicago.

The withdrawal of Awolowo and the prompt proclamations of amnesty and conciliation issued by the new president soothed everyone, even many Smalls. Having won a decisive victory, the leaders of the Small party urged their followers to return to work—for the time being. Life resumed its normal tempo. But in the next test of strength, the world elections of 2129, the Smalls won 588 seats and other parties voicing structural opposition to the Commonwealth took 402. With 994 seats, the World party was forced into an uncomfortable second coalition with the Dignity party and the True Communists.

The history of the next seventeen years is tortuous and painful to relate. In the light of the outcome, few of the details matter. The World party divided into two factions, recalling the days of the Leninists and the Woolyheads. One favored decisive action and abjured compromise; the other hedged. When the Small delegates in the People's Congress appealed for a second round of civil disobedience in 2131, the Intransigents (as the World party hard-liners were nicknamed) succeeded in expelling them from the Congress. The Small party itself was outlawed. Smelling blood in the air, the Smalls cautioned their followers not to rise in protest. The next year, after a vote of no confidence narrowly passed in the Congress, the Council responded by replacing its True Communist president with Walter Lyell-MacKenzie, a ne plus ultra Intransigent from Australasia.

Instead of giving way gracefully, Lyell-MacKenzie declared a state of global emergency and dissolved Congress. A second round of strikes and demonstrations orchestrated by Small agitators convinced him to suspend the constitution of the Commonwealth. He ruled under martial law for the next five years, until his assassination in a museum of antiquities in Esfahan by a Shi'ite guard, who snatched a medieval scimitar from a display case, crying "God is Great!" as the president walked by.

The Intransigents faded quickly in the new decade. In the autumn of 2140, under the leadership of World party moderates, the Council lifted the ban on the Small party, which had only grown stronger during its proscription. In new elections, the Smalls took 41 percent of the seats in Congress. No party won enough seats to form a stable government. Further elections in 2142 gave the Small party 48 percent, and in 2147 it won 67 percent. Its first and last president, Germinie-Constance Vaudésir de Lamothe, arranged a worldwide holovision ceremony to lower the flag of the Commonwealth on 21 October 2147.

I remember the occasion very well. As everyone knows, the flag consisted of a bright red circle on a field of green and white, with a black arrow rising upward from the center of the circle. The red circle symbolized humanity under socialism, the green and white symbolized nature, and the arrow the progressive course of world history. Some feminists called the design phallocentric. Perhaps it was. Many people who watched the ceremony on holovision in stadiums and theaters cheered as the flag slowly and deliberately made its way down the hundred-meter pole on the grounds of the last world government house, situated that year in the Siberian town of Krasnoyarsk.

At the time, I was only sixty-three. Intending to write a biography of Vaudésir de Lamothe, I took the trouble to attend the festivities in person. Would you believe? I began to cry! I laughted at myself, wiped my eyes, smiled at my companion, and looked again. The huge flag had almost completed its descent. Light snow was falling. The Commonwealth was dead. An age drew to its inexorable close Both of us, at that moment, felt a spasm of fear for the future of humankind.

INTERLUDE

Aunt Lucinda had one child by her African husband, Gatsha Mphephu. The child, my cousin Hedvig, joined the Dignity party after her first certification in upper school, represented Cape Department in the People's Congress for several years, and then retired from politics to become an architect and, between 2130 and 2137, a tribune in Table Bay District, which included her home city of Capetown. You know her as "Heddy," although to the best of my recollection she has not visited you since 2197. I found the following exchange of official documents when she let me search through her discs from the Commonwealth years. The first few exchanges were apparently not filed. Her patron was a journalist who had applied unsuccessfully for a supplementary half share of income.

> *District Tribunate*
> *Capetown*
> *SAST 110-9327-JJ*
> *13 March 2132*

Jacobus Piet Hiemstra
Asst. Dist. Secy. for Income Distribution
District of Table Bay
Stellenbosch
SASY 036-1133-VN

Dear Secretary Hiemstra:
  With reference to File 0129-[33PT]-Brin/Port-000027-01-66, as copied to you on 09 Jan., followed 07 Feb. and 28 Feb., we regret that your office has delayed its reply and beg assistance. On behalf of Citizen Nicholas Brinker, W# 55-X-765-768, be assured that I have verified his

bona fides through the District Secretariat of Public Safety and the District Secretariat of Communications, as requested in your memorandum of 15 Feb.

To review, Mr. Brinker is a freelance broadcast journalist, with three other certifications. Mr. Brinker has won the District of Table Bay award for merit in journalism, also awards from Susquehanna Department (North America) and the World Ministry of Communications for independent coverage of family life on Sun Ring Station 12. Professional needs entitle him to a full half-share supplement, pursuant to Title 975, Par. 88(c,f), 2102 Revised Code, and claimed on Form 2277-H3189H. Mr. Brinker cites expenses of cameras, relays, cables, discs, headgear, robotics, and supernumerary earthside and spaceside travel, providing vouchers, receipts, and estimated costs of his next two assignments.

If you need further information, our office will be happy to comply; however, we feel that this case has remained on our books long enough and deserves your prompt attention.

Faithfully yours,
Hedvig Jensen-Mphephu
Associate Tribune
♦

Secretariat for Income
Distribution
District of Table Bay
Stellenbosch
SASY 036-1133-VN
29 March 2132

Hedvig Jensen-Mphephu
Associate Tribune
Tribunate, District of Table Bay
Capetown
SAST 110-9327-JJ

File: 0129-[33PT]-Brin/Port-000027-01-66

Case: Citizen Nicholas Brinker, W# 55-X-765-768

Query: Need of Citizen Brinker for supplementary income in profession of independent broadcast journalism is acknowledged, subject to routine verification, but does citizen need to continue as independent journalist? Under Title 1898, Par.50(m) and Par.51(supp.), 2119 Code, and Title 27, Par.177(a,b,c,d), 2119 Revised Code, regulations specify citizens in professions requiring supplementary income for more than twenty-four consecutive months must apply for recertification of skill under Title 331, Par.2(c,k), 2087 Revised Code (Annex 28b), or present evidence of special circumstances warranting extension (same, Annex 28c). Complete and return relevant forms under same.

Disposition: Recommend patron consider applying for post with Intermedia Cooperative as a field team journalist. However, rehearing will be scheduled if queries are answered satisfactorily.

Reply to: Jacobus Piet Hiemstra, Assistant Secretary.

◆

District Tribunate
Capetown
SAST 110-9327-JJ
05 April 2132

Jacobus Piet Hiemstra
Asst. Dist. Secy. for Income Distribution
District of Table Bay
Stellenbosch
SASY 036-1133-VN

Dear Mr. Hiemstra:
   With reference to File 0129-[33PT]-Brin/Port-000027-01-66, I am in receipt of your memorandum of 29 March, re the case of Citizen Nicholas Brinker, W# 55-X-765-768. Find enclosed Forms 4876-J2129W and X21-4732-K9948M. In our judgment these forms were not necessary since we have already established that Mr. Brinker was not consecutively employed for twenty-four months as a broadcast journalist, having spent three months (from 20 Dec. 2130 to 22 March 2131) as a science teaching consultant at Lumumba Middle School in Lubumbashi, Bangweulu Department. To expedite our request, we enclose the forms nonetheless.
   We continue to press for an early and favorable resolution of Mr. Brinker's request. There can be no serious question of his right to con-

tinue in his profession of independent broadcast journalist, as guaranteed under Title 8712, Par.11(b,d), 2077 Revised Code.

> *Faithfully yours,*
> *Hedvig Jensen-Mphephu*
> *Associate Tribune*

◆

> *Secretariat for Income*
>   *Distribution*
> *District of Table Bay*
> *Stellenbosch*
> *SASY 036-1133-VN*
> *28 April 2132*

Hedvig Jensen-Mphephu
Associate Tribune
Tribunate, District of Table Bay
Capetown
SAST 110-9327-JJ

File: 0129-[33PT]-Brin/Port-000027-01-66

Case: Citizen Nicholas Brinker, W# 55-X-765-768

Query: Receipt of Forms 4876-J2129W and X21-4732-K9948M is hereby certified. However, several entries (Lines 23, 27, and 59) in Form 4876-J2129W were answered evasively. Under Title 765, Pars. 2–3, 2127 Code, your patron is hereby required to resubmit Form 4876-J2129W with full response to queried entries and also submit form 9091-P24P with notarized deposition stating reasons for evasion in full. Failure to comply within ten (10) days of dispatch of this transmission may result in criminal prosecution under Title 765, Par. 3(g), 2127 Code.

Disposition: Review of case tabled pending receipt of Forms 4876-J2129W and 9091-P24P.

Reply to: Jacobus Piet Hiemstra, Assistant Secretary.

◆

District Tribunate
Capetown
SAST 110-9327-JJ
09 May 2132

Jacobus Piet Hiemstra
Asst. Dist. Secy. for Income Distribution
District of Table Bay
Stellenbosch
SASY 036-1133-VN

Dear Mr. Hiemstra:

With reference to File 0129-[33PT]-Brin/Port-000027-01-66, this office continues to protest that our patron, Citizen Nicholas Brinker, W# 55-X-765-768, is not required by law to file Forms 4876-J2129W and 9091-P24P. We have complied, per the enclosures, with the notice given in your memorandum of 28 April, only to expedite these proceedings. The delays have seriously inconvenienced Mr. Brinker and forced him to cancel his plans to produce a documentary program on education at Sun Ring Station 12. Find also enclosed our Memorandum of Procedure J9J-44 notifying you that we have cited your office for unwarrantable delay to the District Secretariat of Justice.

In order to assist our patron, who is facing debt, we respectfully suggest that your office grant him a temporary one-eighth income supplement effective 15 May, pending resolution of File 0129-[33PT]-Brin/Port-000027-01-66. This would not fully meet his legitimate and verified needs, but under the circumstances he is willing, and we are advising him, to seek this relief. I have enclosed his request for relief pro tempore on Form 9339-G117A.

We look forward to your earliest possible response.

Faithfully yours,
Hedvig Jensen-Mphephu
Associate Tribune

◆

Secretariat for Income
Distribution
District of Table Bay
Stellenbosch
SASY 036-1133-VN
15 May 2132

Hedvig Jensen-Mphephu
Associate Tribune
Tribunate, District of Table Bay
Capetown
SAST 110-9327-JJ

File: 0129-[33PT]-Brin/Port-000027-01-66

Case: Citizen Nicholas Brinker, W# 55-X-765-768

Query: Be advised with reference to your letter of 09 May that, since 15
Apr., grants of one-eighth income supplement pro tempore are consid-
ered extraordinary procedures under Regulation 231/234 of Ministry of
Income Distribution. They require submission of Form 9339-G117A-2 to
Subdepartmental Secretariat of Income Distribution. Your Form 9339-
G117A herewith returned.

Disposition: Case referred to District Secretariat of Justice with recom-
mendation to prosecute Mr. Brinker and yourself for obstruction of administrative process under Title 765, Par.3(g), 2127 Code.

Reply to: Vusamazulu Mangope, Deputy Director, Subdepartmental
Secretariat for Income Distribution, Karroo District.

◆

District Tribunate
Capetown
SAST 110-9327-JJ
16 May 2132

Jacobus Piet Hiemstra
Asst. Dist. Secy. for Income Distribution
District of Table Bay
Stellenbosch
SASY 036-1133-VN

Dear Mr. Hiemstra:

With reference to File 0129-[33PT]-Brin/Port-000027-01-66, our office will be in touch with Mr. Mangope in due course. Meanwhile, it is incumbent on me to request, with all urgency, that you place in writing the substance of our video conversation of this morning at 9:35–9:42. For the record, let me state that I regard your action in referring this case to the District Secretariat of Justice as primary harassment of the Tribunate and subject to counterprosecution under Title 19, Par.35(a,b,n), 2078 Code. Our office has filed a protest with the Departmental Secretariat of Justice, and we have requested Congresswoman Kruger to approach the office of the permanent undersecretary of the World Chamber for his obiter dictum.

Faithfully yours,
Hedvig Jensen-Mphephu
Associate Tribune
✦

Secretariat for Income
Distribution
District of Table Bay
Stellenbosch
SASY 036-1133-VN
17 May 2132

Hedvig Jensen-Mphephu
Associate Tribune
Tribunate, District of Table Bay
Capetown
SAST 110-9327-JJ

File: 0129-[33PT]-Brin/Port-000027-01-66

Case: Citizen Nicholas Brinker, W# 55-X-765-768

Query: [None]

Disposition: In response to your memorandum of 16 May, be advised that our office has referred your case to District Secretariat of Justice in light of your failure to resubmit Form 4876-J2129W and submit Form 9091-P24P within limit of ten (10) days set by statute and specified in our memorandum of 28 April. Your reply was dispatched 09 May, as per enclosed copy. Statutory requirement under Title 765, Par.3(g), 2127 Code, pertains to suspicion of evasion and is subject to criminal penalties. Be advised we have also contacted office of Congresswoman Kruger, whose attorneys promise full and unbiased inquiry.

Reply to: Jacobus Piet Hiemstra, Assistant Secretary.

◆

District Tribunate
Capetown
SAST 110-9327-JJ
17 May 2132

Jacobus Piet Hiemstra
Asst. Dist. Secy. for Income Distribution
District of Table Bay
Stellenbosch
SASY 036-1133-VN

Dear Mr. Hiemstra:

   With reference to your memorandum of this morning, be advised that Martinus Hoorn, deputy counsel in the office of Congresswoman Kruger, has now approached the permanent undersecretary of the World Chamber, who expects tribunal action to be filed against your office in the District Court of Capetown tomorrow.

   We regret that matters have taken this turn, but it is our firm intention to protect the prerogatives of the District Tribunate at every cost. I am authorized by the principal tribune to recommend that you withdraw your request filed on 15 May with the District Secretariat of Justice. If this action is taken and verified by independent audit, we are prepared to advise Deputy Counsel Hoorn of your cooperation.

                          Faithfully yours,
                          Hedvig Jensen-Mphephu
                          Associate Tribune

                          ◆

Secretariat for Income
Distribution
District of Table Bay
Stellenbosch
SASY 036-1133-VN
17 May 2132

Hedvıg Jensen-Mphephu
Associate Tribune
Tribunate, District of Table Bay
Capetown
SAST 110-9327-JJ

File: 0129-[33PT]-Brin/Port-000027-01-66

Case: Citizen Nicholas Brinker, W# 55-X-765-768

Query: [None]

Disposition: *Your attempt earlier this afternoon to circumvent adminis-*
trative process is noted and has been copied to Subdepartmental Deputy
Director Mangope, Deputy Counsel Hoorn, Congresswoman Kruger,
and Permanent Undersecretary Wang.

Reply to: [None]

◆

The documents in the case of Nicholas Brinker stop at this point.
I askèd Cousin Heddy how it all came out. She could not recall every
detail, but apparently her superior and Hiemstra's reached an understanding after several days in intergovernmental court, and the
charges were dropped on both sides. When I questioned her about
the hapless Mr. Brinker and his petition for supplementary income,
her memory failed her altogether.

BOOK THE THIRD

THE HOUSE OF EARTH

10

THE SMALL REVOLUTION

Restructuring

When Germinie-Constance Vaudésir de Lamothe, president of the Executive Council, and titular leader of the Small party, saw the Commonwealth flag settle in a soft heap on the great disc of steel at the base of its pole on that snowy afternoon in Krasnoyarsk, she turned to the cameras and smiled. "We have seen the end of empire," she said. "As your last president, I offer you my resignation, and my farewell. Now go, and multiply!"

Her gesture caught the world by surprise. Everyone familiar with the Small program understood that a monumental restructuring of the world system was foreordained. But most of us expected that there would always be a Congress, and a Council, and a president, if for no other reason than to utter proclamations and smile into cameras.

We were mistaken. The Smalls resolved to raze the socialist cosmopolis to the bare ground. Both the symbols and the substance of the world-state had to pass, as quickly and painlessly as could be. The presidency itself was abolished the next morning in Krasnoyarsk, by a special act of the People's Congress. A timetable was drafted by the Executive Council to dissolve all the other structures of the Commonwealth, starting with the World Militia, which was disbanded officially in January 2148.

The Congress itself, along with the Council, stayed on for a number of years to oversee the dismantlement of the world order. The key legislation, at all odds, was the sheaf of Autonomy Laws passed by the Congress in 2150. The new laws abolished the departmental system, calling it "artificial" and "inhumane." Groups of citizens who wished to establish communities were invited to submit prospectuses to the Congress for chartering. Small party agents fanned out through the world to discuss plans and help mediate between groups contending for the same land or populations.

Agents were also dispatched to the habitats in space. They had next to nothing to do. The typical habitat was already largely self-sufficient and, as a rule, opted for autonomy with little debate. Few spacefolk took much notice of the changes on the bright blue world below them.

The early 2150s were a frantic time for earthside community organizers. In several instances, the departmental structure was retained more or less intact, under some other name. Small party agents did what they could to promote dismemberment, but, if the local population honestly preferred things as they were, the party had no legitimate grounds for complaint.

Here and there, two or three departments even chose to federate, much to the dismay of the Smalls. Thames Department, which included 3.6 million people living in the southeastern corner of the island of Great Britain, voted in a referendum to amalgamate with the southern half of Dartmoor Department, to the west. Perhaps recalling the prophecy of "Ecotopia" in the twentieth-century novel by Ernest Callenbach, the 3.9 million citizens of Columbia Department, in northwest North America, joined forces with the 3.1 million of Redwood Department, to the south. Other sizable polities emerged in northeastern Asia among the Han peoples of old China, in English-speaking Australasia, and in the Hindi-speaking lands of the Indian subcontinent. The largest polity chartered by the Congress during the 2150s was Nihon, comprising three departments in the former empire of Japan, with a total population of 11.9 million people.

Another possibility was for a given district within a department to declare its independence. Under the Commonwealth, every department had been subdivided into a dozen or more districts, each with its own bureaucratic apparatus and a population of roughly 250,000. Many district boundaries had been drawn quite arbitrarily. But here and there districts cohered well, coming in time to think of themselves as authentic political entities. The best of them voted to continue under the new order, now as sovereign states.

In the world as a whole, communities even of this size were exceptional; those of only one or two thousand were not rare. The typical community consisted of an urban neighborhood, village cluster, or experimental society, bound by a common written or customary law, and composed of people linked by religion, race, ideology, language, or historical tradition. The number of intentional communities rose sharply after the 2150s but even in that first decade exceeded five thousand. Although, like the utopias of past centuries, they had a tendency to disaggregate after a few years, some endured and still flourish today.

When the chartering process was finally complete, late in 2157, the Council reported that 41,525 autonomous communities now existed on earth and in space, ranging in size from Nihon to a tiny group of 250 Druse in the mountains of the former Al-Jabal District in the Middle East and an equally small band of self-styled Apocalyptic Bible Baptists settled along the banks of the Yazoo River near Vicksburg in southern North America.

Each community was required to select its own form of government, economy, and social structure. Orthodox Muslims were at last able to live strictly by the *shari'a,* although only a few dozen Koranic communities were actually established, thanks in part to the resourceful opposition of women in the Muslim lands. Capitalism on a small scale was introduced in many communities. Taking a leaf from the book of the League of Space Cooperatives (despite—or perhaps because of—its small size, an influential force in the new age), some communities experimented with neofeudal economies not unlike the system adopted in the space habitat of Hightown.

There was less variety in modes of governance. More than 85 percent of all communities opted for direct democracy. The larger ones had to settle for one form or another of representative democracy, including "demarchy," the system of government by representative sample first proposed in the twentieth century by the Australian scholar John Burnheim. A few of the newly designed intentional communities practiced matriarchy or patriarchy, while some attempted to get along without any form of government at all.

At the other end of the spectrum, one community in twenty chose hereditary or elective monarchy. Uniquely, Nihon contrived a complex system of indirect democracy presided over by a hereditary emperor. The first man to serve as emperor was a collateral descendant of the last emperor of Japan, discovered in a sea-farming village near Toyohashi by a team of enthusiastic genealogists.

In certain unusually heterogeneous regions with histories of ethnic or religious conflict, intercommunitarian peace councils were formed to keep an eye on relations between communities The peace councils often played a major role in mediating disputes, although they were not invariably successful. Their chief function in the early days was to ensure safe passage out of one community and a warm welcome into another for members of minority groups uncomfortable in their original place of residence.

Apart from the Autonomy Laws, the task of the Small Revolution in the 2150s was simply to disassemble the world system, piece by piece. The machinery of global economic planning and interdepartmental trade and transfer, the income distribution regime, the elaborate network of public schools with their standardized curricula and certification processes, the creative arts juries, and the intelligence-gathering operations of the ministry of public safety were all terminated, in stages. The world currency system, based on the Commoncent, finally disappeared in 2158, one of the last fixtures of the old order to take its leave.

The Commoncent was an old friend, difficult for many to relinquish. Although humankind had long commanded the technological resources to make even relatively small communities self-sufficient, the governments of the Commonwealth routinely did their best to foster interdepartmental trade, on the premise that autarky would lead to lawlessness and strife. Now, with the help of AI robotics, communities learned to produce everything they needed themselves. If people craved something made or grown elsewhere, they could readily obtain the know-how to make or grow it for themselves.

In order to obtain such know-how, all they required was an open channel of communications, which the Smalls persuaded most communities to provide and maintain. As in the years of the Commonwealth, every individual and community in the global communications net had access to every other by interactive holovision, computer links, and radio service. Reference materials, instructions, plans, and blueprints could be exchanged back and forth between communities. It took implausibly little time to wean humankind from its dependence on intercommunitarian trade and the almighty Commoncent.

To oversee the communications net and keep it in good working order, the ministry of communications recommended that the Congress organize several permanent self-sustaining communities of engineers who would take the necessary responsibility and find their own replacements, as required. The ministry of transport filed a similar set of recommendations to maintain terrestrial and interplanetary public travel. The Congress approved the plans of both ministries and recruited the appropriate number of hardy volunteers.

But the most impressive single engineering project of the Commonwealth, the solar power satellite system, did not survive. It was an article of faith with the Smalls that communities should not rely, whenever possible, on facilities located outside their lands and centrally managed by global authorities. Dependency, they argued, was also control. If communities continued to receive all or most of their energy from the Sun Ring, they would be vulnerable to manipulation by whoever operated the Ring, its receiving stations along the Equator, and the underground superconducting cables linking each station to communities throughout the world.

The Sun Ring did not, of course, come down. We can still see it with binoculars in the night sky. It provides useful staging areas for the docking, assembly, and launch of spaceships, not to mention its value to astronomers. But its solar cells were removed, the stations on the Equator were closed, and the cables no longer transmit power. We found other ways of meeting our energy needs (as I will explain later).

The Sun Ring stopped beaming solar energy to earth in the late spring of 2159. Turning off the Ring was the final major undertaking of the new central government. Without ceremony of any kind, the People's Congress dissolved both the Council and the tribunate and then legislated itself out of existence. Its only concession to symbolism was its choice of dates. The last institutions of the Commonwealth closed shop on 14 July 2159, the 370th anniversary of the storming of the Bastille in Paris.

The End of the Party

During the twelve-year interregnum between the lowering of the flag of the Commonwealth and the final adjournment of the Congress, the guiding force in the world was unquestionably the Small party. I have thus far said very little about the structure of the party. It prided itself on having no formal organization, no supreme leaders, and no interest in power or self-perpetuation. To some extent, its image of itself was quite accurate. But it could not have toppled a great polity such as the Commonwealth and installed its own revolutionary world order without cohesion and discipline.

Numerous biographies have been written of the most prominent Smalls, which give us some hints of how they managed to accomplish so much. For one thing, the leadership consisted largely of very young men and women of extraordinary intelligence, compassion, and empathy. Ninety-five percent of them were products of the Genetic Initiative. Their high sociability quotients saved them from tendencies toward megalomania, and they worked together easily, with a kind of selfless intuition of one another's feelings and wishes. As many as one-quarter of the total membership of the party consisted of individuals who, in any other political formation, would have surely reached the pinnacles of command and influence.

Here and there, a figure stands out briefly. Vaudésir de Lamothe, for whom I conceived a short-lived passion, although we met only twice, had been chosen president of the Council precisely because she lacked ambition and was happy to be a graceful symbol. Several other Small "celebrities" were of the same sort. More cerebral individuals, such as Masha Toradze, or Yao Shaoqi, or Stanko Christov, or Bidú Chaves de Mendonça, have produced eloquent, succinct memoirs of the Small Revolution, memoirs, however, that say little about their personal lives or their idiosyncrasies, assuming they had idiosyncrasies at all. In this respect, they resemble most of the superchildren of the Genetic Initiative, including, I do believe, my own dear Ingrid! Your generation surpasses even theirs, but you both evince that same wise, mysterious mix of imagination, logic, and warmth of feeling intended by the bioengineers who designed your genomes. In the new mix, the fascinating but ultimately destructive vanity of the great man or the great woman, the vanity of a Vassily Kravchenko or a Gina Mascagni, rarely if ever rears its head.

In any event, the Smalls worked together almost effortlessly. They had in mind a single, clear, unambiguous outcome, for which they needed to toil like Trojans, but which they firmly believed would come to a sudden end and liberate them for other, more personal tasks. They invested all their energies in the revolution. When they won, they joyfully let the reins of power slip from their hands.

Initially, in the days of the Commonwealth, the Smalls set up an informal global directorate of some five hundred men and women, which convened occasionally in person, but more often by videophone. World party wits teased the Smalls mercilessly for being "a party of centralized decentralists." Cadres operated at every level of the Commonwealth administrative hierarchy, in the towns, districts, departments, and central instruments of governance, but almost always pursuing policies voted by the directorate, whose members they picked in special party elections. Later, when the Smalls took charge of the Commonwealth, they staffed the Council exclusively with members of their party directorate.

It is all the more astonishing that the party was able, as it had promised, to disband. But disband it did, in the late autumn of 2139, just four months after the dissolution of Congress. The central directorate abolished the party, declared itself adjourned, and vanished without a trace, except that many of its veterans joined with other Smalls in their local communities in forming modest social and political clubs that exerted a variety of influences in public life for years to come. Some of these clubs still thrive, and I sometimes attend the meetings of one or two of them myself, although I had never belonged, or wanted to belong, to the Small party.

Of all the other parties that once frisked and capered on the broad stage of global politics, few survived the interregnum. Deprived by death of Gina Mascagni, the Free Trade party sputtered out in 2151. The Democratic Rally for Neocapitalism stuck to its guns but, like the Free Trade party, lacked a raison d'être after the legalization of capitalist economies by the Autonomy Laws and shrank to a tiny stubborn remnant that habitually opposed all government bills in the People's Congress until the dissolution of 2159.

The minor parties on the left, such as the Dignity party and the True Communists, fragmented along both regional and ideological lines, weakening themselves irrevocably. One branch of the Dignity party, representing a few of the poorest regions of Africa and South Asia, did persist for years after the dissolution of Congress. It hit on the ingenious idea of sending its members around the world clad in dhotis and ragged shawls and armed with wooden begging bowls, to remind the more fortunate citizens of the new order that some parts of the world had been "condemned" to enduring poverty by the fall of the Commonwealth.

Once all ethnic and religious groups had a chance to form their own self-governing communities, most of the political parties that catered to their causes disintegrated swiftly. The only parties that survived belonged to evangelical faiths, for whom world conversion was a duty enjoined by their respective gods. But as major forces in world politics they had no future. World politics itself had ceased, for all practical purposes, to exist.

All this, of course, brings us to the World party, the party of my father, the party of the Commonwealth, the party that had united all humankind and helped bring us seventy-five years of peace. As you must know from everything I have said, I am of two minds about the World party. I am critical of the disrespect shown to its leaders and policies by the scholars of our own time. Yet I share their fear that the course it took in its later years could have resulted in the petrifaction of human society and culture.

Leadership and membership alike, the soldiers of the World party were wholly unprepared for the events of the second quarter of the century. They had not yet grown fat and complacent, but managing the world suited them. Although their chief philosophers freely speculated about the eventual dying out of the state, as foreseen by Friedrich Engels, they argued that the world needed a long "tutelage," perhaps of five centuries, before the state became dysfunctional. Without the services of the World party, humankind would fragment and regress.

Clearly, the party was not prepared for the disillusioning events of the 2130s and 2140s. Overwhelmed by its own world-historical obsolescence, the World party not only lost power: it shattered into several bitterly contending factions. By 2150 there were ten, ranging from the Intransigents on the far left (or far right?), who plotted the recall of the World Militia and armed counterrevolution, to a circle of moderates favoring alliance with the Free Trade party. One faction drew nearly all its support from cadres in North America, another was based in Africa, a third in Asia. Thousands of stalwarts left altogether and joined the Dignity party. Reversing an old taunt, several Smalls jokingly referred to their fallen rivals as "a decentralized party of centralists."

But for lifelong World party members, the humor had long since fled from politics. After years of floundering, a congress of leaders from seven of the ten factions met quietly in a lodge on the shore of Lake Louise in the former Canadian province of Alberta. They discussed their differences. They discussed the prospects of their party. Tempers flared at first, and a few of the delegates departed angrily.

But, after two days, a spirit of calm resignation settled on those who remained. Bearing in mind the long and honorable history of their movement, they resolved to end the party without further delay, rather than prolong its unseemly agonies. They drank a final toast, embraced one another, and went their separate ways. From that day forward, 5 December 2153, the World party ceased to exist.

The Logic of Decentralization

By the smiling blue waters of Lake Louise, party leaders asked one another over and over again, "How did the bastards do all this? How did the Smalls conquer the world? Why are their strategies working?" Various answers were given, turning chiefly on the expectation that sooner or later the people would "wake up," after they had paid "a heavy price" for trusting charlatans and ecomystical fools. If we can believe the recollections of the two attendees who wrote their autobiographies, no one present professed to understand, in any visceral or conclusive way, how so much change could have been set in motion with so little heat and strife.

As we prepare to enter the seventh decade of the era inaugurated by the Smalls, we do have answers to those questions asked at Lake Louise in 2153. They may not be correct, or they may not be the whole truth, but a consensus has been reached among historians, which I share with you for what it may be worth, together with one conclusion of my own.

The consensual view hinges on the observation that humankind in the middle of the twenty-second century had changed profoundly from the race that fought and strove and endured through all the previous millennia of history. Its tools, societal structures, genetic endowment, and world outlook were qualitatively unlike anything known in earlier times. The human race had not been "perfected," but it had been fundamentally altered. The mechanisms once needed to make collective life possible, along with the conventional wisdom about human nature and original sin, had outworn their usefulness. Humankind still *had* a nature and was still quite capable of what its theologians liked to call "sin," but the rules of the game were no longer what they been before, just as one cannot compare the civilization of *Homo sapiens* in the late Pleistocene to the civilization of *Homo sapiens* in the twentieth century.

Of the four great transformations that had created a new humankind—in tools, societal structures, genetic endowment, and world outlook—the one that facilitated all the others was the first, which was also the first to occur. By progressing from stone tools to mo-

lecular tools, from a Paleolithic to a postmodern technology, humankind did not merely acquire more power over nature. Humankind
became independent of nature, and of the labor required to achieve
such independence in the first place.

Even more remarkably, humankind became independent—to a
significant degree—of itself, liberated from the need for complex social machinery to organize and carry out the production of goods
and services, liberated from the need to design in painstaking detail
new technologies and the supporting economic tissue to bring their
fruits to market. Although human inventiveness remained indispensable, the arrival of AI and the moltech revolution meant that most of
the labor, even the creative and intellectual labor that at one time
only men and women could perform, could be assigned to tools rather
than workers. The tools themselves became so versatile, inexpensive,
durable, miniaturized, self-maintaining, self-replicating, and self-
designing that the cumbersome apparatus of global government contrived by the architects of the Commonwealth lost all justification.

In short, why employ a thousand million human beings to "manage," "administer," and "organize" a system that, in its raw essentials,
could be duplicated in any town of five thousand competent postmodern men and woman? Why, for example, rely on a Sun Ring
when a solar farm, a fusion generator, or a matter-antimatter blender
can do the job on native soil with the oversight of two or three technicians? Why install a plant geared to manufacture a thousand spaceplanes a week on the other side of the planet when you can have a
microfactory in your backyard industrial park producing the two
planes your community actually needs once a decade? Why import
bananas from Central America when you can grow them in your
own cybernetic greenhouse in Anchorage?

In all fairness, the degree of independence from nature, society,
and labor attained by technology was not really great enough even
in the early twenty-first century to warrant the sort of radical decentralization instituted after 2147. If one takes into account only
technological factors, so much decentralizing would have been im-
practicable until at least the last quarter of the twenty-first century,
and perhaps later still. But, by 2147, the time had arrived, and more
than arrived.

The second metamorphosis that historians hold responsible for the
success of the Small Revolution involves the structure of human society itself. We have noticed the long, much interrupted progress

through history of the democratic idea. In early riverine civilizations power was wielded by a minuscule elite. In the bourgeois democracies of the nineteenth to the twenty-first centuries, some of it was shared (less in reality than in constitutional theory) with the middle and even the lower classes. Under the Commonwealth, the people held substantially more power, but they still did not govern themselves in the fullest sense of the word. The day-to-day tasks of government were performed by a few thousand congresspersons and ministers, a host of bureaucrats, and the principal functionaries of the World party.

But, as the years went by, the social and economic power of the people increased almost inconceivably. The equalization of wealth and the razing of the system of mass exploitation built by the lords of capital ensured that in the future no person would find it easy to extract profit from the labor of another. The Commonwealth's program of universal public education from lower to upper school added further to the skills, self-esteem, and sophistication of its people in every part of the planet. If the resurrection of private enterprise in some regions of the world opened opportunities for a few citizens to grow richer than their fellows, they would owe their good fortune to their own skill and industry, not to the legalized swindling of others.

Of almost equal importance was the re-creation of *Homo sapiens* by prenatal gene surgery. The Genetic Initiative of the Commonwealth had transformed more than ten million children between 2096 and 2147. The majority of communities in the decades that followed authorized the same or still more radical surgery to enhance intelligence, sociality, and empathy. Genetic modification became as routine as immunizations for childhood diseases in earlier times. As you know from the modest example of your grandfather, even adults could benefit (although much less so) from modification.

Many students of the Small Revolution contend that the leavening effect of the new human type, *Homo sapiens altior,* on the population as a whole was a pivotal factor in the revolution. Such claims are inherently unverifiable, but no one disputes that the Small leadership was predominantly *altior.* Some of its most enthusiastic and charismatic lieutenants were *altiores* as well. As the numbers of the modified grew, so did support for the new order, from the 2150s onward.

But, even if the modified had been uniformly hostile to the Small Revolution, their very existence could only have helped the Small cause. Sharp witted, yet outgoing and cooperative, the young members of *Homo sapiens altior* fashioned a new model of human behavior ideally suited for life in autonomous communities. They were less inclined than the old human type to take advantage of others and too intelligent to be taken advantage of themselves. Their extraordinary powers of mind and heart were another form of wealth, shielding them, as ample personal incomes and education helped to shield everyone, from the age-old tendency of most of *Homo sapiens* to fall victim to predators.

Finally, the Smalls succeeded because value structures had changed fundamentally in the late twenty-first and twenty-second centuries. For half a millennium and more, Western civilization had reared its children to believe in gain, treasure, ownership, profit, accumulation, credit, capital. The West had also converted most of the world's non-Western peoples to its eminently bourgeois scale of values. The man or woman with the greatest number of fine homes, fine vehicles, and fat investment portfolios was the man or woman "of distinction" in bourgeois society, whom everyone sought to emulate. Eventually, no matter how noisily people waffled about such "higher" things as love and faith and art, they could not in all honesty imagine a society in which material wealth was of secondary importance.

As we noted in chapter 7, plutomania became rare and almost extinct in the days of the Commonwealth. People lost the habit of valuing possessions over personal relationships, the pleasures of mind and body, productive labor, and all the other good things of life. Even the Free Traders and other parties styling themselves neo-capitalist stressed the joys of enterprise, not accumulation. The Free Trade party, in particular, expressly supported the income distribution laws, although it worked to liberalize them.

In the period after 2147, a reorientation of values occurred again, but the culture of the Small Revolution had as little use for plutomania as the culture of the Commonwealth. The craving for material possessions was not revived, except by a few eccentric communities. Living in harmony with nature and fellow communitarians took precedence over both the materialism of the age of capital and the substantialism of the Commonwealth. Philosophies grounded in mystical or spiritualist premises enjoyed a new vogue, as did a resurgent feminism that challenged what the North American ethicist Christine Bergonzi of New Chicago termed the "Promethean male ethos of Commonwealth socialism." I shall discuss all this more fully in the next chapter.

But, clearly, neither the Commonwealth nor the decentralized world order of the Smalls extolled acquisitiveness, competitiveness, violence, or the pillage of the biosphere. In its own way each attached the highest importance to the sociable virtues. Philosophers in both argued that hunger for excessive material wealth spurred not only class exploitation but also racial strife, patriarchy, ecocide, and warfare. In short, one of the reasons the Small Revolution prospered is that most people were conditioned by the reigning values of their civilization to prefer social harmony to private gain. Splintering the world into thousands of autonomous polities did not cause the revival of internecine conflict partly because the cultures of postmodern humankind had done their work so well.

Having shared with you the consensus of scholars on the success of the Small Revolution, I wish to add only a single point. You will notice one common denominator in all four explanations: the indispensable contribution of the policies and beliefs of the men and women of the Commonwealth. Without their work, could we have had the technologies, the equality of opportunity, the genetic enhancements, and the ethical culture on which the Smalls built their new civilization? Perhaps, in time. More likely not. More likely a fourth world war among the battered survivors of the third, and the extinction of our genus. Thus, in its own crooked way, history lurches forward.

In any case, the Small Revolution did succeed. Whether humankind deserved such a denouement, I cannot say. But it did succeed. A new world order was born, a world order without a central organ of governance, without a name, without a flag. It is our home. When we do have occasion to speak of it formally, we call it the House of Earth.

INTERLUDE

To give you a sense of the rhythms and dilemmas of life in the early days of the new era, here are selections from the private diary of Eduardo Mistral Ortiz, a North American cardiologist and cardiovascular surgeon, whose father (also a physician) emigrated from Buenos Aires to the Department of the Finger Lakes in 2088. Dr. Mistral has practiced in the same community for fifty-five years and was kind enough to send me a copy of his diary for the year 2159. In spite of his Hispanic name, he is also very much a Jensen. His maternal grandmother Alfonsina was the daughter of your distant cousin Jens Otto Jensen, who, you remember, settled in Argentina in 2017. The community in which Dr. Mistral serves, Cloudland, was once known as Binghamton. Before the Catastrophe, it was an industrial town noted chiefly for its fine university, the alma mater of Mitchell Greenwald. Not a direct target of Soviet attack, Binghamton survived the war more or less unscathed, as did a good part of its population.

3 July 2159

A typical day in the life of a harried and worried man. The Community Gathering finally legislated a new currency this morning, to replace the Commoncent, but I don't imagine they'll get around to minting or circulating any of it for another six months. I suggested they could use the Chenango shekel coined in Norwich, but they won't. Community pride!

This afternoon I saw five new patients. A boy with a leaky valve, nothing serious. An old woman who needs a new heart, which I can't grow in time to do her any good. A man with chest pains caused by eating too many raw beans. So it goes.

Met Wisp tonight, for stargazing. (Our second clear night in a row!) She was wearing a diaphanous red and green sari. I could have eaten her alive, but it was hands off, and pay attention to the stars. We argued for a while about astral influences. Ecomystics don't exactly believe in them, but they don't exactly not believe in them, either. Wisp refuses to take sides, but she was very solemn when she explained the latest theories. I kept a straight face.

◆

4 July 2159

The skies have closed up again, and we had some light rain tonight. The big event today was Will Pepper's appointment. As I suspected when we stressed him last week, he's got almost total blockage of all three arteries. I borrowed Crowley's scanner and did a scan first thing. His percentages are 90-95-85. The collaterals aren't doing much better. Cholesterol is 450 mg/dL, with only 25 HDL, in spite of taking kilograms of that god-damned enzyme blocker and living on bread and water for five years. Poor guy. He hasn't had any blocker since we ran out in April, but it wasn't working too well anyway. Some of these cases of familial hypercholesterolemia are just about incurable. At least with what I've got. Too bad he never had genetic intervention. I could send him to a genetech, but that would only slow down future deposits.

What the man needs now, I mean like yesterday, is a complete reaming in a functional laser cath lab. But Cloudland doesn't have one, and neither does Pocono or Montrose or—why bother to even ask?—the Johnson City Ecomystical Solar Village. When I think we used to have two working cath labs in the area! But you don't dare risk a catheterization if you can't align the sensors, and the sensing equipment in both labs is completely shot.

I have two options. I can send Will to Syracuse with a bag of Chenango shekels and hope the surgeons there accept him, or I can try one more time to induce that unimaginably stupid robot to fix the sensors. Tell me, diary, which is it?

And while you're in the mood to give advice, work on this one, too: by the middle of the month I will have used up the last batch of general medical supplies from the dark days when we groaned under the oppressive yoke of the infamous superstate. Some supplies we can do without, I guess. Some I can beg or borrow from better-stocked colleagues. Some I can buy from the new medical marketing co-op on Hawley Street. Some I can make myself, in spite of being all thumbs. But some I just won't have the time or the wits to scrounge. In fact there's half a dozen things I need that I can't find already. Would you please give me a week of 18-hour days so I can catch up?

But diary just says, Hell, I'm not your medical log, Ed. Stop it! I'm your own personal little book. Have some fun in life. Go persuade Wisp that the stars want you to fuck her. Meanwhile, good night.

◆

5 July 2159

More rain today, and the skies are slate gray. I spent an hour on the net contacting robotics people in Pocono. They showed me how to program Roger to realign the sensors, but I did some tests on a recently deceased collie, and I wasn't satisfied with the results. Of course there's a lot of difference between a live man and a dead dog.

Then when Will came in this afternoon, I scanned him again just to be sure, and the percentages are 75-95-70. Still poor, but the figures don't square with the first set (except for the 95 percent on the circumflex), which means either I didn't perform the scan correctly or Crowley's scanner is misfiring. Crowley wanted it back, but I'll try again tomorrow or the next day. I need a more complete scan anyway for the surgery, if there's ever going to be surgery.

I talked to Nightingale and Fossey on the net about growing a heart for Ms. Parseghian. They wonder if she'd even be strong enough for the operation.

You're getting restless, I can tell, but, yes, diary, yes, I made it with Wisp tonight. She was in a lazy mood. We took an electric raft down the Susquehanna. It was about nine o'clock, the light was fading fast, and just before we docked the boat, Wisp docked me.

◆

6 July 2159

Wisp buzzed at daybreak and we had a long talk. She is so fresh and happy and untroubled, just like everybody in the village. But somehow, in spite of all the differences between us, I can talk to her, open up as I've never done with anyone. I mentioned marriage again, but she dodged the issue. I don't think it's the age difference. What's 20 years out of 200 (if you can believe the geros!)? All she'll say is that when she turns 40 next year she'll think about it. None of her friends is married yet, either. I understand how she feels, but it doesn't offer much consolation. I'm lonely.

I envy the geros, though. They have at least twenty journals still publishing in the net. You can dial through one and believe it's 2140 again. Our people in cardiology have to get better organized. It's embarrassing. Tonight I ransacked the JCS and found only one article on realignment of sensors, and that was published in Chinese in 2149! Took me ten minutes just to get it translated.

◆

7 July 2159

Rain again, and this time a deluge. 3 cm in two hours. Wisp left me a message on my screen. She's gone up to Lake Cayuga with some people from her "pod" in the village. They count squirrels and thrushes and screw all day long. I know I'm not supposed to be jealous of podmates, but it's next to impossible, especially when I need her so very much myself. How is the new age going to handle jealousy? What's the party line? Ah, right. No party. The Smalls barely exist any more, and they've pledged themselves to disappear as soon as the Congress rings down the curtain next week.

When I used to belong to the World party, I believed in answers. Not certainties, perhaps, but answers. You knew things. Diary, tell me. What do we know nowadays? What are we, besides an assortment of bipeds consecrated to our own amusement? Where are we going?

Had to attend a Community Gathering this afternoon, rain or no rain. We met in Ross Park to hear motions on the new antimatter blender. The physics people need to know how big a blender we want, and nobody knows what we want, as usual. With the Sun Ring shut down, we've got to have a more reliable source of power prontissimo. I'm tired of brownouts and fadeouts because the sun's too dark (this is Cloudland after all, what do they expect?) or nobody thought to haul in enough sugar beets for alky. Anyway, only 4,000 people showed up, probably because of all the wet. Just between you and me, diary, I pine for the days when the good old district secretariats did all the work and let us alone.

Almost forgot. Roger the Robot went over the sensors again and this time everything checks. I think we're in business, which is good because Will is showing symptoms of galloping angina.

I write about Will Pepper but my thoughts are really on Wisp Brightfeather and a certain picnic on the shores of Lake Cayuga. If any of those feckless villagers harm her in any way, I will personally arrange to make them fuckless villagers. With one swoop of my trusty laser scalpel . . . !

Don't take me seriously, diary. A man in love is a man in love, and a man in love is a man in no condition to write in diaries. You understand.

◆

8 July 2159

One perseveres. I led a chaste and blameless life today. Saw eight patients in the a.m., ten in the p.m. Ms. Parseghian is getting worse. I've scheduled Will for surgery tomorrow. The full scan confirmed my first diagnosis. I fouled it the second time, somehow or other. There's 90 percent blockage in the distal circumflex, 95 percent in the second and third *marginal branches, and multiple lesions all through the left anterior descending system, including the diagonals. I sent my scanner data to Herskowitz in Buffalo, and he concurs on every point. As soon as Will is okay again, Blumfeld will give him some gene modification to help quiet that hyperactive liver and build up his receptor sites.*

A long talk with Wisp before bedtime. She's learning to read shadows now. The latest spookery. "The way your shadow lies is the way your future flies." So says Ambience, the village guru. Wisp hinted that maybe I should come practice in the village. They have no cardiologist. They don't have a lot of things. Most of the people are young and superbly healthy. They eat only what they grow, and they grow everything to perfection in spite of the stony soil around here. They till several thousand hectares across the river, where the university used to be.

The only problem is, they're slightly mad. Wisp, too. Lovely and radiant, in the full flower of young womanhood, but not entirely connected. For example, they've taught her that the earth (did you know this, diary?) is alive. It has a mind, diffused through all its spheres, planning each step in its evolution to self-consciousness. Did you know?

The ecomystics are great picnickers. I didn't ask about the festivities yesterday, except the usual "Did you have a good time?" but I know how they love to picnic. They maintain communal shelters for the cold weather, but much of the time they just loaf around in the great outdoors in tents.

Living in the J.C. Ecomystical Solar Village would be grand for, say, two weeks, especially if Wisp could fend off her podmates. But moving there is something else. Be honest with me, diary. How would you like to go camping in the woods with all of the folks, forever?

◆

10 July 2159

No time to write yesterday. The laser and the ultrasonics performed beautifully, Will is clean, and he's already on his feet. I'll send him up to Blumfeld tomorrow. It's a good feeling, fixing up a man all by yourself. It's an even better feeling, knowing you did it with equipment that you taught your robot to repair. I suppose that's what the Smalls mean by "autonomy." I could do with less of it sometimes, but when it works, what can I tell you? It works.

I see Wisp tomorrow. She promises me a "treat."

◆

11 July 2159

The treat was learning how to read shadows. Wisp wore her phosphorescent red and green sari again, and learning meant a lot of being close, so I cooperated, but my brain was not the organ principally affected.

It's all drivel. Just between us, it isn't even that good. What makes a beautiful, intelligent, caring young woman devote half her waking hours to the pursuit of rainbows, moonbeams, and cuckoo birds?

I visited Ms. Parseghian in the afternoon. She's quite sick. We don't have the right drugs for her, but I plan to synthesize a few batches tomorrow. The net has the formulas I'll need, and Roger is an old hand at organic chemistry. Together, we'll do it, or bust.

No sunshine for four straight days. And in answer to your question, no, Wisp and I did not, repeat, did not make love, unless you want to count kissing her neck a few times during shadow-throwing lessons.

◆

13 July 2159

Another very busy day yesterday. Slept over at the clinic making drugs. Roger needs an overhaul. Wisp is away again, this time at a podfest in the mountains, which means all her podmates, every last one, will be there and it will take ten days.

We made love just before she left this morning. As she was leaving, she took my hand and smiled and told me what happens at a podfest. She didn't want me to find out from somebody else.

The rumors are true, I guess. It's her turn to podslave. She will help all the men, all hundred and five, to commune with Gaia, the earth mother. You don't want to hear the details. She promises me they will be gentle. I promise myself not to think about it. Not once.

Ms. Parseghian died this evening, without pain. She was 103. I could have saved her with a cloned heart, even a donor heart, but we just don't have the facilities, and anyway she ran out of time. Ironically, the sun was shining brightly all day.

◆

14 July 2159

I took the day off. Will Pepper stopped by, looking fit and happy. We drank a glass of Cayuga together and talked politics.

While he was still here, the holo came on with news about the final adjournment of Congress. They also replayed the scene from twelve years ago when the voluptuous Vaudésir de Lamothe hauled down the flag in Krasnoyarsk. We tried to reflect on the solemnity of the moment, the end of the Commonwealth, the dawn of a new era, and so forth, but all I could do was stare at the president's tits.

I think I'm over Wisp.

◆

There is more, of course, including a temporary revival of interest in the much-soiled Wisp, but what Eduardo wrote on 14 July was essentially his last word on the subject of Wisp, the House of Earth, and life in general. When I showed him the parts of his diary I planned to use, he laughed and laughed.

11

THE AUTONOMOUS SOCIETY

The Politics of Progress

When the Smalls persuaded humankind to decentralize in the 2140s, one of their many slogans was "governance without government." They anticipated that most people would choose to live in small communities and adopt a form of direct participatory democracy. As the general will of each community matured, the need for permanent institutions of government would pass. Every citizen would take his or her turn in drafting legislation and managing public business, usually on a part-time basis. Monday's judge would be Tuesday's artist, Wednesday's village councillor, Thursday's student of Arabic, and Friday's swimmer of the Hellespont. Politics—in the old sense of the struggle to wield public power—would evaporate.

Politics on a world scale, including the major worldwide parties, did evaporate, more or less on schedule. But in the communities decisions have to be made. Although a politics of class interest cannot flourish in classless societies, differences remain, even within communities of modest size—differences of age, gender, ability, temperament, ideology, training, and experience. What needs to be done? Where shall we do it? When and how? From the first, people divided along many lines, and the result has been politics.

But what makes politics so vital as well as so ubiquitous in communitarian life is the pace of social change dictated by incessant progress in science, technology, scholarship, and all the arts and crafts. If decentralization had been followed by "an epoch of rest"

253

(the subtitle of William Morris's utopian novel, *News from Nowhere*), a time without significant innovative change, there might still have been politics, but it would have mattered no more than rites of passage or games of chess.

In sum, the engine of the lively politics of our House of Earth has been progress: the same reckless, onrushing, almost mindless force that propelled humanity from feudalism to capitalism, from capitalism to the Catastrophe, from the Catastrophe to the Commonwealth, and from the Commonwealth to our patchwork world of today. If stability and continuity are the hallmarks of a great civilization, humankind has not lived in a great civilization for many centuries; perhaps it never did.

The only difficulty for the world historian is that we no longer have, properly speaking, a world history. There is no central data bank, no planetary bureau of statistics, no world ministries to require standardized record keeping. Some communities abound with historians who publish remarkable collections of primary sources, voluminous general histories, and detailed monographs on a broad range of topics. Other communities (the greater number) are too small, too insular, or too present-minded to nourish the historical imagination at all.

All we can do, under the circumstances, is generalize from the limited archival resources available in the global communications net. This is no small task! Thousands of communities have contributed their records to the net, records of every imaginable sort. But many thousands more have contributed relatively little. Some attach a higher priority to the visual and performing arts than to the culture of words and numbers. The citizens of still others lead contemplative lives, keeping their silence.

In any case, it is clear that, from the 2150s onward, humankind turned to political and social experimentation on a scale without precedent in its history. Politics flourishes as never before, and in greater profusion. In larger communities, such as the Northwest Republic (comprising the federated departments of Columbia and Redwood in North America), there are as many as a hundred contending political parties and movements. At the other extreme, Novy Rus (the area between Leningrad and Moscow) has only one party and the Constitutional Empire of Nihon only three.

Even the quite small communities often buzz with political activity and debate. When we were discussing his diary, my cousin

Eduardo told me that in his beloved Cloudland a dozen political factions participate in the Community Gathering. They run candidates for town offices and press their legislative agendas wherever they can find a warm ear to bend, all this in a community of only thirty-five thousand souls. The Johnson City Ecomystical Solar Village, next door to Cloudland, has fewer than ten thousand inhabitants but at least ten political parties and fifty religions.

By way of illustration, I could relate the political history of one or two exceptionally well documented communities, but I am not sure what this would tell us about all the rest. It is time to explore other matters.

Ecomysticism and the Zeitgeist

The same diversity that characterizes politics in the new age also characterizes its ideational and aesthetic culture. Or nearly. At first glance, what strikes the eye is diversity, but the diversity is not infinite, and there are overarching tendencies that distinguish the spirit of our times—our zeitgeist, if you please—from the spirit of earlier ages.

The most obvious shift in the climate of opinion has been the virtual abandonment of the neomaterialist or substantialist worldview of Commonwealth culture and its replacement by an outlook suggestive of the irrationalism of the twentieth century or even the nihilism of the mid-twenty-first, but without their darkly negative aspect. The pendulum has swung again, away from the consecration of reason and its powers to a consecration of heart, feeling, and spirit.

As substantialism was the reigning philosophy of the World party, so the philosophy most often associated with the Smalls and their intellectual progeny is known as ecomysticism. This is the least systematic and scholasticized of philosophies in the history of our millennium. I hardly know how to define it. The word is on every pair of lips, but what does it mean?

For most it means the belief that the earth, not just the biosphere, but the whole earth, is alive and—in some transcendental sense—conscious of itself. Universalist ecomystics say the same of the whole cosmos. Both factions agree that the deification of the forces of nature by prehistoric men and women struck much closer to the truth than the arid theories of modern physics. In the ecomystical vision, "matter" is nothing more than a show projected onto our sensoria by the indwelling spirits of being, like images in a holofilm.

It follows that human beings should live in a style that conforms as much as possible to the rhythms of nature, rising with the sun, avoiding artificial light whenever possible, eating only natural and unprocessed foods, practicing ahimsa (noninjury of other living things, except plant life expressly grown for sustenance), living mostly outdoors, renouncing the ego, and using technology only to make life simpler and more natural. Some ecomystics oppose all forms of genetic engineering; others just as enthusiastically favor it, if engineering can be shown to bring the human type closer to the model of humankind formed in the beginning of time by the earth spirit. Virtually all ecomystics practice ego denial, which includes the refusal to attach one's name to any work of art, science, or scholarship. For this reason we do not know the name of a single master of ecomystical thought. Without exception, ecomystical treatises are published anonymously.

But the varieties of ecomysticism are legion. Besides the geists (earth worshippers), the universalists (cosmos worshippers), and the friends and foes of bioengineering, there are neoplatonic, phenomenological, reincarnationist, and charismatic ecomystics; syndicalist, communist, tribalist, and gerontocratic ecomystics; and many others.

The zeitgeist has also proved hospitable to several older philosophies. The Proto-Marxists, a sect that stresses the work of Marx and Engels in the early and mid-1840s, have a small but widely diffused following. The philosophies of Plotinus, Chuang-tzu, Sankara, Jalal ud-Din Rumi, Leibniz, Schelling, Vivekananda, Husserl, Heidegger, Whitehead, and Marcel have all enjoyed revivals.

Not quite a philosophy, but surely a characteristic thought system of our time, is the militant neofeminism of Christine Bergonzi of New Chicago. She has written a trenchant critique of the worldview of the Commonwealth era, *The Ideas of Men* (2175). Here she attacks the Prometheanism of Commonwealth institutions and beliefs and also the allegedly Promethean character of much contemporary public life. She subjects phrases like *the conquest of space* and *the march of history* to neofeminist analysis, arriving at the conclusion that a life-denying, earth-denying stratum exists, indelibly, in the male psyche that renders the whole sex unfit for public service. Maleness is summed up, she writes, in the myth of Prometheus, who stole fire from heaven and inspired "the pseudo-heroic trampling of nature and womankind that men call the 'march of history.'" Bergonzi does not condemn technology as such, but she deplores the mentality that attaches the highest value to "productive" labor rather than to nurture and healing.

The new worldview has given rise to a bewildering mélange of arts, literatures, crafts, and multimedia creative spectacles, even richer than those of the preceding age, but typified by an underlying mystical sensibility in striking contrast to the neorealist trend of Commonwealth art. One of the most distinctive products of our aesthetic culture is the all-day Geistfest, a festival of electronic mantras, aleatoric holoplasty, and demonstrations of hypnotrance technique linked to a text in Mandarin, Sanskrit, and classical Greek declaimed by children. The members of the audience wander through the stadium and participate spontaneously in every event.

Spontaneity is a critical element in the new arts. Many works are designed to be created in performance. Critics lament the several centuries of "fossil art" that preceded our time, when theater and music directors struggled to achieve a precisely faithful re-creation of the original writer's or composer's intentions, when every word of every text was scrutinized for authenticity, and every painting was deeply analyzed to be certain of its genuineness. Contemporary artists reject most of the products of modernism and early postmodernism in favor of the styles and models of medieval, folk, and primitive art.

Yet, in spite of all these clearly emergent trends, there is a still deeper, still more pervasive current in contemporary culture now acknowledged by many scholars as the dominant mode of thinking in our time, surpassing even ecomysticism. It is not incompatible with ecomysticism or with any of the movements I have surveyed. Strictly speaking, it is incompatible with nothing. But it grows organically out of the matrix of the social philosophy of the Small party, and it gives every indication of sweeping everything before it in the twenty-third century.

I refer to the school of thought (and aesthetic criticism) known most familiarly as Absolute Relativism. We associate it with the popular tracts of Jacques Duboeuf of Bourges and Sutan Widjojo of Jakarta, which impart its essence, but there are many Absolute Relativists in colleges of higher learning throughout the world who have expounded its tenets in far greater depth and precision.

Briefly, the new philosophy takes the "relative" relativism of the nineteenth and twentieth centuries, which yielded the credicide discussed in our first chapter, and turns it upside down. Instead of proclaiming the death of belief and the impossibility of truth, it assumes that all truth claims are true until and unless proven false. Until now, critical thought has been concerned with puncturing illusion and unmasking fraud, on the assumption that all philosophers lie, except the critics themselves, who know that all philosophers lie. "Once upon a time," says Widjojo in the first paragraph of his *Pansophy* (2191), "the task of philosophy was unraveling. Today let us ravel the threads again and enjoy the infinity of truth."

Absolute Relativists adopt an almost Bacchic stance with respect to truth claims. "They intoxicate us," writes Widjojo. Although men and women may stumble over their own feet and contradict themselves with loose thinking, more often they speak with a cosmic voice. The inspirations that invade them are literally inspirations, "breaths from Heaven." Each deserves to be studied with awe and open-heartedness. Each may help us shrink "the margins of unknowing."

But Widjojo, quoting Cecília Ruiz of Havana, does not flinch from the final reckoning implicit in Absolute Relativism. Just as most ideas are true, so no idea is absolutely true. "All science is hypothesis, all philosophy is metaphor, all art is fantasy, all truth is myth. All exist in relation to otherness, even these truths, and even this admission, and even this admission of the prior admission, worlds without end." Or, in another familiar maxim, now from Duboeuf, "Thought is play."

Not that we contemporaries indulge ourselves only in games of the mind and spirit. Many of us indulge in games of the flesh. I have lived to see a worldwide renascence of both individual and team sports. The Olympic Games, which had become orgies of nationalism and megacorporate commercialism in the last age of capital, were discontinued under the Commonwealth because of their bad odor. We started them up again in 2188, staging separate tourneys every four years on every continent. Before, nation competed against nation, sponsor against sponsor; today, all the entrants are individuals, who come to the games representing only their own personal prowess. No one who passes the qualifying tests is denied participation.

But the Olympics are only one example of the sporting events that take place in our society every day. Most of them occur in our home communities, among friends and neighbors, without protocol.

Some commentators foresee a time, not far away, when *Homo sapiens* (who is also *Homo ludens*) will devote nearly all its energies to play. By *play* they mean not only sport but art, letters, dance, music, treks through wilderness, all the ways in which we celebrate and preserve the genius of youth. Future historians may spend as much time on play as I have spent on the grim "business" of politics and economics.

Appropriate Tools

Also implicit in the playfulness of *Homo ludens* is the delight we take in tools and how they work and what they can do. A few of the most radical ecomystics forego all but the meagerest tools and live like Neolithic savages, but in our House of Earth the zeitgeist has never really been hostile to technology.

Many World party faithful had foreseen quite a different outcome, warning that a vote for the Smalls was tantamount to a vote against technology and against progress. To judge by what we have seen so far, they were ludicrously wrong. Although the Commonwealth supported technical innovation far more vigorously than, let us say, the Chinese empire in the Ming Dynasty, when the mandarinate actively discouraged change in order to protect its imperial prerogatives from the schemes of upstarts, the evidence suggests that between 2125 and 2150 the rate of technological progress slowed almost to a standstill. It is implicit in the dynamics of great bureaucracies that no apparatchik welcomes disruption of routine or shifts in political power from center to periphery.

But in the decentralized world that followed the fall of the Commonwealth, the brakes on technical progress subtly applied by the bureaucrats of the cosmopolitical ancien régime were released. Interacting freely in the global communications net, scientists, engineers, and technicians relished their new-won freedom. Progress has resumed. The technologies introduced in the twenty-first and early twenty-second centuries have been refined, to make them more efficient and less cumbersome for use in small communities. New systems have been built to the same scale. It has been an era of light, elegant, fluid design.

One immediate priority was to find a source of energy to replace the power microwaved from the Sun Ring. As a stopgap measure, some communities resorted to fusion reactors and solar farms in wastelands. Most rejected both strategies, preferring to recover the energy they needed from dams, geothermal sources, and liquid fuels distilled from biomass crops such as sugar beets.

The solution ultimately arrived at was the matter-antimatter blender, developed by particle physicists and engineers in the Northwest Republic in 2153 as an experimental drive for spacecraft. It was introduced into local communities in 2159 and 2160.

Commonwealth scientists had worked on such a device for years. They learned how to synthesize infinitestimally small batches of antimatter for use in nuclear weapons, but they could not manufacture enough for the needs of a civilian energy program. Tested under laboratory conditions and never marketed, their experimental reactor would, in any case, have employed antimatter only as a trigger for controlled hydrogen fusion.

In the matter-antimatter blender invented in 2153, a particle-beam generator produces the antimatter, which is then injected through pipe-shaped magnetic fields into a furnace fueled by liquid hydrogen. The antimatter, released molecule by molecule from magnetic containment, fuses with the normal matter, discharging energy in a continuous fierce stream. Since each meeting of particles and antiparticles results in the total conversion of both into energy, the yield is many times greater than in nuclear reactions. A single blender of the original design of 2153, no bigger than a small house, could pump enough energy in one hour to supply the needs of a town of five thousand people for a year. Today's even smaller blenders produce ten times as much energy in half the time.

In many other fields, the chief innovations have been simplifications of older technologies. The baroque array of robots produced in the Commonwealth (over 200,000 models) has shrunk to a dozen compact yet versatile types capable of almost any function except what robotics engineers call "original volition." That is to say, they can reason, invent, express preferences, generate emotional and sensory responses to stimuli, direct subintelligent robotics systems, and make complex decisions, but they have no wishes or goals of their own, no purposes, no plans for their future or ours. As if to underscore the point, our engineers have generally refrained from giving robots any resemblance to the forms of human beings or animals.

We have also simplified the communications net inherited from the Commonwealth. In those days, great systems of fiber-optic cables handled much of the material broadcast across distances, but today virtually all transmissions to terminals and receivers are wireless, carried by short waves. The only major task of the global communications communities is to oversee, maintain, and (if necessary) replace the maze of orbiting satellites that connect all parts of the earth with one another.

One simple standardized product familiar to all of us, based in this instance on another developed early in the years of the Commonwealth, is the so-called record cube, a black ceramic microarchive measuring 21.5 centimenters on every side. In your school you probably consult smaller, abridged versions of the same unit, but, in the chips of the 21.5-centimeter model, information engineers have managed to store all the written and electronic records of humankind, including every book, journal, newspaper, government document, media transmission, film, and recorded performance surviving from earliest times down to at least 2147. Of course it can no longer be claimed that a record cube contains all the records. With the discontinuance of systematic planetary record keeping after the middle of the twenty-second century, new editions of the cube are woefully incomplete for the recent period.

In one sense our House of Earth can be accused even of diminishing the technological capacities of humankind. Economystics have created a climate of opinion in which many goods and services once deemed essential to a civilized way of life are no longer valued, or even available. The trend is clearly away from what ecomystics term "overdependence on prostheses." One noteworthy example is the replacement, almost everywhere, of hydroponic farms, synthafood factories, and large aquaculture systems by small, traditional dirt farms.

There is even a widespread inclination, which may prove stultifying, to avoid long-distance personal travel. The bright-eyed camera-wreathed tourist, so commonplace a figure from the nineteenth to the mid-twenty-second centuries, is nowadays seen less and less. The immense world transportation network of earlier ages has shriveled to a few meager floater mainways and air and space services, which carry almost no goods and only a quarter of the passengers carried just a hundred years ago.

Yet, on the whole, we remain a technological civilization. Our technology—to use the word popularized by the ecodecentralist social philosopher of the twentieth century E. F. Schumacher—is "appropriate" to our needs. If these needs are somewhat more modest than they used to be, it does not mean we have ceased to be tool users.

Nor has humankind abandoned large-scale innovative projects, despite all the difficulties involved in carrying them through in a decentralized world. In the twelfth chapter, I want to tell you about four, in particular: the Darwin and Samsara Projects, the terraforming of Mars, and the Interstellar Expeditionary Service.

Breaking the Cycle of Dependency

Before examining these great collaborative efforts, I must say a few words about families, children, the relations of men and women, and personal life in the new autonomous society of the House of Earth. Much of it is disquieting, even to the doughtiest defenders of our civilization. We have paid a price for our autonomy.

At the time of the formation of the Small party government in 2147, the population of the earth and its colony worlds in deep space stood at 3.75 billion. As the death rate continued to drop because of ever-longer life spans, various communities were heard to complain on the world communications net of overcrowding. Demographers combing through the available records estimated in 2165 that the earth would soon have four billion people, and might already.

The word was therefore passed from community to community that, although everyone had the right in the new era to reproduce to his or her heart's content, responsibility to the biosphere dictated restraint. Communities that exceeded the carrying capacity of their land found gates closed everywhere when they tried to export their human surplus.

A reaction against childbearing itself set in. The neofeminist militants, led by Christine Bergonzi, argued that endogenic reproduction was a device adopted by men to perpetuate the subjection of women. "Poor, powerless, and pregnant!" she wrote. "That is how men want us to be, and how, even after our 'liberation' in the twenty-first century, we have lived throughout history." But, she continued, the reproductive cycle was also a "cycle of dependency" afflicting all members of the family. Children were raised in the long shadow of their parents and lived like slaves. Both parents took sadistic pleasure in ruling them, as husbands enjoyed ruling wives. When the former slaves earned the chance, they became slave masters themselves. In some cultures both parents and children were in turn dominated by grandparents; in others the grandparents formed a subclass of the enslaved.

In the neofeminist analysis, only two solutions offered themselves: ectogenic reproduction, with the fertilized egg nurtured in an artificial womb and the child raised in learning cooperatives without knowledge of its natural parents, or childlessness. Of the two, the neofeminists recommended the latter, but they recognized it could not be a solution for every woman if humankind were to carry on. Adapting the technology used by Commonwealth scientists to grow clones, a task force of female biologists from London Lea (the community replacing Thames and southern Dartmoor departments in the British Isles) perfected a safe, inexpensive ectogenic reproduction system used by hundreds of thousands of women in recent decades. Ecomystics deplore a method of childbearing so alien to nature, but the new mothers have not complained.

The main thrust of neofeminist agitation, however, has been directed against reproduction itself and against the nuclear family. "A woman is complete in and of herself," writes Bergonzi. "Neither she nor any man needs a child or a mate to find absolute fulfillment as a human being." Many ecomystics and other groups agree, for a variety of reasons. Chief among the arguments one hears is the imperative of adjustment to the balance of nature. If people live for two centuries, instead of one, their obligation to the biosphere is clear. One child in a lifetime is quite enough.

Not everyone by any means concurs; hence the Mars project, which we will discuss later. But, from the scanty available evidence, we have managed to keep the population of the earth from growing unconscionably in the past quarter century. At the present time, in 2200, it is probably no more than 4.1 billion.

If population is under control, the same cannot be said of family life. We noted the decline of the family under the Commonwealth; in the House of Earth, it is all but extinct. One reason is the curtailment of reproduction and the influence of neofeminism. But that is not the principal reason. As people live longer, they appear to have lost the obsessive interest in mating that once characterized the human race. Even those who choose to reproduce in the natural manner do not really raise their offspring, in any sense familiar to earlier ages. They are raised by the community, chiefly in schools, meeting parents only on special occasions, as children once met distant cousins from other lands. Many never meet their parents at all.

In the typical community (if there is such an oddity), men and women no longer pair. They have *passades*. They have many friendships, with each other and their own sex. They participate vigorously in community affairs. But they seldom pair. Communities in which marriage is normal do exist. Some attract curious visitors, who are given tours of actual "connubial domiciles" in which actual husbands and wives live together as we see them in the motion picture "films" of the twentieth century. Nevertheless, all the data at our disposal indicate that the family has disintegrated, once and for all. Group marriages, often attempted under the Commonwealth, are even more rare than traditional monogamous pair bonds. Most contemporary ecomystics regard any form of marriage as unnatural, violating the aboriginal instincts of man and woman to live in hunting-and-gathering tribes without separate nuclear families.

An unforeseen by-product of the decline of the family is the gradual emergence of womankind as the new "dominant" sex. I put *dominant* in quotation marks because women have not assumed the role long taken by men. They do not rule the domestic roost, which has disappeared in any case. They do not occupy all the leading positions in community councils or in the arts and professions. They are not hero worshipped, like a Lenin, a Lincoln, or a Greenwald. But their influence has, almost imperceptibly, grown with a steadiness that I think at one time took even neofeminists by surprise.

The principal reason, perhaps, is that, just as the culture of earlier centuries was shaped by and for men, so today's culture, although not created by women alone, is more attuned to female capacities and proclivities. It is a society devoted exclusively to the arts of peace. It is a society of relationships rather than functions, where sociality counts for more than pure intellect or pure feeling.

To speak anatomically, it is a society in which neither the left nor the right half of the brain is supremely valued. Our ideal is the behavior possible only when both halves interact productively; and, as we have long known, women possess a richer network of neurones linking the lobes of the cerebrum than men. Their hormonal system, free from what neofeminists call "testosterone poisoning," is also better suited to the kind of society in which we now live, a society without violence, ruthless competition, empire building, or the "Promethean ethos." All things considered, women's biological advantage endows them with greater practicality, flexibility, and common sense than men; more and more, we look to women for leadership and models of civic virtue, as centuries ago we looked to men.

But the growing ascendancy of womankind has not solved all problems or ushered us into a social paradise. The imminent disappearance of family life, once the glue that held society together, gives many of us a sense of unease, even foreboding. Will bachelorhood lead ultimately to self-centeredness and the erosion of charity? Can children without parents form appropriate visions of their place in society and their future? Are *passades* suitable substitutes for enduring passion and lifelong commitment to a beloved spouse? Even if we assume that only one person in ten was happily married in earlier societies, might not that one person have contributed indispensably to the health and wholeness of his or her society? We shall know the answers to these questions only after the passage of many years, if then.

Another problem is what Dinu Grigorescu of Ploieşti (parodying Khader Barakat) labels "the illiberalism of liberty." We have our freedoms, our autonomous societies, our right to live and do much as we please, free of ministers and bureaucrats. But dissidents in many close-knit communities have noted that, the smaller the community, the more difficult it becomes to escape from watchful eyes and open ears. The unwritten law may grow even more onerous than the law enforced by apparatchiks.

Also relevant is the model of sociality provided by the genetically modified and by womankind, which stresses cooperativeness, not personal achievement, and consensus, not rampant individualism. Grigorescu, like several other recent commentators, finds all too many contemporary men and women "bland, undaring, almost ovine. . . . Today's smart sociable smiling faces foretell a future race of human sheep."

A further threat on the horizon is described by sociologists as "the coming gerontocratic revolution," the gradual passing of all real authority in the world to the elderly, especially to elderly women. One needs no global census returns to see that the world's population is growing older by the year. Long lives and few births can have no other outcome.

Already there is clearly a generational problem in most communities, as the old tend to monopolize influence and political power, forcing young people to wait many years for the opportunity to be heard. To be sure, the aged today are hale and youthful by contrast with their counterparts in modern times. Their bodies age much more slowly, their minds stay fresh and keen, and they are not afraid to learn new tricks.

But gerontologists who have studied the typical man or woman over the age of ninety report disturbing tendencies that specialists from earlier centuries would not have been surprised to hear. For example, it remains as true as ever that most minds are programmed by the experiences of the first thirty years of life to think in terms of certain problems, categories, and concepts, to reason in one distinctive personal way, and to be stretched or limited by a particular complex of behavioral patterns. It also remains true that most minds continue throughout adult life to think, reason, and be stretched or limited along the same lines, no matter how open they are to new ideas, no matter how much new information they assimilate, and no matter what new experiences they may have. They can modify their thought processes up to a point, but the imprinting that occurs during the plastic years of childhood and early maturity is too deep and powerful to allow anything like a fundamental reconstruction.

It has even been seriously suggested that what the new elderly need most is a "mind sweep" that can remove programming and allow centenarians to start life over again without all the hobbling preconceptions acquired during the first thirty years. Brain surgeons have shown how the job could be done, at least in theory, but the cost of such an operation would be the virtual elimination of identity or selfhood. Whether it will someday be possible to remove the imprinting without removing a person's inward essence and memories remains to be learned. Specialists are not sanguine.

Meanwhile, the warfare between the classes in the modern era is echoed (however faintly) in ours by the struggles of young and old. I feel much sympathy for young people today, knowing they will have a more difficult time making their mark on the world than my generation did.

And there is one other reminder of class struggle in our contemporary life, the even more muted struggle between the genetically modified and the "ordinaries." Through no fault of their own, the modified are simply brighter and more competent on the average than the best of us ordinaries. We ourselves are bright enough to recognize their superiority but not altruistic enough to avoid occasional dark feelings of resentment, distrust, and even chagrin, which sometimes translate into blatant discrimination against the modified, doubled if they also happen to be younger than we are. This is a problem that will presumably vanish toward the end of the twenty-third century, when the last ordinaries die out—if, indeed, we do! But it may well recur as the modified themselves begin encountering the still abler superchildren of your generation

Yet I sometimes wonder if the greatest obstacle to the prospering of our new society is not metaphysical. One of our younger social philosophers, the substantialist Khorn Som of Phnom Penh, laments the loss of direction that she sees in the dismembered civilization of the House of Earth. "It is only a rooming house," she writes, "a cell block without connecting doors, a labyrinth of sealed exits. We have places to stay; but we have no home." The end, Som foresees, will be a gradual spiraling return to the old modern world, without tribal wars perhaps, but also without a redeeming sense of world mission or purpose.

Khorn Som is a substantialist, unusual for someone of her relative youth. Her views are widely dismissed as "anachronistic," but they keep turning up in commentaries one reads in the net. Somehow she has struck a sensitive nerve. As the Proto-Marxist Avner Eshkol of Jerusalem writes, "Perhaps the pendulum has swung too far." Eshkol ventures the guess that by 2250 we may find it necessary to restore the Commonwealth, not in all its baroque glory, but in a humbler re-incarnation, to serve as a meeting ground and symbol of the under-lying historic unity of humankind. I share some of his nostalgia for the Commonwealth, but I am dubious of his forecast. By 2250, I sus-pect the human race will be too busy in the starlanes to trouble itself with yet another cycle of rearrangements on earth.

But who knows? I am a historian, not a prognostician. You will say I should stick to my last, and you may be right!

INTERLUDE

My son Hans supplies the material for our last interlude, selections from a debate that he moderated in 2198 at the Small club in his town, the Republic of Svendborg. You know Hans as a father, the man whose seed helped to give you life. Although your home is far away in Aarhus, I take a certain atavistic pleasure in thinking that, on every Earth Festival Day, you and he, and your mother, and your mother's second child Bertel, spend time together and talk about our family. Such occasions are rare these days, but we who share common ancestors owe them remembrance. We would be poor citizens of the House of Earth if we learned no history and poor human beings if we had no knowledge of the people whose blood fills our veins. In the discussion that follows, Hans is the moderator, Yoon Sok My of Pyongyang speaks against the proposition that "the House of Earth is the first utopia," and Helen Smith-Carlsen of Svendborg defends it. Yoon was invited to Svendborg because of his rising reputation as a Relativist dialectician. Smith-Carlsen enjoyed a brilliant career as a Small party orator of the 2130s and 2140s. We enter the proceedings at the beginning of the second hour.

Moderator: *Let me recapitulate. In our discourse to this point, we have heard a history of the idea of utopia, tracing it as far back as the Bible, the* Republic *of Plato, and the* Tao-te-ching. *We agree that utopias are images of the good society, where the common life is all that it should be. By definition there has never been a utopia in the temporal world; utopias are implicit indictments of the present order, explaining how it falls short. But, paradoxically, some of us today contend that we now live in a true utopia, that our House of Earth, although not flawless, has fulfilled the dreams of the ages. Ms. Smith-Carlsen so affirms. Mr. Yoon says nay. Let me pose to each of you a question: is the House of Earth the* best *society known to humankind, even though it may not be the best* possible *society?*

Smith-Carlsen: *I so affirm, but I reject your speculation that it may not be the best possible society. The best possible society, as I have already argued, is one that allows all communities to do as they wish. Whatever they wish is ipso facto good because it expresses their general will. They may wish a thousand different things, and do, and should, but what makes the House of Earth a utopia is that it grants full autonomy, at a time in the evolution of our species when violation of the autonomy of others has become unthinkable.*

Yoon: *I answer nay. There is no criterion external to history to judge what is good or better or best. But if you like, I will so affirm.*

Moderator: *Please explain.*

Yoon: *I will grant that the House of Earth is the best society known to humankind if Ms. Smith-Carlsen will grant that all the others were best as well.*

Smith-Carlsen: *I answer nay. As usual, Mr. Yoon is speaking in riddles. How can all societies be the best?*

Yoon: *Because they are all the expressions of the general will of their age.*

Smith-Carlsen [scowling in disbelief]: *Does this mean that the general will of Rome was expressed by Caligula and that the Soviet general will was expressed by Stalin?*

Yoon [laughing]: *No, the Roman general will and the Soviet general will expressed themselves! The people always do the best they can, but what they can do is not always the same. Let me pose a question of my own. Are all communities of the Commonwealth equally good?*

Smith-Carlsen: *I so affirm.*

Yoon: *Ah! If there is good-better-best in human affairs, how can you account for the astonishing fact that in forty thousand communities the general will has expressed itself to precisely the same degree with precisely the same qualitative result? Is the constitutional empire of Nihon morally equal to the patriarchy of Palermo or the matriarchy of Madras? Do you weigh every society on your scales until we reach the contemporary epoch and then tip the scales into the incinerator?*

Moderator: *One question at a time, Mr. Yoon, please.*

Smith-Carlsen: *You are deliberately distorting what I said: I said the new world order is a true utopia, not its component communities. It is a utopia because it allows them all to be what they are.*

Yoon: *Are you saying that the Rome of Caligula was not what it was?*

Smith-Carlsen: *It was not all it could be.*

Yoon: *Is the empire of Nihon all it can be?*

Smith-Carlsen: *Perhaps not, but it has the freedom to be more.*

Moderator: *Let me take us off this particular treadmill and rephrase my question. Assume for the moment that utopias are not impossible societies after all. Assume that in a few favored epochs, however brief, a utopia is achievable and has been achieved. Can you name one such other epoch, leaving aside the question of the credentials of the House of Earth?*

Smith-Carlsen: *The only arguably utopian epoch in history was the prehistoric, before slavery and empires. However, I answer nay because prehistoric communities lacked independence from the iron laws of nature and from the predations of their own sister communities. They had not yet learned to live in dialogical harmony with their environment or with each other.*

Yoon: *In reply to your question, Mr. Jensen, I so affirm. Every epoch is a utopia, although not in its own eyes. Every epoch fulfills the aspirations of its ancestors. Every epoch is viewed through a golden haze of nostalgia by its progeny. Utopia is both hope and homesickness, both quest for omnipotence and regression to the half remembered haven of the womb.*

Moderator: *But can you give us an example?*

Yoon: *All ages are "examples."*

Moderator: *Just one please.*

Yoon [laughing]: *Why not? I could hardly miss! Consider the eighteenth century in Europe. Men of the "Enlightenment" like the marquis de Condorcet looked forward to a time when the world would be a single rational community, when all peoples would be equally civilized and prosperous, when everyone would receive an education at public expense, when trade and enterprise would be free, when the mechanical arts would greatly abridge the labor required of workers, when women would be the legal peers of men, when a scientific system of welfare insurance would protect everyone from life's hazards, when wars would end, when the conquest of disease, malnutrition, and filth would enable all citizens to live long and healthy lives. Most of his vision had already come true by the second half of the twentieth century. If he could have visited Paris and all the world in 1950, he would have been delighted. But how many people living in 1950 thought of themselves as denizens of utopia? How many millions living in 1950 looked yearningly back through time to the fair Brigadoons and Wakefields of the eighteenth century and pined for their blue skies, their clean waters, their pure and simple splendors? Every society is some other society's utopia, in prospect or retrospect, or both.*

Moderator: *Do you wish to comment, Ms. Smith-Carlsen?*

Smith-Carlsen: *Mr. Yoon is a self-proclaimed Relativist, so we must expect these sophistries. All I would say is that our society does fulfill the expectations of many utopographers of the past. But let me ask a question in return. If people do not realize they once lived in utopia until their society has turned to dust, why do so many of us toiling in the traditions of the Small party so earnestly believe that our society, here and now, is indeed a utopia?*

Yoon [smiling broadly and bowing]: *Ah! You have me!*

Smith-Carlsen: *You yield the point? With all due respect, I cannot quite believe what I am hearing.*

Yoon: *You do have me. You have me in a quandary. The difficulty is that no one can use words except as they are defined, and our genial moderator attempted to change the rules by changing the definition of a utopia. He asked us to consider that utopias are objective possibilities, which may at one time or another have actually existed. I cannot accept the premise. As I use the term, a utopia is always a far better society than the one in which the utopographer happens to live, which is precisely what qualifies it to be called utopian. To be sure, from Aristotle, Bossuet, and Hegel to the present day, many people have declared themselves citizens of utopia. But they were all apologists, like yourself, Ms. Smith-Carlsen, publicity agents for the status quo. Who believes them? Would you believe me if I said I was the best person who ever lived? The difference between a utopia that one labors to achieve and a utopia in which one pretends to live already is the difference—as the German sociologist Karl Mannheim wrote in the early twentieth century—between utopia and ideology. You are an ideologue, Ms. Smith-Carlsen, and no doubt utterly sincere. At one time in the days of the Commonwealth, you were an ardent utopographer. You gave us the stirring vision of a good society at the end of history's rainbow. But today, Ms. Smith-Carlsen, please forgive me, today you are just another ideologue.*

Smith-Carlsen [flushing]: *An "ideologue" who has retracted not one of the values and beliefs she held in the first half of this century!*

Moderator: *I apologize for changing definitions in midstream. Let us try a different tack. Ms. Smith-Carlsen, you maintain that our House of Earth is a utopia because it allows all communities to be autonomous. Autonomy means, if it means anything, self-government, in which every constituent self speaks with an equal voice. But some of our critics insist that in fact we have privileged orders. They say that a new class system has taken the place of bureaucratic or megacorporate tyranny, a new feudalism based on age, genetic endowment, and gender. How do you both respond?*

Smith-Carlsen: *I deny such accusations, on behalf of the people of Svendborg and people everywhere. The critics offer no evidence, only suspicions and hypotheses.*

Yoon: *And do you also deny that large communities like Nihon and London Lea wield a disproportionate influence in science, technology, art, and thought? Do you deny that people are not free to emigrate from their home communities? Do you deny that foreign travel has grown steadily more difficult? Do you deny that communities indoctrinate their children with their collective value systems more effectively than a remote global mandarinate could ever do? Do you deny that female culture and female priorities have stifled the free expression of maleness?*

Do you deny that the old, by virtue of seniority and prolongevity, intimidate the young? Do you deny that the genetically modified discriminate against ordinaries, and vice versa, whenever they can?

Moderator: *The rules state, Mr. Yoon, that a discussant or moderator may ask only one question at a time. You have asked seven. Please choose one of these. As time permits, we may be able to introduce the others later.*

Yoon: *Since I am a man and Ms. Smith-Carlsen belongs to the privileged sex, let me ask her my question about matriarchy. Do you deny that female culture and priorities have stifled the free expression of maleness?*

Smith-Carlsen: *Please do not insult my intelligence, Mr. Yoon. I deny it categorically. The sexes are equal, in law and in custom, in almost all communities. We know of patriarchies, such as the one in Palermo, and we know of matriarchies, but, of the communities registered in the world net, fewer than 1 percent refuse absolute equality to both sexes.*

Yoon: *You speak of legalities. I speak of realities. Every responsible psychologist and anthropologist in the net will tell you the realities. Through no fault of women, the culture of our age, unlike the cultures of the past, prioritizes qualities peculiar to your sex. The result is that men are at a palpable disadvantage, in a society that no longer attaches high value to their temperaments and skills.*

Smith-Carlsen: *Even if you are correct, which I dispute, it would be an easy matter for genetic surgeons to devise a program of modifications to relieve men of their "deprioritized" assets.*

Yoon [wincing]: *Ouch! Your surgical shears are cold! In fact several programs have already been devised, but no geneticist can guarantee that the men would still be recognizably male. And no male has volunteered to test their theories.*

Smith-Carlsen: *As I said earlier, we do have problems, and progress is yet to be made. I use the word* utopia *in its dynamic sense, as process, not finality. But do I have the right to reply with another question, Mr. Jensen?*

Moderator: *You answered Mr. Yoon's question. It is surely your turn.*

Smith-Carlsen: *Thank you. I will respond to all your earlier points when the time comes, Mr. Yoon, because many people share your prejudices and preconceptions about our society. But my question is this. Why do you see only problems in our society? What prompts such negative thoughts? I realize that my remarks are ad hominem and for this reason out of order. Please do not answer if you find them offensive.*

Yoon [laughing]: *No, no, please! We Relativists have been accused of many things, but not negativism! Not that! I have no negative thoughts about the House of Earth. Nor will you ever do better than you do now. You are already doing your best. This is our philosophy. We refuse to judge or compare. How can a civilization that admits so many possibilities displease us? I have just reminded you that it cannot be a utopia, in its own time. By one idea of the good, it passes muster; by another, it may not. So it has been with all societies, all the works of men and women. When you understand, deeply and fully, the futility of judgment, you will cease to fret about progress and utopia and destiny, and you will rejoice in the sublime now, the twinkling of eternity reserved for you!*

◆

Your father at this point called a recess for luncheon. The debaters returned for another round, but they added little substance to their arguments of the morning. He tells me that, despite the wit and bonhomie of Yoon Sok My, most of the audience clearly preferred Helen Smith-Carlsen and declared her the winner by a vote of 115 to 27. Absolute Relativism may nourish the mind, but, in the words of Pascal, the heart has its reasons that reason does not know.

12

TRANSHUMANITY

Life and Death

For growing numbers of citizens, especially young citizens, the most tremendous question before humankind in this age is not war or peace, wealth or poverty, faith or unbelief, patriarchy or matriarchy, community or cosmopolis, or any other issue ventilated in the previous two chapters, but the question of life: life or death? They see all the travails of humankind down to the late twenty-second century as a preparation, a mental and physical schooling, for the ultimate challenge that confronts our species. The true test of our mettle, they say, comes now, as we decide whether or not to live.

For many of us in older generations this seems almost an impertinent question. Whether or not to live? Who chooses death? Who—apart from a few unfortunates with painful, debilitating, and incurable diseases or deformities—would ever choose death?

But the answer we receive is persuasive. Given current knowledge of human biology and current biotechnical capacities, death has become a matter of choice. Humankind has the opportunity to live. Not just for a century or two, which by the clock of the cosmos is a mere blink, but forever. Shall we seize that opportunity or let it slip away? Most young people today agree that the chance must be taken, and taken boldly and promptly. If one believes that life is precious, irreplaceable, and unique, it must be conserved. As a species, we have lost our excuse to die.

So, as you hear these words, in the year 2200, the question uppermost in many minds is whether to share the results of the Samsara Project with all humankind. Do we know enough? Have we conducted enough tests? Will biotechnically aided reincarnation give us true immortality—not a renewal of life but deathlessness?

In every other area of life preservation, we have done well. There has never been a time when so many people enjoyed good health for so long as during the last five decades. The greatest single advance has been the development of the all-purpose medical robot, the "medrob," which now handles (with the help of a human nurse or technician) nearly every medical problem encountered in everyday practice. Each medrob is equipped with a full array of diagnostic scanners capable of cell and fluid analysis, imaging of tissue, and measurement of vital functions. Medrobs of various designs have been available everywhere since the late 2170s. Most surgical procedures have also been fully automated, using medrobs equipped with millions of branching microscopic fingerlets.

Of course medical problems are comparatively rare. New communicable diseases do sometimes appear, which require attention and treatment, but the old ones disappeared or were brought under control long ago. The genetic modification of embryos, greatly improved diets, and routine exercise have eliminated most instances of degenerative disease, and we can cope surgically with cases that do appear if people see their local medrob or clinic for regular diagnostic tests.

The longevity bioengineering of the Commonwealth era has stood the one test that matters, the test of time—but only up to a point. Excision of the DNA responsible for halting cell reproduction delays the aging process, according to our best current estimates, by approximately fifty-five extra years. Careful tests of the cells, tissues, and physiology of persons who received longevity surgery through the Genetic Initiative in the period from 2097 to 2107 indicate that they will probably live until about 2270. Ninety-five percent of them are still with us, in 2200, and in excellent health.

Also, persons like your grandfather who have undergone genetic modifications in adulthood are living at least thirty years longer than they could have expected to live without them. At 116, although I am close to my extended natural limit, I do have older friends who received the same treatments and are now in their 120s. But in a larger sense we are a dwindling breed since nowadays the vast majority of human beings receive genetic modification for longevity during the first days of embryonic life.

All this has been disappointing to contemporary longevity bio-engineers. Techniques have been further refined since the days of the Genetic Initiative, but it appears that nature long ago devised a whole series of limits to the powers of animal DNA. We have surmounted some of these limits in our manipulations over the years. Yet, every time we eliminate one limit, we encounter new ones. The chemical released in senescence identified as the cause of the signals transmitted to DNA molecules to halt reproduction is only one obstacle. Removed from the system, it can no longer wreak its havoc, but we have discovered, deep in the programming of all DNA molecules, an "absolute" limit that can be removed only by disturbing the timing mechanisms of the body so fundamentally that no researcher dares make the attempt. With the considerable knowledge we now possess, it would appear that 175 years is nature's final sentence, without further appeal.

Of course 175 years is not ninety. The extra time has been put to good use. People from the twenty-first century would have great difficulty telling anyone's age. For those genetically modified at conception, puberty seldom occurs before the age of twenty. Most continue to look, feel, and act like young adults until they reach their mid-sixties, and middle age stretches well beyond one hundred. No modified female has so far experienced menopause until her late seventies. The modified not only look younger; they *are* younger in every respect: in stamina, imagination, energy, joie de vivre, all the qualities attributed to youth, except—perhaps—plasticity of mind.

But the modified, we are quite sure, will someday die. After 175 years of thought, emotion, sensation, creativity, memory, all the comings and goings of a full life, they will close their eyes for the last time and die. Just as surely as the men and women of the Stone Age, who were old at fifty, just as surely as any of us now alive, they will die.

Unless! Unless we learn how to transfer human consciousness from one body to another, human or artificial. For millennia the peoples of South Asia believed in the transmigration of the soul after death into a new body. Some of them still do. But the soul is not the same as consciousness. Human consciousness is the secretion of living brains, the only unambiguously verifiable reality known to us. Descartes said it well. Of one thing we may be sure, if nothing else: *cogito, ergo sum.* We are conscious; therefore we exist. The irreducible "I" of experience, present in all our waking moments and all our dreams, the protagonist of all our stories, exists. When the bodily medium in which it flourishes dies, consciousness dies with it.

But, if it were possible to make a copy of consciousness and install it in a new supportive medium, then the "I" would—perhaps—continue. This is the premise of the Samsara Project, from the Sanskrit for *transmigration*. The germ of the idea goes back to the late twentieth-century robotician Hans Moravec, but no twenty first-century research group was able to accomplish what Moravec had proposed. Imaging in precise detail every neurone of the human brain, converting that image into the language of a computer, and installing the computerized model into an electronic brain proved too overwhelming a task.

Even when the task *was* substantially carried out in the early 2020s by several North American scientists, they failed—as almost everyone had foreseen—to achieve the transmigration of consciousness. Instead, they created a machine that possessed the memories of the donor's brain and exhibited the donor's ways of reasoning, without in any way sharing the donor's personality, will, or identity. The machine represented the worst of both worlds: the slowness of the human mind and the lifelessness of the machine mind.

Attention then shifted to direct brain-to-brain transfer technology. Secret experiments with cloned human beings as recipients of the donor's consciousness began in 2093 and were abruptly canceled the next year when word of the illegal procedure reached the Commonwealth minister of health, Qian Gundi.

The Samsara Project picked up the threads of this older research from the Commonwealth era in 2177. It took years to mobilize because no single community had the human resources needed, and ethical opposition to the cloning of whole human beings is still robust. In the end, scientists and support personnel from ten communities scattered across three continents became involved. The contributions of each of the ten communities were vital to the success of the project, although it is likely that scientists from Beijing Commune and from the Ganges Valley Federation played the leading role.

The cloning operation itself, ethical considerations aside, is quite simple. Anyone can have an exact replica grown in a liquid medium up to any desired chronological age. The replica is not allowed to gain consciousness, so that its mind is a perfect Lockean tabula rasa.

But the central innovation of the Samsara Project is the mind-net technique. In mind-netting, the donor's brain is scanned over a period of at least one month, twenty-four hours a day, until every combination of neural impulses has been recorded and collated. Imaging by psychoholography permits the transfer surgeons to imprint every impulse pattern on exactly the right portion of the replica's brain. Because the clone has the same physical body, with the same sensorium and glandular system as its donor, its brain then functions in the same way as the donor's brain. Or so project scientists claim.

The first "netting" of a complete human mind was demonstrated in 2189, and the first successful transfer of memory and personality from a donor to a clone (in the parlance of the Project, *charging*) occurred just seven years ago, in 2193 in New Patna.

This was only prefatory to the final task. Bioengineers theorize that, when the brains of the donor and its already "charged" clone are connected by a dense lacework of electrodes at the time of the donor's death, the consciousness and identity as well as the mental characteristics of the donor will flow intact into the clone's mind. But this will happen, they say, only if the clone has had no opportunity to develop an identity of its own after being charged. In short, the clone must return to biostorage or enter a hibertube until the time of its donor's death.

As you know, the hibertube is a device originally designed to enable interstellar cosmonauts to spend part of their long voyages in diminished animation. It lowers pulse, respiration, and other processes to one-fiftieth of their normal rate and induces a deep trance state. Since 2188, we have also used hibertubes for forward time travel. Persons entering diminished animation in a hibertube may emerge many years later, not appreciably older in a physiological sense, and resume their lives. There has not yet been time to test hibernations of more than a decade in length, but no subject has suffered lasting ill effects from the experience, and the procedure is now generally recognized as safe and suitable for general use.

As I speak these words, more than a hundred human replicas with fully charged minds are sleeping in hibernation. But no donor is on the verge of death, and none has thus far attempted to transfer his or her identity into the mind of a charged clone. Nor, in the communities where hibernating clones are stored, has a consensus been reached on next steps. It is entirely possible that, if a donor does die, he or she will not attempt transfer in the final hours.

The problems involved are of many orders and levels of complexity. Project scientists are divided on the issue of whether a dying subject is an appropriate candidate for identity transfer. Some argue that the only fit candidate is someone in relatively good health, with a clear mind, who elects to die several years ahead of his or her time and signs a euthanasia contract to that effect. Others oppose euthanasia on both ethical and logical grounds.

Still others question the whole enterprise because of its dependence on clones. Clones, critics contend, are human beings. Charging them with the consciousness of another human being, even an exact twin, is a violation of autonomy and a reversion to slavery in its most abusive form. The Samsara researchers must, they say, redirect their attention to the charging of artificial brains, despite the formidable biotechnological difficulties entailed and the severe disadvantages for donors of being reborn in an artificial body.

Objections are heard as well to the assumption that the immortal mind can ever be a healthy or even truly human mind. Nature, some insist, made us to die. Once set in its ways, a mind matures and then declines into futile and ultimately meaningless repetition. Faced with eternity, minds might become diseased, suicidal, or perhaps even paranoid and dangerous to others.

But almost all of us agree that the greatest problem is verifiability. How will anyone know if identity transfer has actually occurred? The theories supporting it are cogent. Yet in the final showing, since identity is a purely subjective reality, no one except the donor would be able to verify transfer, and the donor would (assuming failure) no longer exist. The clone might think that it was the donor. The clone might be able to "prove" its authenticity by drawing on all the donor's memories and psychophysiological traits. But under the circumstances its deposition could never be taken at face value. The clone might be deluded or lying to save its own identity. Who could tell?

The one argument on the other side that compels attention and safeguards the Samsara Project is hope. Hope for a life that spans millennia, hope for self-endowed immortality in genetically identical (or even genetically improved) bodies, youth perpetually renewed, consciousness growing in widsom and knowledge from age to age. We cannot know, unless we try, whether reincarnation will give us eternal life or not.

Is the fulfillment of such hope worth all the effort, the doubting, and the sacrifice? Who among us is sage enough to pronounce judgment? Who among us should decide?

The Darwin Project

Rivaling the Samsara Project in some minds is the continuing effort of genetic engineers to improve or at least modify the human type. Their work has met with deep hostility. Although quite a few ecomystics suggest that fresh advances in gene surgery may actually help bring *Homo sapiens* closer to its original essence, the majority of ecomystical texts clearly oppose any further "meddling" with the human genome, except to prolong life or prevent disease and deformity. Some of the smaller sects concur with their views.

I freely confess that these views make little sense to me. The increases in intelligence and the behavioral alterations achieved by the bioengineers of the Commonwealth era were in such general use by 2146 that during the past half century only the most intransigent of ecomystical parents have refused to give their embryos the same treatment. But, if this much embryonic gene surgery is acceptable, why stop there? Clearly, the Commonwealth surgeons did far more than "meddle" or "tinker" with *Homo sapiens*. As we know, they created a whole new variety of humankind, *Homo sapiens altior*. I conclude that, if ecomystics can tacitly approve the creation of a new version of humankind, they have no grounds in their own philosophy for refusing to sanction further progress in the same field.

The central enterprise in species modification today is known familiarly as the Darwin Project, after the author of *The Origin of Species*. The project was initiated in 2169 by teams of geneticists and other scientists primarily from just three communities, the Huanghe Valley Cooperative in East Asia, the Northwest Republic in North America, and the Vilayet of Ankara. Its director is Rahsan Feyzioglu of Yozgat. Her co-director, Gholam Razmara of Shiraz and Xi'an, is responsible for much of the basic science of the project, Feyzioglu for coordination and oversight.

Briefly, the Darwin Project has set for itself the task of constructing new genetic models for humankind, models that elevate the varieties of intelligence to still higher levels than the Genetic Initiative, with a broader range of behavioral modifications enhancing not only empathy, sociability, and altruism but also a spectrum of extrasensory faculties.

The existence of so-called extrasensory faculties was challenged and for all practical purposes disproved in the twenty-first century. But studies from the 2130s onward disclosed that the earlier critique of extrasensory perception, rooted in neomaterialism, was premature. Extensive studies conducted by Maamoun el-Din Hassan of Cairo, Salim Ahmed Pervez of Rawalpindi, Fyodor Bakhtin of Tomsk, Emma St.-John Peabody of Moose Jaw, and several anonymous ecomystics established by 2160 the authenticity of at least twelve extrasensory powers. Some of these had often been reported in the past, such as the ability to intercept and reconstruct visual images formed by nearby minds or the ability to psychoimmunize oneself against cancer. Others were more exotic, including a faculty for "hearing" shortwave radio transmissions, "reading" the earth's magnetic field and ecosystemic pulse, and stimulating DNA repair.

In most instances, Peabody and her colleagues at the Institute for Hypersense in Saskatoon learned how to enlarge ESP powers in suitable subjects by exercises or by electronic amplifiers. The next step was to find the source of these powers in the human genome, which the Darwin Project began undertaking in 2172. Through detailed comparative analysis of subjects with and without measurable ESP ability, the genetic subunits responsible for each faculty were identified and added to the genomic inventory completed (so we believed) in the previous century. To the credit of the earlier biomappers, no new subunits were discovered in this effort: only unsuspected interactions of subunits with already known discrete functions of their own.

A fascinating by-product of ESP research was the delineation of an array of faculties not involving extrasensory perception and observed in the past only as gifts randomly distributed to geniuses and idiots savants. These gifts had not been included in the genomic inventory because of inadequate evidence. The ability to recall instantly everything ever sensed or learned, the ability to perform complex mathematical operations in one's head, the ability to play musical instruments or sculpt or paint without training, and various other extraordinary talents were studied by Darwin Project researchers, following leads supplied by the investigators of ESP. After testing, many of these "gifts" were added to the genomic model designed by the Darwin Project.

Or should I say genomic models? For there soon came to be more than a hundred, after scientists ascertained that some supernormal abilities, behavioral traits, varieties of intelligence, or ESP powers could not coexist with others in the same individual. As a result, the Darwin Project proposed many alternative editions of *Homo sapiens altior,* each with its own distinctive combination of enhancements. First one community and then another conducted gene surgery on embryos utilizing the models of the Darwin Project. Millions of children were born with a dazzling assortment of higher powers, including you, Ingrid, and little Bertel and perhaps one-quarter of the new members of the human race during the past two decades.

As I presume you know, you have been classified an *altior 4-B* and Bertel an *altior 3-A.* By our way of measuring intelligence, you fall in the upper .01 percent of those who were genetically modified prior to the Darwin Project, Bertel in the upper .02 percent. Given the greatly elevated intelligence of the modified themselves, these are miraculous scores. Your psychologist tells me that you now have a mental age of twenty-five, as I can well believe from our talks. When you reach fifteen, you will surpass anything possible for *Homo sapiens,* and by twenty-one you will have grown far beyond all but an insignificant fraction of the *altiores.*

Another aspect of the genetic revolution wrought by the Darwin Project is the discovery that some of these new strains of *Homo sapiens altior* cannot mate successfully with others or even with the original *Homo sapiens.* In short, the researchers have—without intending it—created new species of humankind, not just variations on the human theme. Physical anthropologists are working on a revised taxonomy, which will recognize the existence of at least fifteen distinct species of the genus *Homo* in addition to *Homo sapiens.*

In these same years, roboticians have sketched plans for new artificial entities (one hesitates to call them robots) that may be capable of original volition. In theory, all that separates a robot from a human being is the absence in robots of circuits linking the faculties of preference, reason, and action. Robots have been taught to feel and desire, to think and solve problems, and to perform a variety of physical tasks. An integrated robotic system in which these faculties are interwoven as in human brains might well be capable of self-generating purposes, goals, and the power to originate volition.

In the face of such prospects, bitter disagreements have broken out in innumerable communities concerning the destiny of our species. Do we still have a species, or are we fragmenting into scores of new ones that will soon go their separate ways? Will our chief competitors in times to come be artificial beings? Will the new superraces, human or robotic, share our humane values? Even if they share such values at first, what will prevent them from modifying themselves and arriving, in due course, at priorities or purposes hostile to our own and even dangerous to the survival of *Homo sapiens?*

I suspect that many individuals who take the conservative position in these debates are more jealous than fearful. But undeniably the future does not look bright for the traditional model of humankind. It will almost certainly become extinct by choice, sooner or later. Nor will any single new race inherit the stars in its stead. As we scatter our seed through the cosmos, it will be a seed of many hues, many shapes, many goals and yearnings. Some of it may be descended only from our minds, not from our loins. As the twentieth-century writer Arthur C. Clarke foresaw, we have come to the end of the childhood of the human race. The old simplicities dissolve. The future seethes with possibilities beyond our ken.

The House of Heaven

The last of the great collective projects undertaken in our time that I must describe are our enterprises in space, which go well beyond anything accomplished during the last age of capital or under the Commonwealth. Although exploration and research continue, the main object of our efforts today is the settlement of space, not by a few million earthlings but by thousands of millions. "In the year 2300," writes Alva Lind of Uppsala, "more than half of us will reside in colonies and habitats beyond the earth. Our House of Earth will become the House of Heaven."

There is no reason to doubt her words. Already we have seen the building of thousands of new habitats in terrestrial, lunar, Venusian, or Martian orbit or in the asteroid belt. The population of these habitats has soared to at least ninety-five million, many times greater than the numbers who lived in space in the days of the Commonwealth. Of special interest is the success of space engineers in hollowing out six large asteroids and fitting them for human settlement. The lunar and Martian colonies have also grown significantly, and the scientific stations built by the Commonwealth on satellites of Jupiter and Saturn have been joined by several dozen new communities circling not only the two largest planets but also Mercury, Venus, and Uranus.

Most of these activities have required little collaboration among earthside communities or, for that matter, among communities in space. Despite the heroic engineering feats involved, even the transformation of the six asteroids was managed fairly easily by construction macrobots from independent spaceside communities, each operating on its own with no outside help.

Other exploits have posed greater challenges. Two, in particular, have drawn the attention of all humankind. Neither could have been carried out by single communities, even our largest. One stems from a historic decision taken on Moon Day, 20 July 2169 (the bicentennial of the first lunar landing), at a gathering of scientists from fifty communities meeting on the site of the former World Space Museum in Cocoa Beach, North America; the second is more difficult to chronicle but originated in the 2150s in consultations among the scientists and cosmonauts of several communities once active in the interstellar programs of the Commonwealth. With these projects, the genus *Homo* enters fully into its future as a starborn people, tied to earth only by the bonds of sentiment, history, and filial piety.

The Cocoa Beach Conference of 2169 revived an ancient dream, broached at a meeting of space scientists held near San Francisco in 1975: the dream of a new earth on the planet Mars. Your generation will be the first to enjoy the fruits of the work begun at Cocoa Beach. I can only apologize, on behalf of all previous generations, for the unconscionably long delay in getting it started. Most specialists in the science of terraforming—or planetary engineering, as it is known to specialists—agree that the Mars project could have been initiated as early as 2030 and finished by the year 2100.

But in 2169 the right moment had arrived at last. The Cocoa Beach meetings lasted from early June to late July, bringing together more than a thousand experts in all the relevant sciences and engineering skills. They discussed a rich variety of experiments in Martin biology, most of them performed on Mars itself by residents of the principal underground colony in the highlands near the Schiaparelli Basin. They discussed climatic and atmospheric engineering, water and mineral resources, energy needs, and demographic objectives. They concluded that, in no more than fifty years of intensive work, roughly 35 percent of the Martian surface could be made habitable. The rest would consist of mountains, canyons, wastelands, polar regions, and huge shallow seas covering much of the northern hemisphere of the planet. Mars has only one-fourth the surface area of earth, but 35 percent of that would still amount to forty-five million square kilometers, the size of Asia, enough land to accommodate one billion people comfortably.

After gaining the full support of the four already established Martian colonies, the forty-three participating earthside communities formed the "Mars Consortium" and set to work in earnest in 2171. Their first priority was to raise the surface temperature of the planet. This feat was accomplished by placing immense sodium mirrors in orbit around Mars to increase its share of solar radiation and by thickening the Martian atmosphere with chlorofluorocarbons, oxides of carbon and nitrogen, and other gases manufactured in Martian or space factories. These are precisely the gases that helped warm the earth so disastrously in the late twentieth and twenty-first centuries, but now the warmth was welcome, on a planet where the temperature even in equatorial regions seldom rose for more than a few hours a day above the freezing point of water and dropped at night to 175 degrees Kelvin.

Not surprisingly, the most valuable additions to the Martian atmosphere were the chlorofluorocarbons, which had been lethal to the ozone layer on earth (nonexistent on Mars) and much more effective than CO_2 in contributing to the greenhouse effect. One molecule of certain chlorofluorocarbons traps as much heat as ten thousand molecules of CO_2.

By 2188, the engineers of the Mars Consortium had brought the surface temperature of Mars in the temperate and equatorial latitudes to tolerable levels. The water ice in the polar caps had melted, along with fields of permafrost lying just under the Martian soil. The lowlands of the northern hemisphere began to flood, lakes and oceans formed, rain and snow fell, rivers ran, and the atmospheric pressure rose steadily, as gases were released not only from factories but also from the thawing of polar and underground ice. The long Martian summer came to resemble early spring in North America or Siberia.

At this point it was time for the bioengineers to take their turn and provide the greenery of spring as well. New varieties of salt-resistant algae and lichen requiring little or no oxygen and relatively impervious to the abundant ultraviolet radiation that stings the face of Mars were coaxed to grow in a wide range of Martian terrains; thousands of metric tons of topsoil were imported from earth containing the microorganisms, annelids, and other fauna needed to condition the land for supporting higher forms of plant life. The fauna required oxygen, available in minute but adequate quantities from the per-

nitrates in the Martian soil as well as from the algae themselves. In any event, they thrived and multiplied until they covered the planet.

As I speak these words, all the preliminary stages in the terra-forming of Mars have been completed. Factories are hard at work enriching the atmosphere with nitrogen and oxygen. An ozone layer has begun to form high in the Martian stratosphere. Fields of coarse crops adapted to the Martian climate and soil are releasing more oxygen into the air. In a few more decades, it will be possible to grow hundreds of varieties of edible grains, tubers, and vegetables. Already Martians and their visitors from the Consortium can walk about in the open air equipped with nothing more elaborate than winter clothing and oxygen masks. The pink sky has begun to turn blue.

The older Martian settlers often lament the passing of the world they came to love. It is characteristic of the genus *Homo* that we adapt to almost any environment with relative ease, even an environment experienced mostly through the window of a space helmet or a periscope protruding from a habitat buried in the sand. To a surprising degree, we take life as we find it, and learn to be happy; so it has been with the old Martians in their icy desert home.

But visitors to Mars agree on one thing. Whatever regrets or resentments native Martians express, only a few actually oppose the terra-forming of their land. Like the rest of us, they know that someday they will roam Mars as their ancestors once roamed the earth, tilling its soil, basking in its sun, swimming in its lakes, tramping its woods and fields and mountains. Terraforming will not spoil Mars. It will only bring its beauties and treasures within easy reach of everyone.

We hope that terraforming Mars will also furnish a haven for the multitudes of long-lived and perhaps immortal earthlings who now begin to crowd our home planet. Demographic pressure will inevitably mount throughout the twenty-third and twenty-fourth centuries. The migration to Mars and the space habitats will relieve that pressure for many years to come.

Yet the only lasting solution is to find new homes for our genus in the vaults of interstellar space. Under the Commonwealth, you remember, drone ships propelled by nuclear fusion were sent out to tour the stellar "neighborhood." Even earlier, in the first half of the twenty-first century, astronomers received a maze of radio and neutrino-stream signals from distant solar systems, proving the presence of intelligent life in other parts of the universe.

Interest in these signals eventually faded. Nearly all of them originated in inaccessibly remote portions of this or other galaxies. The closest confirmed source was 7,222 light years from earth. Nearly all the messages were also indecipherable. Even when we could understand some of the message, it typically contained little information of value.

The most haunting example, received millions of times between 2038 and 2040, originated in a seemingly empty quarter of the galaxy 58,550 light years away. Translating its digital codes into human language, scientists read a cry for help from the bear-like inhabitants of a colony world under attack by virulent microbes. Each automated cry ended with the symbols for "Mother . . . Death . . . Reproduction . . . Never."

We still listen to such messages, but there is little point in attempting communication with beings so far removed from us in space and time. Our attention has shifted in recent decades to the immediate stellar neighborhood, stimulated by the discovery in the 1150s of half a dozen planets of earth's mass and distance from their suns, all within twenty light years of the solar system. The chief tool in this search has been the 125-meter telescope on the moon, which examines infrared wavelengths and can detect the presence of oxygen in planetary atmospheres. We learned that all six of the terrestrial planets do have an atmosphere rich in oxygen, which makes it nearly certain that all six are alive.

Inspired by this knowledge, in 2162 a group of nineteen communities formed the Interstellar Expeditionary Service to encourage and subsidize manned flights to the nearest stars orbited by earth-type planets.

The key to their success, as everyone recognized from the first, was the development of a system of propulsion much more powerful than the nuclear fusion engine invented by Commonwealth engineers. Everyone also knew from the first that the likeliest candidate for such a system was the matter-antimatter blender, perfected in the Northwest Republic in 2153. Its chief designer, Tom Cadwallader of Spokane, had always intended it to be used as an engine for spacecraft, although by a quirk of timing it achieved its first practical application in the generation of energy on earth.

In 2163, a modified matter-antimatter blender with a hundred times the capacity of the standard model was installed in a fusion-powered space drone and allowed to fire after the ship passed beyond the orbit of Jupiter. A charged deflector shield guarded the hull of the vessel from cosmic dust. The system performed flawlessly, and all later tests were equally successful.

Traveling up to 80 percent of the speed of light after leaving the solar system, the first manned interstellar ship departed in 2166. Its crew of two hundred spent most of the voyage sleeping in hiber-tubes. They visited the single terrestrial planet in the Alpha Centauri system, returning in glory in 2178 with the loss of only two lives. The planet, Elysium, is thick with life, but most of it is marine, and all land creatures are of the vegetable kingdom. Geologists estimate that Elysium has reached the same approximate stage as earth in the late Devonian period, some 340 million years ago. It could readily support a population of two billion souls, and perhaps more.

Without awaiting the return of the first expedition, the directors of the Interstellar Expeditionary Service dispatched a second to Barnard's Star, at a distance of 5.9 light years, and a third to Sirius and Procyon, 8.6 and 11.4 light years away. Volunteers, you may be sure, were not wanting, including your cousins Carl and Otto Brandt, crew members in the voyage to Barnard's Star. A fourth expedition is on its way back from Omicron and Epsilon Eridani, a fifth is en route to Wolf 359, and three more are being organized.

As I am sure you know, the greatest finds were on the small planet circling the white dwarf companion of Procyon. By contrast with Elysium, this planet (known to most of us as Hecatomb) is now largely dead, having been struck by asteroids twice in its recent geologic history. Hecatomb's dominant intelligent species, anthropoids of great ingenuity and energy, left the planet at least seventy-five million years ago without furnishing a forwarding address. But archeologists studying their remains in artificial caverns deep under the surface report a highly advanced civilization from which we have much to learn. The Sirius-Procyon expedition will not return to earth until 2209, but the first detailed radio transmissions from the expedition arrived last month. They promise a wealth of historical, technical, and scientific information that may revolutionize life in the solar system.

Much work remains. More expeditions. More monitoring of signals from distant stars and galaxies. Above all, the dispatch of colony ships bound for Elysium and the other inhabitable planets of our stellar neighborhood. The Interstellar Expeditionary Service has commissioned designs for spaceworthy vessels that would carry from five to twelve thousand persons each. Service directors are also considering a third option, a powered hollow planetoid that would transport half a million colonists to any selected star.

Scientists in communities not participating in the Interstellar Expeditionary Service are often critical of its efforts. Citing the prophecies of the American writer George Zebrowski in his novel *Macrolife* (1979) and its various sequels, Axel Hutter of Kufstein and his associates in the Belt habitat of Bulero (one of the six modified asteroids) see no point in producing ships to colonize distant planets. Why not live in the "ships" themselves? They look forward to an age when humankind will shake itself free of dependence on the grit and grime of planets and live in self-propelled "macroworlds" engineered from bodies like Bulero itself or from captured moons. Planets will one day be seen, writes Hutter, as reservations, or museums, or parks, fascinating to visit, but too fragile and unwieldy to serve as homes for our peripatetic genus. Like Zebrowski, he imagines a universe of gypsy macroworlds, questing silently through the black-bright halls of heaven until the end of time.

The Bulerans may be right. Who knows? All I can say is what I see. I see an earth that resembles more and more an egg about to hatch. Cracks appear in its shell. The egg heaves and rocks to and fro. A new humanity strives to be born, and we who watch tremble in fear and joy.

ENVOI TO INGRID

I have finished at last! I hope you followed my advice and did not play all the spools in one day. Not that your grandfather is so very deep! But these two hundred years have been deep indeed. At one time our race nearly committed suicide. Then we built a world empire so high and huge it collapsed under its own weight. Now we prepare to say farewell to earth and our old humanity. Sometimes I think we have lost our way.

My own time grows short. This history is my last gift to you because I have decided to sleep, my dearest Ingrid. I shall miss you—more perhaps than you will miss me—and I shall miss Hans and all my friends and companions. But the restlessness of this age has infected me, too! So I have contracted to enter a hibertube tomorrow, for the maximum term of one century.

When I awake, the world may have changed again, and who can say what will happen? I catch myself wishing that the Interstellar Expeditionary Service and the Samsara and Darwin Projects and the Mars Consortium may be harbingers of a new integration of humankind. I lived too long in the Commonwealth, despite all its stupidities, to feel entirely comfortable in the House of Earth. But I have also lived long enough to know that, with time and patience, all things are possible.

Keep well, and visit your father and mother sometimes. They will always have an interest in your well-being no matter how far you wander. Forgive an old man's sentimentality, but I hope to see you

again, too, when you are a grown woman and a radiant star in the fir-
mament of your new species.

But be sure of this. I do not retire from the world in despair or
rage. I love life as tenderly as I ever did. On my hibertube the technicians will inscribe these lines from Walt Whitman's "Passage to India," the song most dear to my old heart:

O brave soul!
O farther, farther sail!
O daring joy, but safe! are they not all the seas of God?
O farther, farther, farther sail!

A LAST NOTE TO THE READER

When I came to Peter's foolish goodbye, I shook my head in disbelief. He had given me this wonderful book, for wonderful it is, although there are many better ones, and then he left me. I could not understand why for years. I do now, but it still hurts to think that I shall not see him again until the next century, and perhaps not ever, if he dies in his hibertube. Although people age slowly in tubes, they continue to age. But we must respect his wishes and let him sleep.

I trust that readers will overlook Peter's obsession with family history. It helps prove his own point that the elderly cannot rethink their premises. In the same way, someone of my time and generation finds it difficult to grasp, at the deepest psychic levels, what he understood by "family life." I loved Peter because he happened to be a good friend of my childhood, not because he inseminated the woman who gave birth to my father!

Yet in one respect he did underestimate us. People today recognize that the Commonwealth and the World party, which Peter revered to his last days, supplied the indispensable bridge between capitalism and liberty. Such is the course of world history: from liberation to liberation, through trials to the stars. Each stop along the way is essential. None can be passed by.

Still, let us remember: the object of all our striving is not capitalism or socialism or anarchy. We do not live for world orders. World orders exist for us, to help us live for ourselves in the fathomless flux of being.

Sail on, brave soul! Peter Jensen, I love you. Sleep in peace, and farther, farther sail.

Ingrid Jensen
20 March 2210

AFTERWORD   by Immanuel Wallerstein

We are all, or most of us, fascinated with the future. That is why science fiction is such a popular genre. This book claims, however, to be not fiction but a history of the future. The line is thin, but nonetheless worth trying to assert. None of us can of course know for sure about the future. But then none of us can know for sure about the past, or even about the present. We take what we think we know and try to make a coherent interpretation out of it, addressing our concerns, our anxieties, our hopes. We can probably do that almost as well about the future as about the past. At least, that is the implicit premise of this book.

What appeals to me in this history of the future is that it offers us both reality and choice. The book has three parts, and each is a plausible projection of the present. Book 1 is an attempt to pursue the most obvious current trends in the operation of the capitalist world-economy to their logical conclusions, or at least one possible set of conclusions. Book 2 is an attempt to envisage the working out of the major utopian vision of the last two centuries of what might constitute an alternative world-system, a socialist world-government. Book 3 is the working out of the second great utopian alternative, the one that emphasizes smallness, decentralization, and the sentiment of community and that, unlike the first utopian vision, is antiproductivist.

For each of the two utopian visions, and even in a sense for the description of the present world-system projected ahead, Wagar puts its best foot forward. That is why this is a book of history. There is a serious attempt to envisage three social organizations of the world in their complexity and in their human honesty. There is no obfuscating name-calling. This is an interpretation of a real future.

For each of the three visions, our present system projected ahead and the two utopian visions, there is also no saccharine coating. Each has its merits, but each has its very serious drawbacks. Each utopian vision solves the problem of the social order it has replaced only to come up against quite new ones, which turn out to be impressively awesome.

One might suspect an Augustinian pessimism. But there is no fire and brimstone in the way the world is presented to us by Wagar, even as he describes the darkest of catastrophic moments in his future. There is a kind of resolute optimism, which seems to say at each point, Back to the last, and try again. We end the book on "farther, farther sail."

Is the book then one long sermon? Perhaps, but it is certainly not a mere reiteration of a nineteenth-century faith in progress. The message is not that progress is inevitable, only that it might be possible. Possible it might be, but easy to achieve it will not be.

This is a work of reflection, sobered by the failures of our system and the failures of the utopian movements it has thus far bred. But it is also a work that interprets the contemporary world-system as one that cannot, for structural reasons, continue in its present form for very long. It therefore brings to the fore the fact that we face historical choices, choices that cannot be avoided, choices that are real—in the double sense of not being predetermined and of having significant consequences—choices that can be made more wisely or less wisely.

One would think that this is an obvious truism or at least a message that would be well received. We are being told in effect that, at least now in the wake of systemic crisis, we collectively have something that approximates free will. But I expect few hosannas. Free will, even when thrust on us by forces beyond our control, is not very welcome. It endows us with a great deal of responsibility. And with responsibility comes the possibility of error. Errors of judgment can be grave, and Wagar spares us none of the reasons to be wary.

Nonetheless, the sobriety of tone is in its way very reassuring. It urges us on, and it urges us to use our historical sensibilities to render more coherent and more intelligent our political choices. That is why this book is not science fiction, in which the author in the end makes the choices for us, but a history of the future, in which the author indicates to us some of the choices we will have to make.

GENEALOGY OF THE JENSENS AND BRANDTS

Otto Jensen
(1968–2044)

Carl Jensen
(1973–2044)

Arne Jensen
(1980–2045)

Jens Otto Jensen
(1988–2095)
m. 1. Lonnie Glick
2. Cecilia Castro
Schmidt

Regine Jensen-Brandt
(1993–2089)
m. Mogens Brandt

Thomas Jensen
(2007–2044)

Harry Jensen
(2011–2044)
m. Olivia Rogers

Dina Geijer
(2002–2044)

Alfonsina Jensen
(2032–2141)

John Brandt
(2025–2129)

Lucinda Jensen
(2038–2134)
m Gatsha Mphephu

Poul Jensen
(2041–2128)

Peter Jensen
(2084–)

Gabriela Ortiz
(2063–2189)

Arne Brandt
(2058–2173)
m. Jeanne Wang

Knud Brandt
(2063–2150)

Hedvig Jensen-Mphephu
(2080–)

Hans Jensen
(2147–)

Eduardo Mistral Ortiz
(2100–)

Carl Brandt
(2097–)

Otto Brandt
(2097–)

Ingrid Jensen
(2190–)

Note: Spouses are shown only if mentioned in the text.
Persons whose names appear in italics supplied material for an interlude or note.
The name of the author (Peter Jensen) appears in a box.

CHRONOLOGY

1995 Beginning of severe worldwide depression.

1997 American intervention in the Philippines. Soviet-American confrontation in Yugoslavia brings world to the brink of a third world war.

1998 Vienna Conference produces East-West detente, signature of comprehensive arms limitation protocol, demilitarization of East and West Germany. Vaccine against AIDS introduced.

1999 Japan acquires nuclear weapons.

2001 Sharp economic upturn. Formation of the Arab Islamic Republic in Cairo.

2002 Preemptive war launched against Egypt by Israel in collaboration with Britain and France.

2004 Mexican Revolution. United States intervenes.

2008 Founding of the Global Trade Consortium (GTC) in Zurich by mega-corporate businessmen in the advanced countries. Cancer largely eliminated by immunization.

2011 First secret understandings between the GTC and elements in the Soviet Union, China, Poland. American strategic defense shield fully operational.

2012   Brazilian Revolution. First commercial fusion plant opens in Tokyo. Founding of the International Data Storage Center.

2013   Black uprising in Republic of South Africa followed by European intervention. The GTC wins confrontation with Soviet authorities over its operations in Moscow.

2014   Establishment of black-ruled Southern African Republic.

2016   Arab People's Republic of the Holy War seizes power in Riyadh. Islamic Republic of Palestine proclaimed in Amman.

2017   Attempted Islamic invasion of Israel. Timely intervention by American, Soviet, and Israeli forces.

2018   Soviet strategic defense shield operational.

2019   The GTC authorizes project to design improved human type by gene surgery.

2020   United Nations lunar base founded. Second Mexican Revolution.

2022   The United States invades and reorganizes rest of Mexico and Central America. The Soviet Union annexes Iran.

2023   First satellite colony ("Moontown") built.

2025   Sino-Soviet border war. GTC-U.N. quarantine of China. Birth of first children altered by GTC gene surgery.

2026   China capitulates. Second Vienna Conference reconstitutes the United Nations as the Confederated States of Earth (CSE).

2027   First signal received from extrasolar civilization, transmitted by neutrino stream; never decoded.

2030   Colony world ("Beltworld," later renamed "Atlantis") built in the asteroid belt.

2032   World economy suffers relapse. Bankruptcy of Standard Energy Corporation triggers depression.

2033   Mars colony established by the GTC.

2035   The World party formed. Mars colony abandoned.

2036   Lunar colony abandoned.

2038   The Church of the Purification founded.

2039   Aided by a cyclone and tidal wave, rising sea levels inundate 10 per-
       cent of Bangladesh. Other coastal areas hard hit in this and suc-
       cessive years.

2041   Death of Soviet premier Vassily Kravchenko signals end of East-
       West detente.

2042   Publication of *The Service of Being*, the "bible" of the World party, by
       Mitchell Greenwald and Carolina Ocampo.

2043   The United States secedes from the CSE over unilateral Soviet oc-
       cupation of Israel. GTC-CSE quarantine of the United States.

2044   Rebellion of Israelis in Autonomous District of the Jordan Valley
       crushed by Soviet forces. World War III. Collapse of the United
       States, the Soviet Union, the United Kingdom, northern Europe,
       East and South Asia.

2045   Death toll in war and its aftermath reaches at least 5.8 billion.

2049   World party issues Declaration of Human Sovereignty. Completion
       of second beltworld ("Lemuria").

2050   Mundialization of Chile and Australia.

2051   Mundialization of South Indian Federation.

2056   With thirty-five countries mundialized, the CSE disbands.

2057   End of the GTC, formation of the Provisional Trust.

2058   Pitched battles between Crusaders of the Church of the Purification
       and World party defense battalions in North America. Mundializa-
       tion of China and Russia.

2061   Mundialization of Argentina.

2062 Proclamation of the Commonwealth.

2063 World Militia authorized to quell resistance to rule of the Common-
      wealth by armed force wherever necessary. Beginning of six years of
      counterrevolutionary wars.

2068 Last skirmishes between Commonwealth militias and local resis-
      tance groups.

2070 Representatives of all nations ratify the Declaration of Human Sover-
      eignty in Melbourne.

2073 Planetary Restoration Authority created by the People's Congress to
      oversee the Great Housecleaning.

2075 Islamic guerrilla force in Middle East disarmed by swift action of the
      World Militia.

2078 Establishment of the tribunate.

2079 Commonwealth engineers reclaim flooded portions of Florida.

2085 Melbourne's last year as permanent capital city of the Common-
      wealth. No successor appointed, but various other cities are desig-
      nated as temporary ceremonial capitals by rotation.

2086 Completion of biomap project.

2090 Satellite solar power collection system ("Sun Ring") begins opera-
      tion. Proclamation of Energy Day. Death of Mitchell Greenwald and
      Carolina Ocampo.

2091 Reclamation of coastal Bangladesh concludes world program of
      restoring areas lost to rising sea levels. Meeting in Chongqing be-
      tween delegates of the League of Space Cooperatives and the
      Commonwealth.

2092 Free Trade party, founded by Gina Mascagni and associates, cap-
      tures 11 percent of the vote in congressional elections. Preamble to
      annual report of the ministry of arts and letters declares war on cul-
      tural avant-gardes.

2093   Goal of two to one ratio between rich and poor citizens in all departments of the Commonwealth achieved.

2095   Genetic Initiative, including program of raising intelligence by gene surgery, legislated by the People's Congress.

2097   Goal of two to one ratio between rich and poor departments achieved in world economic system.

2099   Proclamation of Earth Festival Day. Scientists confirm falling CO_2 levels, end of desertification, air and waters and soil free of industrial contamination, forests replenished.

2105   Resettlement of lunar colony.

2109   Sabbatical Law takes effect, guaranteeing all workers twelve months of educational leave every seven years.

2110   Transition to zero population growth worldwide completed.

2111   Resettlement of Mars colony.

2115   Accident destroys most of Mars colony.

2117   The Small party founded. Mars colony fully restored.

2120   Fission-to-fusion drive in service for space travel.

2123   The People's Congress votes to make gene surgery developed by the Genetic Initiative available to all prospective parents.

2124   Coalition of Free Trade and Small parties wins 31 percent of the vote in congressional elections.

2125   Oppositional movements in Middle East and Indian subcontinent crushed by Commonwealth rapid deployment troops.

2127   Passive resistance campaigns instigated by Small party cadres worldwide.

2129   First interstellar drone launched.

2131   Outlawry of the Small party.

2132 No-confidence vote in People's Congress. Council president Lyell-MacKenzie declares state of emergency and dissolves Congress.

2135 Second wave of popular resistance and demonstrations against the Commonwealth. Lyell-MacKenzie suspends constitution, rules by martial law.

2140 Assassination of Lyell-MacKenzie in Esfahan. Small party allowed to function again. Global elections and restoration of constitutional law.

2142 New elections. Small party elects 48 percent of representatives to the People's Congress.

2147 Small party elects 67 percent of representatives to the Congress and forms first government. Flag of the Commonwealth lowered in ceremony in Krasnoyarsk.

2148 Disbandment of the World Militia.

2150 Autonomy Laws vest all governmental authority in chartered local communities.

2151 Free Trade party disintegrates.

2153 Last congress of the World party, by the shores of Lake Louise; leaders agree to dissolve the party. First successful tests of matter-antimatter blender.

2158 Elimination of the Commoncent.

2159 Solar power satellite system disconnected. Dissolution of all remaining governmental institutions of the Commonwealth. Self-abolition of the Small party.

2162 Formation of the Interstellar Expeditionary Service.

2163 First test of matter-antimatter blender in spacecraft propulsion system.

2166 Departure of first interstellar expeditionary ship, with crew of two hundred aboard.

2169   Initiation of the Darwin Project, directed by Rahsan Feyzioglu. Cocoa Beach Conference plans the terraforming of Mars.

2171   Mars Consortium begins terraforming of Mars.

2177   Initiation of the Samsara (Transmigration) Project.

2178   Return of first interstellar expeditionary ship from Alpha Centauri, reporting exploration of planet Elysium.

2188   Resumption of Olympic Games. First use of hibertubes for forward time travel.

2189   Mind-net technique attempted with first human volunteer.

2193   First successful human mind transfer.

2200   Detailed radio transmission from third interstellar expeditionary ship, returning from Sirius and Procyon, reports major archeological discoveries on planet circling the companion star of Procyon.

STUDIES OF THE FUTURE

SUGGESTED READING

The literature of futures studies has grown prodigiously in the past quarter century. The selected bibliography that I compile for my course at the State University of New York at Binghamton currently lists over a thousand books and journals. *Future Survey,* a monthly journal published by the World Future Society since 1979, has supplied annotated abstracts of more than ten thousand new books and articles on futures-related topics. But what follows is only a brief bibliographic sampler to help orient readers who may be unfamiliar with the field. It includes a number of "classic" texts from the 1960s and 1970s as well as more recent material.

I have divided the sampler into four sections: journals that specialize in futures inquiry; studies of futures methodology and its history; studies of alternative world futures; and scenarios of future history that fuse the techniques of fiction and nonfiction in much the same way as *A Short History of the Future.*

Journals

Future Survey: A Monthly Abstract of Books, Articles, and Reports Concerning Forecasts, Trends, and Ideas about the Future. Bethesda, Md.: World Future Society, 1979–.

Futures: The Journal of Forecasting and Planning. Guildford, Surrey: Butterworth Scientific, 1968–.

Futures Research Quarterly. Bethesda, Md.: World Future Society, 1985–.

Futuribles. Paris: Association Internationale Futuribles, 1975–.

The Futurist: A Journal of Forecasts, Trends, and Ideas about the Future. Bethesda, Md.; World Future Society, 1967–.

Technological Forecasting and Social Change. New York: Elsevier Publishing Co., 1969–.

Methodologies

Cazes, Bernard. *Histoire des futurs.* Paris: Seghers, 1986.

Cornish, Edward, with Members and Staff of the World Future Society. *The Study of the Future.* Washington, D.C.: World Future Society, 1977.

Fowles, Jib, ed. *Handbook of Futures Research.* Westport, Conn.: Greenwood Press, 1978.

Helmer, Olaf. *Looking Forward: A Guide to Futures Research.* Beverly Hills, Calif.: Sage Publications, 1983.

Hughes, Barry B. *World Futures: A Critical Analysis of Alternatives.* Baltimore: Johns Hopkins University Press, 1985.

Jouvenel, Bertrand de. *The Art of Conjecture.* New York: Basic Books, 1967.

Linstone, Harold A., and W. H. Clive Simmonds, eds. *Futures Research.* Reading, Mass.: Addison-Wesley, 1977.

Makridakis, Spyros, and Steven C. Wheelwright, eds. *The Handbook of Forecasting: A Manager's Guide.* New York: John Wiley & Sons, 1982.

Marien, Michael, and Lane Jennings, eds. *What I Have Learned: Thinking about the Future Then and Now.* Westport, Conn.: Greenwood Press, 1987.

Martino, Joseph P. *Technological Forecasting for Decision Making.* 2d ed. New York: Elsevier North-Holland, 1983.

Meadows, Donella H., and J. M. Robinson. *Groping in the Dark: The First Decade of Global Modelling.* New York: John Wiley & Sons, 1982.

Polak, Frederik. *The Image of the Future.* Leyden: A. W. Sythoff; New York: Oceana Publications, 1961.

Sachs, Ignacy. *Development and Planning.* Cambridge: Cambridge University Press, 1987.

Schwarz, Brita, Uno Svedin, and Björn Wittrock. *Methods in Futures Studies: Problems and Applications.* Boulder, Colo.: Westview Press, 1982.

Wagar, W. Warren. *The City of Man: Prophecies of a World Civilization in Twentieth-Century Thought.* Boston: Houghton Mifflin Co., 1963.

World Futures

Asimov, Isaac, ed. *Living in the Future.* New York: Beaufort Books, 1985.

Barney, Gerald O., ed. *The Global 2000 Report to the President.* Washington, D.C.: U.S. Government Printing Office, 1980.

Bell, Daniel. *The Coming of Post-Industrial Society: A Venture in Social Forecasting.* New York: Basic Books, 1973.

Bell, Daniel, ed. *Toward the Year 2000.* Boston: Houghton Mifflin Co., 1968.

Bell, Wendell, and James A. Mau. *The Sociology of the Future.* New York: Russell Sage Foundation, 1971.

Beres, Louis René. *Apocalypse: Nuclear Catastrophe in World Politics.* Chicago: University of Chicago Press, 1980.

Bernard, Jessie. *The Future of Marriage.* 2d ed. New Haven, Conn.: Yale University Press, 1982.

Boulding, Kenneth. *The Meaning of the Twentieth Century.* New York: Harper & Row, 1964.

Brown, Harrison. *The Human Future Revisited.* New York: W. W. Norton & Co., 1978.

Clarke, Arthur C. *Profiles of the Future.* Rev. ed. New York: Holt, Rinehart & Winston, 1984.

Cole, H. S. D., Christopher Freeman, Marie Jahoda, and K. R. Pavitt, eds. *Models of Doom: A Critique of "The Limits to Growth."* New York: Universe Books, 1973.

Ehrlich, Paul R., and John P. Holdren, eds. *The Cassandra Conference. Resources and the Human Predicament.* College Station: Texas A&M University Press, 1988.

Ehrlich, Paul R., Carl Sagan, Donald Kennedy, and Walter Orr Roberts. *The Cold and the Dark: The World after Nuclear War.* New York: W. W. Norton & Co., 1984.

Falk, Richard A. *A Study of Future Worlds.* New York: Free Press, 1975.

Ferguson, Marilyn. *The Aquarian Conspiracy: Personal and Social Transformation in the 1980s.* Rev. ed. Los Angeles: J. P. Tarcher, 1987.

Francoeur, Robert T., and Anna K. Francoeur, eds. *The Future of Sexual Relations.* Englewood Cliffs, N.J.: Prentice-Hall, 1974.

Gouldner, Alvin W. *The Future of Intellectuals and the Rise of the New Class.* New York: Seabury Press, 1979.

Harman, Willis W. *An Incomplete Guide to the Future.* New York: W. W. Norton & Co., 1979.

Harrington, Michael. *The Twilight of Capitalism: A Marxian Epitaph.* New York: Simon & Schuster, 1976.

Harwell, Mark A. *Nuclear Winter: The Human and Environmental Consequences of Nuclear War.* New York: Springer Verlag, 1984.

Heilbroner, Robert L. *An Inquiry into the Human Prospect.* Rev. ed. New York: W. W. Norton & Co., 1980.

Henderson, Hazel. *Creating Alternative Futures: The End of Economics.* New York: Berkley Publishing Corp., 1978.

Kahn, Herman, William Brown, and Leon Martel. *The Next 200 Years: A*

Scenario for America and the World. New York: William Morrow & Co., 1976.

Levi, Werner. *The Coming End of War.* Beverly Hills, Calif.: Sage Publications, 1981.

McHale, John. *The Future of the Future.* New York: George Braziller, 1969.

Meadows, Donella H., Dennis L. Meadows, Jørgen Randers, and William W. Behrens III. *The Limits To Growth.* 2d ed. New York: Universe Books, 1974.

Mendlovitz, Saul H., ed. *On the Creation of a Just World Order: Preferred Worlds for the 1990's.* New York: Free Press, 1975.

Mesarovic, Mihajlo, and Eduard Pestel. *Mankind at the Turning Point.* New York: E. P. Dutton, 1974.

Mische, Gerald, and Patricia Mische. *Toward a Human World Order: Beyond the National Security Straightjacket.* New York: Paulist Press, 1977.

Repetto, Robert, ed. *The Global Possible: Resources, Development, and the New Century.* New Haven, Conn.: Yale University Press, 1985.

Roszak, Theodore. *Person/Planet: The Creative Disintegration of Industrial Society.* Garden City, N.Y.: Doubleday & Co., 1978.

Schell, Jonathan. *The Fate of the Earth.* New York: Alfred A. Knopf, 1982.

Simon, Julian L., and Herman Kahn, eds. *The Resourceful Earth: A Response to Global 2000.* New York: Basil Blackwell, 1984.

Stine, G. Harry. *The Hopeful Future.* New York: Macmillan Publishing Co., 1983.

Teich, Albert H., ed. *Technology and the Future.* 4th ed. New York: St. Martin's Press, 1986.

Thompson, William Irwin. *At the Edge of History: Speculations on the Transformation of Culture.* New York: Harper & Row, 1971.

Toffler, Alvin. *Future Shock.* New York: Random House, 1970.

Toffler, Alvin. *The Third Wave.* New York: William Morrow & Co., 1980.

Wagar, W. Warren. *Building the City of Man: Outlines of a World Civilization.* New York: Grossman Publishers, 1971.

Walford, Roy L. *Maximum Life Span.* New York: W. W. Norton & Co., 1983.

Wallerstein, Immanuel. *The Capitalist World-Economy.* Cambridge: Cambridge University Press, 1979.

World Commission on Environment and Development. *Our Common Future.* New York: Oxford University Press, 1987.

Scenarios of Future History

Callenbach, Ernest. *Ecotopia.* New York: Bantam Books, 1977.

Cowley, Stewart. *Spacebase 2000.* New York: St. Martin's Press, 1984.

Dixon, Dougal. *After Man: A Zoology of the Future.* New York: St. Martin's Press, 1981.

Hackett, Sir John. *The Third World War: August 1985.* New York: Macmillan Publishing Co., 1979.

Hackett, Sir John. *The Third World War: The Untold Story.* New York: Macmillan Publishing Co., 1982.

Hawken, Paul, James Ogilvy, and Peter Schwartz. *Seven Tomorrows: Toward a Voluntary History.* New York: Bantam Books, 1982.

Jay, Peter, and Michael Stewart. *Apocalypse 2000: Economic Breakdown and the Suicide of Democracy, 1989–2000.* New York: Prentice-Hall Press, 1987.

Macrae, Norman. *The 2025 Report.* New York: Macmillan Publishing Co., 1984.

O'Neill, Gerard K. *2081: A Hopeful View of the Human Future.* New York: Simon & Schuster, 1981.

Prehoda, Robert W. *Your Next Fifty Years.* New York: Grosset & Dunlap, 1980.

Stableford, Brian, and David Langford. *The Third Millennium: A History of the World, AD 2000–3000.* New York: Alfred A. Knopf, 1985.

Stapledon, Olaf. *Last and First Men.* London: Methuen & Co., 1930.

Theobald, Robert, and J. M. Scott. *Teg's 1994: An Anticipation of the New Future.* 2d ed. Chicago: Swallow Press, 1972.

Wells, H. G. *The Shape of Things to Come.* New York: Macmillan Co., 1933.

Wells, H. G. *The World Set Free: A Story of Mankind.* New York: F. P. Dutton, 1914.

INDEX OF PERSONS

In this index the names of characters from the future appear in italics; all other names belong to past or living persons

313

INDEX OF SUBJECTS